AFRICAN ISSUES

Series Editors Alex de Waal & Ste

D1388755

Mozambique & the
Great Flood
of 2000*
FRANCES CHRISTIE & JOSEPH HANLON

Killing for Wildlife Policy
Conservation in Zimbabwe
ROSALEEN DUFFY

Angola From Afro-Stalinism
to Petro-Diamond Capitalism
TONY HODGES

Congo- Transnational
Paris Traders on the
Margins of the Law
JANET MACGAFFEY & RÉMY BAZENGUISSA-GANGA

Africa Disorder
Works as Political
Instrument
PATRICK CHABAL & JEAN-PASCAL DALOZ

The Criminalization
of the State
in Africa
JEAN-FRANÇOIS BAYART, STEPHEN ELLIS
& BEATRICE HIBOU

Famine Politics & the
Crimes Disaster Relief Industry
in Africa
ALEX DE WAAL

Above titles
Published in the United States & Canada
by Indiana University Press

*forthcoming

**Peace
without
Profit**

How the IMF
Blocks Rebuilding
in Mozambique

JOSEPH HANLON

**The Lie
of the
Land**

Challenging
Received Wisdom on the
African Environment

Edited by

MELISSA LEACH & ROBIN MEARNS

**Fighting
for the
Rain Forest**

War, Youth
& Resources in
Sierra Leone

PAUL RICHARDS

*Above titles
Published in the United States & Canada
by Heinemann (N.H.)*

AFRICAN ISSUES

Angola From Afro-Stalinism
to Petro-Diamond
Capitalism

AFRICAN ISSUES

Angola

TONY HODGES

From Afro-Stalinism to Petro-Diamond Capitalism

The Fridtjof Nansen
Institute &
The International
African Institute
in association with

JAMES CURREY
Oxford

INDIANA UNIVERSITY PRESS
Bloomington & Indianapolis

The International
African Institute

Fridtjof Nansen Institute
Fridtjof Nansens vei 17
1324 Lysaker
Norway

in association with

James Currey
73 Botley Road
Oxford OX2 0BS
&
Indiana University Press
601 North Morton Street
Bloomington
Indiana 47404
(North America)

British Library Cataloguing in Publication Data
Hodges, Tony
Angola: from Afro-Stalinism to petro-diamond capitalism. – (African issues)
1. Angola – Economic conditions – 1975 – 2. Angola – Politics and government – 1975 –
I. Title II. International African Institute
967.3'04

ISBN 0-85255-851-1 (James Currey Paper)
0-85255-850-3 (James Currey Cloth)

Library of Congress Cataloguing-in-Publication Data available
A catalog record for this book is available from the Library of Congress

ISBN 0-253-21466-1 (Indiana Paper)
ISBN 0-253-33939-1 (Indiana Cloth)

Typeset by
Saxon Graphics Ltd, Derby
in 9/11 Melior with Optima display
Printed and bound in Great Britain by
Woolnough, Irthlingborough

For Sylvette
&
Sébastien

CONTENTS

FIGURES

MAP

TABLES

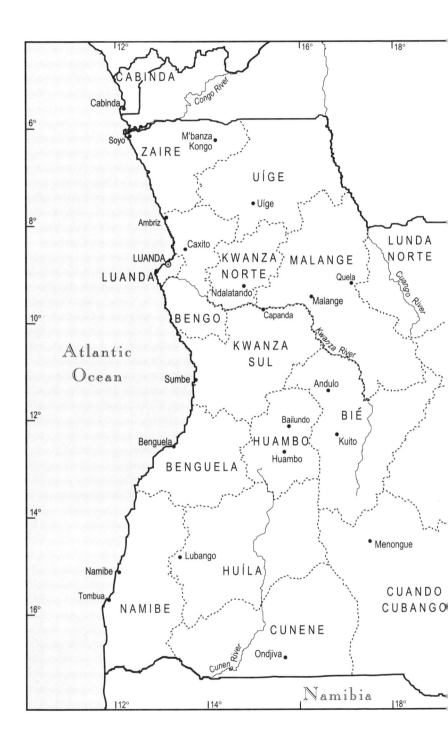

ACKNOWLEDGEMENTS

This study on Angola was undertaken as part of a comparative programme of research on the nature of 'oil states', sponsored by two Norwegian research institutions, ECON Centre for Economic Analysis and the Fridtjof Nansen Institute. The purpose of the programme was to understand better how a large oil industry impacts on a developing or transitional country's system of governance, economy and society and ultimately affects the status of civil, political, economic, social and cultural rights.

Special thanks are due to Helge Ole Bergesen (Fridtjof Nansen Institute) and Torleif Haugland (ECON), who directed the research programme and personally encouraged the study. I am particularly indebted to them for their valuable methodological advice and suggestions in the course of my research and writing. I should also note that valuable comments on the first draft were made by participants in a seminar held in Stavanger, Norway, in September 1999.

Much of the material for the study was gathered while I lived and worked in Angola in 1996–98, and during a special research visit to Angola in 1999. Numerous Angolans and expatriates resident in Angola contributed indirectly to the study, by providing access to documents and data, as well as their thoughts and ideas. It would be impossible to list all these persons and, given the sensitive nature of some of the information and analysis contained in the book, many of them might not wish to be acknowledged in public. I therefore thank them anonymously and collectively, while extending the usual disclaimer that I alone am responsible for the views expressed in the book.

Tony Hodges
Mauritius

During the 1990s, the agenda facing the international oil industry operating in the developing world has changed significantly. First, the issue of
environmental consequences resulting from oil exploration had to be
taken on board. Second, the challenges arising from the human rights
implications of petroleum-led development could no longer be brushed
aside as irrelevant to business. Third, the whole range of questions related
to economic and social development had to be incorporated into the
official vocabulary of a number of trend-setting multinational corpora-
tions, inside and outside the oil industry. The days are gone when an oil
company could simply state that its job is to find and produce oil and get
away with it. Whether the industry likes it or not, it will continue to be
questioned on its track record on the environment, human rights and
socio-economic development.

This new, expanded agenda requires a different understanding of the
predicament of developing countries that are critically dependent on oil for
their future prospects. They are no longer primarily resource-rich territories
but, equally important, countries caught in a development phase replete
with social tensions, economic challenges and political contradictions.
This is a challenge not only to the strategic planning of oil companies, but
also to academic analysis. We need both better tools for understanding the
interaction between economic and political variables and more empirical
knowledge. In order to improve the situation, the Fridtjof Nansen Institute
has initiated a series of studies on the political and economic development
of petro-states, with particular focus on human rights, in close co-operation
with ECON Centre for Economic Analysis, Oslo. The intention is to develop
a framework of analysis that integrates political science and economics in a
coherent fashion and to produce free-standing country studies that are of
interest in their own right, while simultaneously contributing to a better
general understanding of the issues.

This current study of Angola authored by Tony Hodges is an excellent
illustration of the complexity and severity of the problems facing petro-

states. Some of them are unique to Angola, while others can easily be recognized in other oil-producing countries. With this book, Hodges has therefore made a significant contribution to the study of this war-torn country, as well as to the dynamics and failures of petro-states in general.

Helge Ole Bergesen
Fridtjof Nansen Institute
Stavanger

ACRÓNYMS

AAD	*Acção Angolana para o Desenvolvimento* (Angolan Development Action)
ACR	*Africa Contemporary Record*
ADRA	*Acção para o Desenvolvimento Rural e Ambiente* (Action for Rural Development and Environment)
AI	Amnesty International
BNA	*Banco Nacional de Angola* (National Bank of Angola)
BBC	British Broadcasting Corporation
b/d	Barrels per day
BP	British Petroleum
CAP	*Caixa de Crédito Agro-Pecuário e Pescas* (Agro-Livestock and Fisheries Credit Bank)
CBO	Community-based organization
CCF	Christian Children's Fund
CIES	*Centro Informazione e Educazione allo Sviluppo*
CRP	Community Rehabilitation and National Reconciliation Programme (*Programa de Reabilitação Comunitária e de Reconciliação Nacional*)
CSO	Central Selling Organization
DIAMANG	*Companhia de Diamantes de Angola* (Angolan Diamond Company)
DNIC	*Direcção Nacional de Investigação Criminal* (National Directorate for Criminal Investigation)
DPT	Diphtheria, pertussis and tetanus
DRC	Democratic Republic of Congo
DW	Development Workshop
EIU	Economist Intelligence Unit
ENDIAMA	*Empresa Nacional de Diamantes de Angola* (Angolan National Diamonds Company)
EU	European Union
FAA	*Forças Armadas de Angolanas* (Angolan Armed Forces)

FAO	Food and Agriculture Organization of the United Nations
FAPLA	*Forças Armadas Populares de Libertação de Angola* (People's Armed Forces for the Liberation of Angola)
FESA	*Fundação Eduardo dos Santos* (Eduardo dos Santos Foundation)
FLEC	*Frente de Libertação do Enclave de Cabinda* (Front for the Liberation of the Enclave of Cabinda)
FNLA	*Frente Nacional de Libertação de Angola* (National Liberation Front of Angola)
GARE	*Gabinete do Redimensionamento Empresarial* (Office for Enterprise Restructuring)
GDP	Gross domestic product
GNP	Gross national product
GRA	*Governo da República de Angola* (Government of the Republic of Angola)
GRAE	*Governo Revolucionário de Angola no Exílio* (Revolutionary Government of Angola in Exile)
GURN	*Governo da Unidade e da Reconciliacão Nacional* (Government of Unity and National Reconciliation)
HDI	Human Development Index
HIV/AIDS	Human immunodeficiency virus/acquired immune deficiency syndrome
HRW	Human Rights Watch
ICRC	International Committee of the Red Cross
IDP	Internally displaced person
IMF	International Monetary Fund
INAROEE	*Instituto Nacional de Remoção de Obstáculos e Engenhos Explosivos* (National Institute for the Removal of Explosive Obstacles and Ordnance)
INE	*Instituto Nacional da Estatística* (National Statistics Institute)
IOM	International Organization for Migration
Kz	*Kwanza* (Kwanza)
Kzr	*Kwanza Reajustado* (Readjusted Kwanza)
LAC	*Luanda Antena Comercial*, radio station
Libor	London inter-bank offer rate
MAPESS	Ministry of Public Administration, Employment and Social Security
MED	Ministry of Education
MICS	Multiple Indicator Cluster Survey (1996)
MINADER	Ministry of Agriculture and Rural Development
MINARS	Ministry of Social Welfare and Reintegration
MINFIN	Ministry of Finance
MINPLAN	Ministry of Planning

MINTAPSS	Ministry of Labour, Public Administration and Social Security
MINSA	Ministry of Health
MONUA	United Nations Observer Mission in Angola
MPLA	*Movimento Popular de Libertação de Angola* (People's Movement for the Liberation of Angola)
MPLA-PT	*Movimento Popular de Libertação de Angola-Partido do Trabalho* (People's Movement for the Liberation of Angola–Labour Party)
NKz	*Novo Kwanza* (New Kwanza)
OGE	*Orçamento geral do Estado* (General state budget)
OPV	Oral polio vaccine
PIP	Public Investment Programme
PAG	*Programa de Acção do Governo* (Government Action Programme)
PEE	*Programa de Estabilização da Economia* (Economic Stabilization Programme)
PEG	*Programa de Emergência do Governo* (Government Emergency Programme)
PER	*Programa de Recuperação da Economia* (Economic Recovery Programme)
PES	*Programa Económico e Social* (Economic and Social Programme)
PIR	*Polícia de Intervenção Rápida* (Rapid Intervention Police)
PNEAH	*Programa Nacional de Emergência para a Ajuda Humanitária* (National Emergency Programme for Humanitarian Assistance)
PRIMA	*Programa de Reforma Institucional e Modernização da Administração* (Programme of Institutional Reform and Administrative Modernization)
PROESDA	*Programa para Estabilização do Sector Diamantífero em Angola* (Angolan Diamond Sector Stabilization Programme)
PRS	*Partido de Renovação Social* (Social Renewal Party)
PSA	Production-sharing agreement
RNA	*Rádio Nacional de Angola* (Angolan National Radio)
RPA	*República Popular de Angola* (People's Republic of Angola)
SADC	Southern African Development Community
SADF	South African Defence Force
SCF-UK	Save the Children Fund (UK)
SEF	*Programa de Saneamento Económico e Financeiro* (Economic and Financial Clean-Up Programme)
SEPLAN	State Secretariat for Planning

SIGFE	*Sistema Integrado de Gestão Financeira do Estado* (Integrated State Financial Management System)
SINPROF	*Sindicato Nacional dos Professores* (National Teachers Union)
SONANGOL	*Sociedade Nacional de Combustíveis* (National Fuels Company)
SWAPO	South West African People's Organization
TPA	*Televisão Pública de Angola* (Angolan Public Television)
UCAH	*Unidade de Coordenação das Ajudas Humanitárias* (Humanitarian Assistance Co-ordination Unit, of the United Nations)
UNACA	*União Nacional dos Camponeses de Angola* (National Peasants Union of Angola)
UNAVEM	United Nations Angola Verification Mission
UNDP	United Nations Development Programme
UNESCO	United Nations Educational, Scientific and Cultural Organization
UNHROA	United Nations Human Rights Office in Angola
UNICEF	United Nations Children's Fund
UNITA	*União Nacional para a Independência Total de Angola* (National Union for the Total Independence of Angola)
UNITA-R	*União Nacional para a Independência Total de Angola-Renovada* (National Union for the Total Independence of Angola-Renewed)
UNTA	*União Nacional dos Trabalhadores de Angola* (National Workers Union of Angola)
UPA	*União das Populações de Angola* (Union of Peoples of Angola)
UPNA	*União das Populações do Norte de Angola* (Union of Peoples of Northern Angola)
USAID	United States Agency for International Development
USSR	Union of Soviet Socialist Republics
VOA	Voice of America
VORGAN	*A Voz da Resistência do Galo Negro* (Voice of the Resistance of the Black Cockerel)
WFP	World Food Programme

Introduction **1**

Angola presents a terrible, shocking paradox. One of the best resource endowments in Africa has been associated not with development and relative prosperity, but with years of conflict, economic decline and human misery on a massive scale. Few countries present such a stark contrast between economic potential and the state of their populace.

Angola's resource mix is quite remarkable: petroleum, diamonds, numerous other minerals, plentiful land and a generally favourable climate, and huge hydroelectric resources. Its oil industry has grown rapidly in recent years and is now the second largest in Sub-Saharan Africa, pumping out almost 800,000 barrels a day. Angola is also the fourth most important source of diamonds in the world.

If these resources were managed properly, Angola's economy would be among the most dynamic in the developing world. Its people would be amongst the best fed, best educated and healthiest on the African continent. The reality is quite the opposite. Outside the oil and diamond sectors, the economy has been in deep recession for a quarter century, devastated by the destruction and disruption of war and by economic mismanagement. Once self-sufficient in food, the country now has to import half its cereal needs. As Figure 1.1, shows, GNP per capita has been declining in tandem with the rise in oil revenue.

Much of the population has been uprooted by the fighting, swelling the population in the cities, where most scratch a meagre living in the informal economy. Social services such as health and education are in a state of advanced decay, resulting in widespread rising illiteracy and appalling health conditions. Angola now has the second highest child mortality rate in the world: almost a third of children die before they reach the age of five.[1]

---

[1] The under-5 mortality rate is 292 per 1,000 live births, second only to Sierra Leone, another mineral-rich, war-devastated African country (UNICEF, 2000).

Figure 1.1: Oil export revenue and GNP per capita, 1960–97 (constant 1987 dollars)

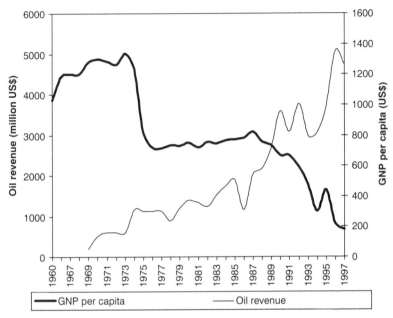

Source: Adapted from Le Billon (1999); World Bank, Africa database CD-ROM

Perhaps the juxtaposition of abundance and misery is not a paradox at all. Could it be Angola's very wealth that has brought it to its current wretched state? One analyst has described Angola as 'a land cursed by its wealth' (Le Billon, 1999: 6). Another has argued that 'oil and diamonds are the twin pillars of the country's wealth and the reason for its poverty' (Munslow, 1999: 551). These writers, and many Angolans too, believe that by engendering conflict, mismanagement and corruption, mineral wealth is ultimately responsible for the country's decline and the plight of its people.

These views are consistent with a body of evidence emerging from comparative studies on the relationship between resources, governance, conflict and development. Surveying the historical evidence, Bergesen and Haugland (2000: 2) have concluded that it is 'clear and indisputable' that

> ...natural resource endowment has not been positively correlated with economic development and social progress. Rather the contrary, international statistics show that countries rich in natural

resources have had a performance which is markedly poorer than those countries that have possessed few natural resources.

In particular, countries rich in minerals have done worse than non-mineral resource-rich countries. A traditional explanation of the poor economic performance of such countries, in particular oil exporters, has been the 'Dutch disease' phenomenon, which results from the negative impact of exchange-rate appreciation on other sectors of the economy. A commodity boom, resulting in a temporary rise in prices and revenue, may also encourage a surge of borrowing, leaving countries with an unsustainable debt burden when prices decline, as happened to many resource-rich African countries, including oil exporters, at the beginning of the 1980s.

However, while the Dutch disease and similar economic phenomena may have serious consequences, including knock-on effects for poverty and political stability, there appear to be other deeper reasons for the poor performance of resource-rich countries, in particular those with mineral resources. Karl (1997) has argued that commodity dependence shapes social classes, the nature of regimes and 'the very institutions of the state'. The fact that the rents from mineral exploitation accrue mainly to the state does indeed suggest that the problems of mineral-rich developing countries are closely related to the relationship between the state and society, including the competition and conflict that may arise to gain or maintain access to these rents through control of the state.

For example, corruption, which has far-reaching effects on economic and social development through its negative impact on tax collection, the rationality of resource allocation, the business climate and growth, appears to be closely correlated with resource endowment and is a notable characteristic of several major oil-exporting countries, including Nigeria, Algeria, Indonesia and Venezuela. Resource-rich countries also appear to be especially prone to conflict: one study has found that a country deriving a quarter of its national income from primary commodities is four times more likely to experience war than one without large primary commodity exports, and has attributed this to the 'looting goals' that motivate rebellions (Collier and Hoeffler, 1999). In Africa, wars in Angola, Liberia, Sierra Leone and the Democratic Republic of the Congo (Zaire), all of which have large mineral resources, would appear to lend credence to the argument.

This book is a case study of a petro-diamond state. By its very nature, this is a multi-disciplinary exercise, crossing the boundaries of history, economics, political science and sociology. Oil and diamonds are not the sole explanatory variables of Angola's many problems. They interact in complex ways with many other factors. The chapters explore these inter-relationships, while also providing a general introduction to the political economy of Angola.

After this brief introduction, Chapter 2 reviews Angola's recent political history, covering the period from the end of the colonial era to 2000. This is to a large extent a history of almost uninterrupted conflict, stretching over four decades, since the start of the armed rising against Portuguese colonial rule in 1961. Chapter 3 assesses the social changes that have transformed Angola over the past few decades. These include massive population displacements, rapid urbanization, deepening poverty and strains on the family structure, changes in ethnic relations and perceptions of identity, the formation of a new post-colonial elite and, since the early 1990s, widening inequality.

Chapter 4 focuses in detail on the nature of the Angolan state and its relationship with civil society. It discusses how political concepts borrowed from the USSR reinforced an authoritarian, bureaucratic system of governance inherited from Portuguese colonialism. A strong presidential system developed, within a formal one-party framework. In 1991, changes in the international environment and the need to achieve peace with UNITA brought about radical constitutional changes, creating a more pluralist political system and greater space for the development of civil society. But the transition was never fully completed, partly because of the return to war, but also due to the weight of old habits and the vested interests of those in power.

This provides a contextual framework for the analysis, in Chapter 5, of the prolonged crisis in the economy, which has resulted from a combination of economic mismanagement and the effects of the war. Problems of economic governance, including entrenched elite interests, the use of patronage as an instrument for the preservation of presidential power, and inadequate transparency and accountability in the management of public resources, together limited the extent, consistency and effectiveness of economic reforms.

Chapter 6 examines the nature of the oil industry, as an economic, geographic and social enclave, and its key role in enabling the regime to build up powerful armed forces, sustain a system of patronage and, through imports of consumer goods, prevent a social explosion in the bloated cities. By contrast, oil revenue has rarely been used for investment in economic diversification or the development of human capital. Lack of transparency in the management of oil revenues is at the heart of the weaknesses in economic governance.

Turning to diamonds, Chapter 7 shows how access to the diamond resources of the north-east enabled UNITA to sustain its capacity for war-making after the loss of international support following the end of the Cold War and the demise of the apartheid regime in South Africa. International sanctions were belated and had only limited effect. On the government side, diamond concessions have become a key mechanism in the patronage system and the formation of the new elite.

Chapter 8 presents final conclusions. A central tenet of the thesis presented here is that predatory characteristics are highly prominent in the distorted form of capitalism that has emerged in Angola since the early 1990s, as a result of the transition from the brief post-independence experiment in Soviet-model socialism, or what might be described as 'Afro-Stalinism'. The enormous opportunities presented by oil and diamond wealth have fuelled the conflict between the government and the rebel *União Nacional para a Independência Total de Angola* (UNITA — National Union for the Total Independence of Angola), providing both a motive to fight for the retention or capture of state power and a means to do so. The Angolan people have been the principal victims of a tragedy that seems to know no end.

2
Four Decades ▌ of War & Upheaval

Angola has been at war for most of the period since nationalists first took up arms against colonial rule in 1961. There were only a few short months of peace in 1974–75, before the country plunged back into war on the eve of independence in November 1975, and two unstable interludes of 'quasi-peace' in 1991–92 and 1994–98. The conflict, particularly since independence, has been hugely destructive, with far-reaching impacts in all domains of Angolan life. A large proportion of the rural population has been uprooted, leading to one of the highest rates of urbanization in Africa. Much of the infrastructure has been destroyed or has been left to decay, and most sectors of the economy are producing less than they did in the early 1970s.

A striking exception to this bleak panorama has been the rise of the oil industry, which has benefited, as the principal means of financing the war, from pragmatic government policies designed to attract foreign investment. Mainly located offshore and so beyond the reach of rebel forces, the industry has also largely escaped the war-related disruption suffered by other sectors. Although more prone to war-related disruption, the diamond industry has also remained a fount of wealth, helping in particular to bankroll the war effort of the UNITA rebels. In recent years, Angola has therefore presented the paradox of immense mineral-based wealth and developmental potential co-existing with economic collapse and social dissolution.

Origins of the conflict

The origins of the Angolan conflict had little specifically to do with the presence of oil or other natural resources. The key causal factors were the nature of Portuguese colonialism, particularly its failure to prepare for a stable transition to independence, and the development of

7

rival nationalist movements, each with different ethno-regional heart-lands, competing external backers and leaderships bent on achieving absolute power at the expense of their rivals.[1]

Unlike the main colonial powers in Africa, Britain and France, which from the mid-1950s began to prepare their colonies for nationhood, the Salazarist regime in Lisbon regarded its African 'provinces' as integral parts of Portugal. Salazarism was an authoritarian political system at home as well as in Africa, and thus there was no democratic tradition in the African colonies prior to the sudden disintegration of the empire in 1974–75. In three of the Portuguese colonies, Angola, Mozambique and Guinea-Bissau, independence followed an armed liberation struggle.

Three principal nationalist movements took shape in Angola in the 1950s and 1960s, sinking roots among different ethno-linguistic groups. *The Movimento Popular de Libertação de Angola* (MPLA — People's Movement for the Liberation of Angola) was founded in Luanda in 1956 and drew its support mainly from the Mbundu, the country's second largest ethnic group.[2] It also attracted some *mestiço* (mixed race) intellectuals, who were prominent in its leadership until the late 1970s. The MPLA dates the start of its liberation war to an attack on a prison in Luanda in February 1961. The movement was almost wiped out in the capital, but then led a small guerrilla campaign in the Dembos forests, to the north-east of Luanda. Most of its leaders went abroad, to organize guerrilla incursions from across the country's borders. The MPLA's guerrilla army, the *Forças Armadas Populares de Libertação de Angola* (FAPLA), began to infiltrate from Congo (Brazzaville) into Cabinda, from 1963, and from Zambia into eastern Angola, from 1966. These were sparsely populated, non-Mbundu areas and, until the Portuguese Revolution in April 1974, the MPLA had little direct contact with its Mbundu heartland. Unlike the other movements, the MPLA was heavily influenced by Marxist ideas, although it was nominally a broad-based nationalist movement. It received arms and diplomatic assistance from the USSR and other Soviet bloc countries from the 1960s.

In the Bakongo-populated extreme north-west, a rebellion also started in 1961. This was organized by the *União das Populações de Angola* (UPA — Union of Peoples of Angola), which was the direct descendant of an explicitly northern movement called the *União das Populações do Norte de Angola* (UPNA — Union of Peoples of Northern Angola), founded by Bakongo emigrés in Kinshasa in the 1950s. The Bakongo are Angola's third largest ethnic group and also constitute a large part of the populations of neighbouring Congo and Democratic Republic of Congo (DRC, or

---

[1] For an in-depth account of the rise of nationalism in Angola, see Marcum, 1969 and 1978.
[2] For a discussion of ethnicity in Angola, see Chapter 3.

former Zaire). Based in Kinshasa, the UPA set up a nationalist 'front', known as *the Frente Nacional de Libertação de Angola* (FNLA — National Liberation Front of Angola), and a 'revolutionary government in exile', the GRAE, in 1962. The FNLA continued to wage a low-key guerrilla war in north-western Angola, backed up from bases in Zaire, where it enjoyed the support of the former dictator, Mobutu Sese Seko.

The third movement, the *União Nacional para a Independência Total de Angola* (UNITA — National Union for the Total Independence of Angola), came into being in 1966. It had very little external support and concentrated on building up an underground political movement among the Ovimbundu, who, despite constituting Angola's largest ethnic group, had not been mobilized to any significant extent by either the MPLA or the FNLA.

There was also a small fourth movement, dedicated to achieving the independence of Cabinda, an oil-rich enclave separated from the rest of Angola by the thin strip of territory which gives the DRC an outlet to the sea. This was the *Frente de Libertação do Enlave de Cabinda* (FLEC — Front for the Liberation of the Enclave of Cabinda), which subsequently splintered into several fractious groups.

Even during the war against Portugal, the leaderships of the three main Angolan movements proved unable to mount a united front, and at times fought each other. This seriously weakened the anti-colonial movement, which by the early 1970s was little more than a minor irritant to the Portuguese. The colony was experiencing one of its periods of most rapid economic growth and there was also heavy inward migration by Portuguese settlers. It was the success of the liberation movements in Mozambique and Guinea-Bissau, not Angola, that eventually brought about the downfall of the Salazarist regime of Marcello Caetano, thereby paving the way for the independence of all five Portuguese African colonies.

The turbulent transition to independence

When the transition to independence began, following the Alvor Accords between Portugal and the MPLA, FNLA and UNITA in January 1975, the nationalist movements quickly proved unable to work together. Instead, they embarked on a desperate race to achieve supremacy before the scheduled date for independence, in November of the same year. This conflict was exacerbated by external intervention, again, not motivated by Angola's oil or other natural resources, but driven by the geo-political rivalries of the Cold War and by South Africa's determination to weaken Angola's ability to aid nationalists in South African-ruled Namibia to the south (Legum and Hodges, 1976).

South Africa, which pursued a classic 'divide-and-rule' strategy by forging an alliance of convenience with UNITA and the FNLA, invaded southern Angola in August 1975 and, by October, had advanced more than half way up the Angolan coast to within 200 km of Luanda. The Zairean army invaded in the north, in support of the FNLA. The United States meanwhile provided covert support to both UNITA and the FNLA, to counter-balance Soviet military assistance to the MPLA. In response to the South African invasion, Cuba sent thousands of ground troops to Angola, from October 1975. This ensured that, when independence was formally declared in November, the MPLA was in control of the capital, where it proclaimed a 'people's republic' and appointed its leader, Agostinho Neto, as president. Over the following few months, the Cubans helped the MPLA to secure control over the whole country. US intervention halted, following the passage of the Clark Amendment, which barred support for any of the Angolan factions (a manifestation of the post-Vietnam mood at the time in the United States). This left the South African government in the lurch, forcing it to withdraw its forces back across the border into northern Namibia in April 1976.

The outbreak of the civil war in 1975 was accompanied by the mass departure of the Portuguese settler community, which numbered about 340,000 (about 5 per cent of the population). Because of the failure of the colonial regime to invest in African education, this exodus meant the loss of the vast majority of the country's managers and technically qualified personnel. Thousands of small businesses and commercial farms were abandoned, and the country was left with a dearth of skilled human resources. Together, the outbreak of war and the settler exodus plunged Angola into a deep economic crisis from which it has never really recovered.

After gaining power, the MPLA was to adopt Marxism-Leninism as its official ideology in 1976, and to convert itself into a 'vanguard party' as the MPLA-*Partido do Trabalho* (MPLA-PT), in 1977. Propelled initially by the abandonment of settler farms and businesses into nationalizing parts of the economy, the MPLA extended state ownership in the second half of the 1970s and attempted to manage the economy through a Soviet-inspired system of centralized planning. The regime's efforts to build a strong state were undermined, however, by the dearth of skills in the public administration. The main exception was the military sphere where, to meet the varied threats to its security, the regime built up strong armed forces with Soviet aid and oil revenues.

The war and external intervention, 1976–91

The FNLA was virtually destroyed as a fighting force in 1975–76 and subsequently suffered further setbacks when the Mobutu regime in Zaire established more cordial relations with the MPLA government in 1978–79.[3] By contrast, UNITA was able to reorganize after its defeat in 1976, due to the resilience of the political structures it had built up in its Ovimbundu heartland, the fierce determination and charisma of its leader, Jonas Savimbi, and, above all, the support it received from South Africa, which provided rear bases in northern Namibia, training, armaments and logistical support. By the early 1980s, UNITA forces were entrenched in rural areas across much of southern and central Angola, and were beginning to expand their operations into the north. By the mid-1980s, they had reached the Zairean frontier and begun to use Zaire as a rear base for guerrilla activities in northern Angola.

In addition to assisting UNITA, South Africa sought to weaken the Angolan regime and the Namibian nationalists by intervening directly in southern Angola. The South African Defence Force (SADF) periodically attacked Angolan military defences and economic infrastructure, bases of the South West African People's Organization (SWAPO) and Namibian refugee camps. Increasingly during the 1980s, South African forces also participated alongside UNITA in large set-piece confrontations with the Angolan and Cuban armed forces, notably by providing heavy artillery and air cover for UNITA troops.

Following the repeal of the Clark Amendment in July 1985, the United States resumed covert assistance to UNITA, thereby once again establishing a de facto alliance with South Africa (Minter, 1994). Along with the Reagan Administration's similar interventions in Nicaragua and Afghanistan, this was part of a global strategy aimed at sapping the resources of the Soviet bloc by fuelling insurgencies against Soviet 'client states' in the Third World. The threats to the MPLA from UNITA, South Africa and indirectly the USA led to large Soviet arms transfers to Angola in the second half of the 1980s, while also prompting Cuba, with Soviet support, to keep up to 50,000 ground troops in the country.

Given this very extensive external involvement, it is not surprising that the main impetus for attempts to settle the conflict came from changes in the external environment, which began at both the international and regional levels towards the end of the 1980s. Under President Gorbachev, the USSR started to extract itself from its costly involvement in civil wars in the Third World. By the end of the 1980s, South Africa too was keen to cut its losses in Angola and find a solution to the Namibian problem. The first concrete step towards external disengagement came in December 1988, when Angola, Cuba and South Africa signed the New York Accords, under which Cuba promised to withdraw all its troops from Angola, in

---

[3] After democratization in Angola in 1991, the FNLA was to resurface as a minor civilian party, its historic leader Holden Roberto winning 2 per cent of the votes in the presidential elections in September 1992.

return for South Africa's withdrawal from southern Angola and UN-supervised elections in Namibia. Implementation of the accords was monitored in Angola by a small UN mission of unarmed military observers, the UN Angola Verification Mission (UNAVEM). The withdrawal of the Cuban troops began in January 1989 and was completed by May 1991. Meanwhile, Namibia proceeded to elections and independence. During this period, the radical changes in the USSR and Eastern Europe, which brought about the collapse of the Soviet bloc and the break-up of the USSR itself, undermined the MPLA's strategic relations with its historical allies and encouraged the MPLA-PT to reassess its ideological commitments.

The ideological shift, 1985–91

These changes in the external context of the conflict coincided with the emergence, within the MPLA regime, of voices calling for a shift away from a centrally planned economy to one based on market forces. This reorientation, which began rather tentatively at the party's second congress in December 1985, appears to have reflected not only unease at the poor performance of Angola's planning system, but also emergent class interests. The leading Luanda families felt constrained by the dominance of the state in the economy and by the official ideology, and began to seek more latitude for the development of private business interests. Although the process of change was at first quite slow, it appears to have enjoyed the support of José Eduardo dos Santos, who had succeeded to the Presidency after President Neto's death in 1979. The first economic reform programme was launched in 1987. In addition, the growing recognition of the impossibility of a military victory over UNITA encouraged political reforms that would permit compromise and reconciliation.

At a meeting of its Central Committee in June 1990, the MPLA-PT decided to abandon the one-party system and allow open political competition between different political parties. This was followed by the formal abandonment of Marxism-Leninism and the 'PT' addendum to the party's name at its third congress, held in December 1990, and the speeding up of economic liberalization under the *Programa de Acção do Governo* (PAG), launched in August 1990. In May 1991, a constitutional revision law (law 12/91) defined Angola as a 'democratic state based on the rule of law' and introduced a multi-party system (RPA, 1991).

As Chapter 4 discusses, these radical reforms brought about a significant democratization of political life and created space for the development of the private sector and civil society, which had been severely circumscribed under the former system. The contraction of the role of the state was accompanied, however, by a weakening of the state's capacity to carry out its remaining core functions, apart from defence, which continued to receive priority in the allocation of resources. Administrative capacity was further eroded by a steep real fall in the value of public sector wages in the first half of the 1990s.

At the same time, the vestiges of administrative intervention in the economy, along with weak systems of transparency and accountability, encouraged cronyism, distorting the transition to a market-based economy. Taking place in an ideological and moral void, left by the abandonment of Marxism-Leninism, this produced a rogue form of capitalism in which a handful of prominent families, linked politically to the regime (now firmly anchored in the presidency rather than the once 'vanguard party'), exploited opportunities for self-enrichment.

The Bicesse peace process, 1991–92

The political reforms within Angola, along with the changes then taking place in the external environment as a result of the end of the Cold War and the demise of apartheid in South Africa, provided a favourable framework for the first serious peace negotiations between the government and UNITA, which took place in Portugal in 1990–91. For the first time, the world powers were pushing their respective clients towards compromise. The USSR was in crisis at home, following the fall of the Berlin Wall and the loss of its Eastern European empire, and could no longer afford to pursue its costly rivalry with the United States in Angola and other parts of the Third World. Meanwhile, South African support for UNITA came to an end, as a result of the radical political changes that followed the assumption of power by F.W. de Klerk in 1989 and the liberation of Nelson Mandela in February 1990. South Africa was in a process of rapid reform, which would culminate in the first multi-racial elections in April 1994.

The talks in Portugal culminated in the signing of the Bicesse Accords in May 1991. The Accords provided for a ceasefire, the quartering of UNITA troops, the formation of new unified armed forces, the demobilization of surplus troops, the restoration of government administration in UNITA-controlled areas and multi-party parliamentary and presidential elections. The peace process was to be overseen by the parties themselves, through a Joint Politico-Military Commission (*Comissão Conjunta Político-Militar*) with back-up support from a new UN mission, UNAVEM II. The Cabindan separatists were not involved in the peace talks and were not a party to the agreement, so a low-level war continued in the enclave. Three external actors were to play an important behind-the-scenes role during the post-Bicesse peace process, as officially designated observers.

This 'troika' consisted of Portugal, as the former colonial power and broker of the Bicesse Accords, and the two superpowers, the United States and the USSR, by virtue of their previous role as the main external backers of the opposing sides.

Despite the improved external and domestic context, however, the period of peace ushered in by the Bicesse Accords was to prove short-lived. Implementation of crucial military components of the Accords proceeded months behind schedule and the new unified armed forces, *the Forças Armadas de Angola* (FAA), were formed only days before the elections were held in September 1992. The two sides still retained large armies of their own, ready for a resumption of the conflict if one side rejected the outcome of the elections. This is what happened, when, despite the UN's certification that the elections were 'generally free and fair', UNITA accused the government of 'stealing the elections', remobilized its forces and went on the offensive, seizing control of numerous small towns and villages in late 1992. The MPLA had won an absolute majority of seats in the National Assembly, with 54 per cent of the votes, compared with 34 per cent for UNITA and 12 per cent for minor parties. In the presidential election, the margin had been narrower, with the incumbent, José Eduardo dos Santos, obtaining 49.6 per cent of the votes and Jonas Savimbi 40.1 per cent. Since neither presidential candidate had an absolute majority, a run-off second round was constitutionally required, but this never took place because of the resumption of fighting.

By the end of the year, Angola was back at war. Analysts of the 1991–92 peace process subsequently highlighted a number of shortcomings in the design of the Bicesse Accords (Anstee, 1997; Saferworld, 1996). First, the UN's mandate and resources had been hopelessly inadequate for the magnitude of the task of restoring peace to a country twice the size of France, with a shattered infrastructure and two heavily armed rival army-parties deeply distrustful of one another. As the head of UNAVEM II, Margaret Anstee, remarked at the time, she had been asked to 'fly a 747 with only the fuel for a DC3'.[4] Secondly, the time-frame for accomplishment of the provisions of the Accords (16 months) had been much too short, considering the number and complexity of the tasks to be carried out, the distrust between the two parties and the logistical obstacles. Thirdly, the elections had not been conditional on the fulfilment of the military tasks and so proceeded in an inherently dangerous context, due to the continued existence of large rival armies. Fourthly, the lack of any requirement for power-sharing under the Bicesse Accords had implied a 'winner takes all' outcome, raising the stakes for both sides.

---

[4] *Financial Times*, 11 May 1992.

Oscillating between war and quasi-peace, 1992–2000

The new phase of fighting which began at the end of 1992 and was to last until November 1994 was the most devastating chapter yet in the Angolan conflict. Because of the disproportionate demobilization of government forces in 1991–92, UNITA was able for the first time (since 1975–76) to occupy and hold large cities. It seized five of the 18 provincial capitals (Caxito, Huambo, M'banza Kongo, Ndalatando and Uíge), while it also subjected some other provincial capitals (notably Kuito, Luena and Malange) to prolonged sieges and artillery bombardments. The UN estimated that about 300,000 people died during this phase of the conflict, either as a direct result of the fighting, the bombardments of civilian areas and landmine incidents, or indirectly because of the acute malnutrition in the besieged cities.

Although UNITA was no longer receiving official assistance from its former American and South African patrons, it still drew considerable logistical advantages from its close relationship with President Mobutu of Zaire. UNITA's main supply lines ran south from the Zairean border. Meanwhile, it was able to adapt to the loss of foreign military assistance by using its control of the main diamond-producing areas to generate substantial revenue from diamond sales. This revenue was used to purchase weapons on the international arms market, which expanded dramatically after the end of the Cold War and the dissolution of the USSR.

Nonetheless, UNITA was not able to sustain its initial military advantage. Rising oil production and revenues enabled the government to rearm, reorganize its armed forces and gradually retake the initiative in 1994. In addition, under Security Council Resolution 864 of 15 September 1993, the UN imposed sanctions on UNITA, banning the sale of arms and fuel to the movement. While these sanctions had little practical effect, the reinvigorated *Forças Armadas Angolanas* succeeded in the second half of 1994 in driving UNITA from most of the cities it had occupied in 1992–93.

Under duress, UNITA finally accepted the terms of a new peace agreement, which had been under negotiation in Lusaka, Zambia, for more than a year. The Lusaka Protocol, which was signed on 20 November 1994, built upon the Bicesse Accords, but introduced some important innovations, including provisions for power-sharing, the postponement of further elections until after the completion of the military tasks, the UN's direct responsibility for overseeing implementation of the peace process and the dispatch of a large UN peace-keeping force. UNAVEM-III had 7,000 troops at its height. The troika also continued to play an important role. Once again, the Cabindan separatist factions were not a party to the agreement.

As in 1991–92, the peace process moved forward at a snail's pace. There were long delays in the quartering of UNITA troops, while their elite units appear never to have been quartered at all and the rebel movement also failed to hand in its heavy weaponry. Most of the more than 70,000 'troops' brought to the UN-administered quartering areas were village reservists or peasants rounded up to boost numbers. The UN failed to call UNITA's bluff and slid down a path of appeasement, which UNITA exploited to procrastinate, resulting in repeated slippage in the timetable for the Lusaka Protocol's implementation. With premature optimism about the outcome of the peace process, the UN decided to withdraw most of its peace-keeping troops in 1997. In June, the Security Council set up a residual mission, the UN Observer Mission in Angola (MONUA), with only 1,500 troops.

On the political front, although the UNITA deputies elected in 1992 were allowed to take their seats in the National Assembly and UNITA ministers were appointed to a Government of Unity and National Reconciliation (GURN) in April 1997, UNITA delayed the extension of state administration to many of the areas under its control. As of May 1998, three and a half years after the Lusaka Protocol had been signed, UNITA still controlled about 60 localities, including its strongholds in the Central Highlands, at Bailundo and Andulo, where Savimbi had established his headquarters.

Growing international frustration with UNITA's foot-dragging finally led to two new rounds of sanctions against the movement. On 28 August 1997, under Resolution 1127, the UN Security Council decided to ban leading UNITA officials from international travel, close UNITA's offices in foreign countries and ban all aircraft from flying to or from UNITA-controlled areas. Following further delays in UNITA's handover of strategic parts of the country, the Security Council voted in Resolution 1173 on 12 June 1998 to subject UNITA to a third set of sanctions. This time, in an attempt to deny it the resources for waging war, the Security Council banned the purchase of Angolan diamonds not accompanied by a government certificate of origin and ordered states to freeze UNITA bank accounts.

By then, the peace process was in crisis. Localized military incidents were multiplying across the country. The UN Observer Mission was drifting rudderless, as a result of the manifest failure of its appeasement strategy. The following month, the head of MONUA (and architect of the Lusaka Protocol), Alioune Blondin Beye, died in an air crash, leaving a void of leadership. UNITA continued to prevaricate and, by the end of the year, the government had lost patience. At the fourth congress of the MPLA, held on 5–10 December 1998, President dos Santos stated that the only path to peace was war. He called for the ending of the Lusaka peace process and MONUA's withdrawal. On the eve of the congress, government forces had begun a military offensive, launching attacks on UNITA's positions in the Central Highlands (UN, 1999b). In February

1999, the UN Security Council decided to withdraw its last remaining peace-keeping forces, because there was no longer any peace to keep. While MONUA was no more, the UN retained a small mission in Luanda, to watch political developments and promote human rights.

Although the government forces at first suffered some serious reverses, by the end of 1999 the FAA had inflicted major defeats on UNITA, driving the movement from both Bailundo and Andulo and from numerous other localities across the country. Unable to defend fixed positions and to continue maintaining heavy armaments, the rebels were obliged to abandon their semi-conventional form of warfare and revert to a more classical form of rural guerrilla tactics. This was a style of warfare to which they had long been accustomed before their seizure of cities and towns in the 1990s, and there was no doubt that they could continue to wreak havoc on rural populations and the economy in many parts of the country.

However, there had been a military turning point in the conflict. The cities were no longer under threat of prolonged siege or seizure. The surrender and desertion of thousands of former UNITA soldiers in 1999–2000 suggested that the movement's morale and cohesion were eroding as a result of the defeats inflicted by the FAA. Meanwhile in Luanda a number of senior UNITA officials had already split from Savimbi in the closing months of 1998 on the eve of the outbreak of full-scale war, forming a breakaway group called UNITA-*Renovada*.

Most important of all, the rebel movement was beginning to suffer from a growing imbalance, relative to the government, in access to resources. It was finding it more and more difficult to supply its forces with arms, ammunition, fuel and other supplies. While the UN sanctions on UNITA's diamond sales had had little effect, due to the ease of smuggling such small high-value goods, the movement had already lost control of its main diamond-mining areas in late 1997 and was running down the accumulated diamond wealth of earlier years.

The transaction costs for UNITA were also rising, because it was becoming much more risky for airfreight companies to fly into UNITA-controlled areas in violation of the UN sanctions. The Angolan government's intervention in the civil wars in the Democratic Republic of Congo (former Zaire) and the Republic of Congo in 1997 had effectively closed off these two neighbouring countries as bases of operation for both UNITA and the Cabindan separatists. With the defeats in late 1998, UNITA had also lost control of its main airfields. These logistical difficulties had their greatest impact on UNITA's fuel supplies, which were becoming a tight constraint on its military capability by 1999.[5]

---

[5] According to a UN report on the effectiveness of sanctions against UNITA, presented to the Security Council on 20 March 2000, there had been instances of UNITA vehicles running out of fuel in battle situations (UN, 2000).

By contrast, the government was not constrained by international sanctions and benefited from a surge in its revenues from oil after the recovery of the international oil market from the collapse in prices in late 1998 and early 1999. It continued to rearm and reintroduced military conscription in 1999, further strengthening armed forces which, with approximately 100,000 troops, are by far the largest in Southern Africa apart from those of South Africa.

The driving forces of conflict

Overall, during the 1990s the oscillation between periods of peace (1991–92), war (1992–94), peace (1994–98) and war (since late 1998) has been driven mainly by internal political factors. Clearly, a major factor in the breakdown of both the Bicesse and Lusaka agreements was the depth of distrust between the two sides. Each has assumed that the other is prone to cheating and bent on absolute power, and has acted accordingly, tending to confirm the suspicions on both sides. The breakdown of the Bicesse Accords could, of course, only accentuate the climate of mutual distrust during the second attempt at restoring peace, after the Lusaka Protocol.

For all its intractability, the war has neither a real social basis, even in terms of ethnicity (an issue discussed in Chapter 3), nor substantive ideological motives, at least since the MPLA's abandonment of Marxism-Leninism. Furthermore, since the end of the Cold War and the transition to majority rule in South Africa, it is no longer fuelled by external strategic interests. Rather, it is a war driven by personal ambition, mutual suspicion and the prize of winning or retaining control of the state and the resources to which it gives access.

In the specific case of Jonas Savimbi, the UNITA leader, a messianic sense of destiny has driven him on in a quest for absolute power for more than three decades, whatever the setbacks or hurdles. Within UNITA, he has wielded absolute power, holding sway over his lieutenants in the manner of a cult leader. This is a product partly of his personal charisma and genuine leadership qualities, but it is reinforced by a fearsome security apparatus, a culture of zero tolerance of dissent and a personality cult that has parallels with those of Mao Tse-Tung and Kim Il-Sung.

Savimbi's over-developed sense of self-importance and his political intolerance do not lend themselves to compromise or to playing second fiddle in a regime headed by someone else. These characteristics go much of the way to explaining why he proved incapable of making the transition from guerrilla commander to civilian political leader or of accepting electoral defeat, as in 1992, and why he demonstrated such weak commitment to implementation of both the Bicesse Accords and the

Lusaka Protocol. Savimbi's cavalier attitude to the agreement was evident from the moment of its signing. He felt constrained into accepting it, because his forces were in headlong retreat as the FAA advanced in the second half of 1994, but he refused to attend the signing ceremony in Lusaka, sending instead the UNITA secretary-general, Eugénio Manuvakola. He then made deliberately ambiguous remarks about the agreement and placed Manuvakola under house arrest in Bailundo.[6] Savimbi, meanwhile, refused to move to Luanda throughout the four-year period of the Lusaka agreement — eloquent testimony to his lack of faith in the entire process.

The failure to achieve peace in Angola cannot therefore be explained purely in structural terms. Besides the rivalry over access to resources and the general problem of mutual lack of confidence, a key factor has been the psychological make-up of Jonas Savimbi. His role in the Angolan conflict confirms the importance of the individual in history.

For most of the participants in the Angolan power struggle, however, crude material interests are the main motives. They are engaged in a struggle for control of the state because it is critical for access to the public resources generated by oil and diamonds. In a society such as Angola, opportunities for personal enrichment are seen to be vastly greater through the arbitrary and corrupted administrative mechanisms of the state, than through the market. In the absence of major foreign patrons since the early 1990s, natural resources (oil and diamonds) have enabled the two sides to sustain their military forces at relatively high levels of sophistication, while the increased revenue from mineral wealth, in particular oil, has raised enormously the stakes of their remorseless struggle for power.

---

[6] Manuvakola later fled to Luanda and set up a dissident faction of UNITA in 1999 (see Chapter 4).

3
Ethnicity, Poverty & the Rise of a Post-colonial Elite

Over the two and a half decades since independence, Angola has seen profound social changes. The country has been transformed from a predominantly rural society to one where about half the population lives in the cities.[1] The normal process of urbanization has been accentuated by successive large waves of population displacement from the rural areas, triggered by events in the war.

Rapid urbanization has been one of a number of factors causing important changes in the nature of ethnicity. It has brought about greater interaction among peoples of different origins, now living together in an urban setting, resulting in a certain cultural fusion, highlighted by the rise of Portuguese at the expense of African languages. At the same time, closer contact risks heightening competition for resources and opportunities, thereby increasing the potential for ethnically based conflict, especially in conditions of economic malaise and wide social inequality. Years of economic decline and under-funding of the social sectors, along with rapid population growth, population displacements and urbanization, have pushed millions of Angolans to the borderlines of survival, while at the opposite extreme the dismantling of the former socialist system since the late 1980s and its replacement by a form of unregulated capitalism, distorted by cronyism, have created opportunities for enrichment on a fabulous scale by a small politically favoured elite.

Population displacements and urbanization

The huge war-related population upheavals have transformed Angolan society. The first of these upheavals was in 1961, when hundreds of

---

[1] In the absence of a national census since 1970, discussion of population issues is based on extrapolations from that census and humanitarian agencies' estimates of the large migratory movements resulting from population displacements.

thousands of Bakongo were uprooted in the north-western provinces, following the harsh colonial response to the UPA rebellion, and took refuge across the border in what is now the DRC (ex-Zaire). Other Bakongo, and Africans in some other parts of the country, were regrouped into fortified villages by the Portuguese. During the 1980s, most of the Bakongo refugees returned to Angola, some settling in Luanda, where they became a prominent part of the petty trading class in the then parallel (now just 'informal') market. The second upheaval came in 1975, when more than 300,000 European settlers left the country and politico-ethnic polarization also sparked off large migratory movements by African minorities – notably by Ovimbundu migrant workers from the coffee estates of the north-west back to their traditional heartland in the centre-west.

During the subsequent war, large numbers of rural people were driven by fear or by force to leave their homes and seek refuge. Most were inter-nally displaced persons (IDPs or *deslocados*), who settled in cities or temporary camps within the country, but a minority became refugees in neighbouring countries (Zaire/RDC, Congo, Zambia and Namibia). By the time of the Bicesse peace accords in May 1991, there were about 800,000 IDPs and 425,000 refugees. During the brief interlude of peace, some but not all of these people returned home. Then, during the war in 1992–94, hundreds of thousands more people were uprooted, many for the second time. By August 1994, there were 1.25 million IDPs, as well as some 300,000 refugees. Following the Lusaka Protocol, the IDPs were more cautious about returning home than had been the case after Bicesse, while the continuing insecurity (including the threat of landmines) and the military division of the country made it impossible for many of them to travel to their areas of origin.

As of June 1999, there were still 400,000 IDPs displaced since 1992–94, according to UN data, in addition to 952,202 confirmed new IDPs uprooted since the resumption of fighting in 1998. As in 1992–94, some of these new IDPs were former returnees, forced to flee a second or even a third time. In short, almost 1.4 million people, or just over 10 per cent of the population (estimated at 13.1 million) were confirmed as displaced in June 1999.[2]

It is important to stress that the definition of 'displaced' used by the UN Humanitarian Assistance Co-ordination Unit (UCAH), the source of these figures, excludes people who were displaced in the past but subsequently became integrated into host communities. It is an operational definition, intended to facilitate planning for humanitarian assistance and for IDPs' eventual return home, and thus does not capture the full extent of war-related displacement over the past two decades (Hodges, 1996). In

---

[2] For a breakdown of data on IDPs by provinces, as of June 1999, see Table A-6.

practice what has happened is that large numbers of previously displaced people have never returned to their rural home areas during the brief periods of peace, but have settled permanently in the cities, often with the support of relatives already there. This process of integration has been facilitated by the fact that relatively few *deslocados* (only about one-quarter according to data from 1996) have been accommodated in camps. It also must be borne in mind that in a very youthful, fast-growing population (over 45 per cent of Angolans are under 15 years of age), families that were originally displaced rapidly include children born in the areas of new settlement. These children grow up with no direct knowledge of the rural areas which their parents left.

The integration of large numbers of former *deslocados* into the cities and the birth of their children into an urban environment, plus the normal 'pull' factors promoting urbanization (better access to education and health services and greater income-earning opportunities), have brought about a fundamental reversal in the rural-urban balance of the population. Whereas only 11 per cent of the population lived in the urban areas in 1960 and 14 per cent in 1970 (Amado, Cruz and Hakkert, 1992), the National Statistics Institute estimated that 42 per cent lived in the cities by 1996 (INE, undated). It is generally believed (in the absence of a national census, last conducted three decades ago, in 1970) that at least half of the population now lives in urban areas, with the population of Luanda alone over 3 million, or almost one-quarter of the national population.[3]

Language and ethnicity

Rapid urbanization has been one of the factors altering the ethno-linguistic characteristics of Angolan society. To understand these developments, it is helpful, by way of a brief digression, to note that the country has three main ethno-linguistic groups, together accounting for about three-quarters of the African population.[4] These groups, or clusters since they are not entirely homogeneous linguistically, are the Ovimbundu, the Mbundu and the Bakongo. Several smaller groups make up the balance of the population.

The Ovimbundu, whose language is Umbundu, were historically concentrated in the rich agricultural provinces of Huambo and Bié, in the

---

[3] The population of Luanda is thus thought to have grown more than sixfold in three decades, from the 480,613 recorded in the 1970 census (of whom a substantial proportion were white settlers who left in 1975). The city's population has more than tripled in the 17 years since the last provincial census in 1983, which recorded a population of 927,867.
[4] The 1970 census indicated that 93 per cent of the population was black, 5 per cent white and 2 per cent *mestiço*, or mixed-race. More than 95 per cent of the whites left Angola after independence.

central high plateau (*planalto central*). During the colonial period, they began to migrate, due to land shortages and competition with white settlers, to the coast (in particular the cities of Lobito and Benguela) and on a seasonal basis to the coffee farms in the north-west. For economic reasons, many Ovimbundu men also joined the Portuguese armed forces. There was a certain industrial development in the Ovimbundu region, with Huambo and Lobito becoming the second and third largest industrial centres (after Luanda), and Christian churches made major inroads, converting much of the population and establishing schools. According to the 1960 census, which was the last to provide such a breakdown, 38 per cent of Africans were Ovimbundu. This proportion seems not to have changed much since then, as a nationwide survey in 1996 (conducted in all 18 provinces, in both government- and UNITA-controlled areas) found that Umbundu was the mother-tongue of 36 per cent of the population (INE, 1999).

The Mbundu (language Kimbundu) have historically been dominant in the capital and its hinterland (the present provinces of Bengo, Kwanza Norte, Malange and the northern part of Kwanza Sul). Although the Portuguese established relations slightly earlier with the Kongo kingdom, the Mbundu had the most sustained interaction with them, dating from the time when the Portuguese set up a permanent colony at Luanda in 1575, as a base for slave trading. Luanda was under Portuguese rule for four centuries, apart from a brief period of Dutch occupation from 1641 to 1648. While most Angolan peoples came into contact with the Portuguese directly or indirectly through the slave trade (up to 4 million were exported from the Angola-Congo region from the sixteenth to nineteenth centuries), the western Mbundu were the only major group to be ruled by the Portuguese, until the scramble for Africa in the late nineteenth century.[5] In the seventeenth century, the Portuguese subdued the western Mbundu kingdom of Ndongo.

Luanda's development as the capital of the colony and main industrial centre brought disproportionately more Mbundu into an urban culture, where, because of the heavy Portuguese settlement and a quite large lusophile *mestiço* community, Portuguese was widely spoken. This appears to have resulted in rapid linguistic and cultural change among urbanized Mbundu, particularly in the last decades of Portuguese rule. This process developed further after independence, despite the departure of the settlers, as urbanization accelerated, bringing more and more Mbundu into an already heavily lusophone environment. It is striking that, by 1996, according to the survey cited above (INE, 1999), only 15 per

---

[5] For most of the period from the seventeenth to nineteenth centuries, Portuguese rule was limited to Luanda and its hinterland and a similar enclave extending inland from Benguela, which was occupied by the Portuguese in 1661 (Henderson, 1979).

cent of Angolans spoke Kimbundu as their mother tongue, whereas 23 per cent of the African population had been classified as Mbundu in the 1960 census.

The third largest ethnic group are the Bakongo, who live mainly in the north-western provinces of Zaire, Uíge and Cabinda, and in neighbouring Congo (Brazzaville) and the Democratic Republic of Congo (ex-Zaire). Their language is Kikongo. Until the arrival of the Portuguese in the Bakongo region in the late fifteenth century, they had a strong, unified kingdom, based at M'banza Kongo (now in northern Zaire province). The Kongo kingdom was greatly weakened by defeats at the hands of the Portuguese in the sixteenth and seventeenth centuries, but a strong sense of Bakongo identity remained. Because they straddle the borders of Angola, Congo and the DRC, many Bakongo have historically had closer affinities with their northern neighbours than with other Angolan peoples to their south, and this was reinforced by the exodus of Bakongo refugees into what is now the DRC after the 1961 rebellion. Although many of these refugees later came back after independence as *retornados*, it is striking that the proportion of Angolans speaking Kikongo was only 8.5 per cent in 1996, much less than the Bakongo share of the population in the 1960 census (13.5 per cent).

The 1996 survey showed that Portuguese had become the second most widely spoken language in the country, as the mother tongue of 26 per cent of Angolans, well ahead of Kimbundu and Kikongo (see Figure 3.1). The advance of Portuguese, at the expense of African languages, has been greatest among the Mbundu, but all African groups have been affected. Urbanization has been one of the driving forces of this process,

Figure 3.1 Distribution of languages, 1996
(% speaking as mother-tongue)

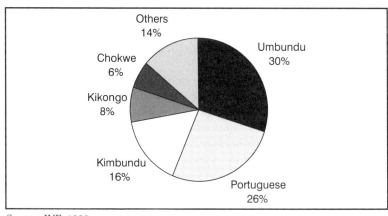

Source: INE, 1999

interacting with other factors, such as the expansion of education after independence and the impact of television. Portuguese has benefited from its status as the sole official language and its promotion by the post-independence government as an instrument of national unity. It has been the exclusive medium of instruction in the schools and has also been the language of the military, providing a common language for generations of conscripts.

The rapid advance of Portuguese is reflected in the age distribution of languages. The 1996 survey found that Portuguese is far more widely spoken by children than among adults. No less than 42 per cent of children under 9 years of age and 34 per cent of those between 10 and 19 speak Portuguese as their first language, whereas these proportions fall to 18 per cent for those aged 20–29 and 10 per cent for those over 40.

The implication is clear: almost half of today's children are being brought up to speak Portuguese as their first language, and Portuguese seems set to outstrip all the African languages, including Umbundu. Although this might pose a long-term threat to Angola's cultural diversity, it could also have the positive effect of helping to develop a stronger national identity at the expense of ethnic particularism. Mandatory military service has also played a unifying role, giving young men from all ethnic groups a shared identity as well as a common language. It has been further argued (Pereira, 1994) that the massive migration into the cities has reduced the influence of the traditional authorities (chiefs and headmen, generically known as *sobas*) and the importance of kinship ties. Last but not least, Zenos (1996: 25) argues that 'sheer exhaustion with 30 years of war is also likely to make most Angolans more interested in peace than in any form of ethnic nationalism that promotes violence'.

To what extent, however, is the war in Angola rooted in ethnicity? As has been noted in Chapter 2, the MPLA and UNITA historically had distinct ethno-regional origins. Although both movements have avowedly nationalist objectives and to some extent multi-ethnic leaderships, it has always been clear where their ethnic loci of gravity lie. The only qualification is that this is more pronounced in the case of UNITA than the MPLA.

UNITA is a fundamentally Ovimbundu party, which has not succeeded to any significant extent in appealing to other ethnic groups. Its leadership is overwhelmingly Ovimbundu.[6] In the 1992 elections, the only provinces where UNITA won more votes than the MPLA were those where the Ovimbundu are the overwhelmingly dominant ethnic group (Benguela, Bié and Huambo) and a fourth sparsely populated province in the south-east (Cuando Cubango) where UNITA had been entrenched since the late

---

[6] A rare exception is the party's vice-president, António Dembo, who is Bakongo.

1970s. In these four provinces, UNITA won 76 per cent of the parliamentary vote and 80 per cent of the presidential vote.

Interestingly, despite the concentration of its support in this part of the country, UNITA has never advocated secession, or the partition of Angola. One reason for this is that the main resources of the country, the ultimate prize in the conflict, are not located in predominantly Ovimbundu areas. The oil resources are concentrated in the north-west, primarily along the coast from Luanda to Cabinda (essentially Mbundu/Bakongo territory), while the main diamond resources are in the Lunda-Chokwe north-east. Nonetheless, in proposals for constitutional revision, submitted to the National Assembly in August 1997, UNITA advocated a federalist system of government, involving the establishment of six regions with a high degree of autonomy, including police forces under the control of regional governments. One region was to be constituted by the predominantly Ovimbundu provinces of Huambo, Bié and Benguela, plus the province of Huíla, which is predominantly non-Ovimbundu except in the north.

Like UNITA, the MPLA swept the September 1992 polls in its 'home turf', winning 85 per cent of the parliamentary vote and 81 per cent of the presidential vote in Luanda, Bengo, Kwanza Norte and Malange. What made the difference for the MPLA was its success in attracting support from other areas where the Mbundu presence is quite limited. In the ten remaining provinces, outside the two parties' core zones, the MPLA did very well, winning 77 per cent of the parliamentary vote and 72 per cent of the presidential vote. Pereira (1994) has concluded that 'it is thus difficult to deny that the 1992 elections revealed strong cross-ethnic support for the MPLA'.

The ambiguity of the ethnic factor in the Angolan conflict is illustrated by the fact that large numbers of Ovimbundu uprooted by the fighting in the *planalto central* have sought refuge in the government-controlled towns. Furthermore, many Ovimbundu are fighting in the government forces, not just because of their numerical importance in the Angolan population as a whole, but because of economic and social factors which have made the people of the *planalto central* a traditional source of recruitment for the armed forces, going back to colonial times. Perhaps most significant of all, the Angolan conflict has rarely been characterized by outbursts of inter-communal violence, acts of ethnic cleansing or communally based massacres of civilians. In this respect, it is quite different from the conflicts in more ethnically polarized African societies, such as Burundi and Rwanda.

Zenos has argued, however, that once economic survival can no longer be guaranteed, there is no certainty that the diverse ethnic groups crowded together in the *musseques* (a reference to the shantytowns built on the sandy wastelands around Luanda) will peacefully co-exist. Warning signs were two outbursts of ethnic violence in Luanda at the start of the 1992–94 war. The first was a pogrom of presumed Ovimbundu supporters of UNITA in November 1992, indirectly encouraged by the government as a way of driving UNITA out of the city following the September 1992 elections. According to Zenos, an estimated 6,000 people were killed. In effect, it was by mobilizing its Mbundu supporters that the government successfully thwarted the risk of UNITA seizing the capital. As Zenos (1996: 18) put it, 'the striking aspect of the November 1992 battle of Luanda is the fact that the ethnically mixed, urban and modern culture of Luanda banded together against a common enemy which was identified ethnically: the Ovimbundu'.[7]

A second round of communal violence came two months later, in January 1993, following government claims that Zaire was assisting UNITA attacks in the north. There were spontaneous attacks in Luanda against Bakongo, transposed by ethnic affinity into *Zairenses* in the popular (Mbundu) mind. About 40 people are thought to have died. Zenos claims that on this occasion the hostility towards UNITA blended with ethnic resentment at the role of Bakongo traders in the informal market, many of whom are *retornados* who came back from Zaire in the 1980s. Together, the events of November 1992 and January 1993 pointed to a 'potential fracturing of the urban ethnic collage' (Zenos, 1996: 25).

The war in oil-rich Cabinda and popular disaffection in the diamond-producing provinces of Lunda Norte and Lunda Sul provide further examples of the potential for ethno-regional conflict – and in the case of Cabinda an overt movement for separation from the Angolan state and nation. In both cases, awareness of the scale of local resources and resentment at their exploitation by outsiders are the motivating factors. In Cabinda, there has been a low-intensity war for years between the government and various factions of FLEC, which at times have benefited from the political complicity of regimes in the neighbouring Congos. In the Lundas, an explicitly regionalist party, the *Partido de Renovação Social* (PRS), appealing to the local Lunda-Chokwe (Angola's fourth largest ethnic group), did well in the 1992 elections, coming second in the parliamentary vote in both provinces, ahead of UNITA. These two cases show the potential risk of ethnic fracturing, and of possible cross-border involvement in localized conflicts by ethnic cousins and/or governments in neighbouring countries, in the absence of effective systems for popular participation and equitable resource management.

Poverty and human deprivation

The backdrop to these actual and potential social tensions is the pauperization of a large part of the Angolan population, alongside the formation

---

[7] For a graphic eye-witness account of these events, see Maier, 1996.

of a conspicuously rich elite, composed of a small number of inter-related families deriving their wealth from their political connections. Although oil gives the country a per capita income ($518 in 1998) that is slightly above-average for Sub-Saharan Africa, much of the population is living in dire poverty. Among the urban population, a 1995 survey found that 61 per cent of households were living below the poverty line, set at $39 per adult equivalent per month, and that 12 per cent were living in extreme poverty, at less than $12 per month (INE, 1996). According to this study, urban households devote 78 per cent of their expenditure to food and 48 per cent to starchy foods, very high levels even by the standards of developing countries and confirmation of the low standard of living.

Most of the urban population is concentrated in the huge informal settlements that have grown up spontaneously around the major cities. These shantytowns have minimal, if any, services or infrastructure, such as electricity, piped water, sewers or rubbish collection, due to the virtual absence of urban planning or infrastructural investment.[8] As a result, the proportion of the urban population with access to piped water and proper sanitation is extremely low, compared with most Sub-Saharan African countries. Data from 1995 show that only 43 per cent of the population of Luanda obtain water from the mains, while 47 per cent have to buy untreated water sold by private vendors from cistern trucks and tanks (INE, 1996). Less than a quarter of the population of Luanda is served by the sewage system (Coopers and Lybrand, 1997).

In view of the decline of the formal sector of the economy and the collapse of salaries in the public administration, most of the urban population depend for their survival on employment and incomes in the informal sector. This sector, which first developed in the mid-1980s as an underground economy during the days of centralized planning, mushroomed during the 1990s, becoming the main source of employment for the rapidly expanding urban labour force. As Figure 3.2 shows, self-employment accounted for 41 per cent of urban employment in 1995, while the civil service was the next main source, at 26 per cent (INE, 1996). However, including those working for others in the informal sector, the sector reportedly accounted for 63 per cent of jobs in Luanda in 1995 (Adauta, 1997).

In fact, for most households, employment in the informal sector has become either the only source of income or the main source, supplementing low wages in the public sector as part of an income-diversifying survival strategy. Most of these informal sector participants, particularly women, are engaged in petty trading, where the barriers to entry, in terms

---

[8] With the exception of a large World Bank-financed project for water and sanitation in the cities of Lobito and Benguela in the mid-1990s.

Figure 3.2 Distribution of urban employment, 1995

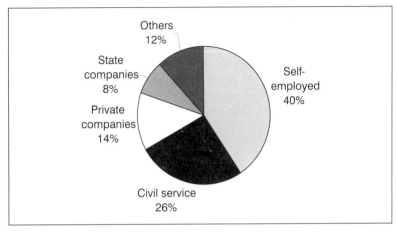

Source: INE, 1996

of literacy, skills and capital, are lowest, but earnings are depressed by a saturated market. The 1995 survey found that 51 per cent of urban families had at least one family member engaged in informal sector trading and that this accounted for 55 per cent of urban households' total income.

There is virtually no formal social safety-net for the vulnerable, apart from the humanitarian assistance provided by international donors through NGOs. Extended family ties provide some kind of informal safety-net, including for those moving into the urban areas for the first time, as *deslocados* or economic migrants. Nonetheless, it is likely that the extended family obligations characteristic of traditional, closely-knit village communities have loosened in large socially heterogeneous urban *bairros*, while poverty limits the scope for supporting needy relatives.[9] Amado and Van-Dúnem (1996) have argued that an intermediary type of urban family structure is emerging, in which nuclear families are becoming increasingly autonomous but retain close ties with other families related by blood and marriage, as a means of providing mutual assistance and solidarity.

As a result of the strains on poor urban families' capacity to cope, new

---

[9] Contrary to commonly held views, the ties and obligations of the extended family have not completely died out in the urban areas, in particular among first-generation migrants. An example of this is given by the finding, in a 1993 survey, that 15 per cent of children in Luanda were not living with their biological parents, but with other relatives, such as uncles and aunts (UNICEF, 1999). In *A Family of the Musseque*, Van der Winden (1996) has described the vitality of extended family ties through the experience of the inter-related members of a cluster of six contiguous households living together in the commune of Ngola Kiluanje, in Luanda.

social problems, which were virtually unheard of in Angola until the early 1990s, have begun to emerge. One of these is the growing phenomenon of children leaving home and living on the streets. It was estimated in 1997 that there were about 1,200 permanent street children in Luanda, in addition to the much larger numbers of children who spend some of their time on the streets hawking or begging (UNICEF, 1999). A parallel development has been the emergence of prostitution, including child prostitution, which has been attributed to the widening of social inequalities in the 1990s (CCF, 1996).

Poverty is more pervasive still in the rural areas, where, in the words of one analyst (Birmingham, 1995: 93), peasants have moved from 'colonial semi-poverty to autonomous self-subsistence of a very low kind'. In much of the country, the peasantry had been integrated into a market economy in the mid-twentieth century, as agricultural labourers and as farmers dependent on a network of colonial 'bush traders' (*comerciantes do mato*). At independence, this system collapsed: both the commercial farmers, who employed cheap African labour, and the traders fled. The state farms and trading companies set up in their place failed to function properly and by the mid-1980s were disintegrating. They were abandoned entirely after the second congress of the MPLA-PT in 1985.

As an urban-based and urban-oriented party, the MPLA-PT had done very little to promote peasant agriculture, and its system of administratively fixed prices, which subsidized urban consumers, discouraged peasant production for the market and gave a competitive advantage to imports. In any case, the war and the constraints on free movement of people and goods prevented a new private trading system from emerging in most rural areas, except on a very limited localized scale. The military division of the country, the collapse of commercial agriculture and the general decline of economic activities also closed off opportunities for the poorer peasant families, with insufficient land to meet their food needs, to supplement their own production with income from employment as seasonal or migrant labourers.[10]

Meanwhile, from the mid-1980s, ever larger numbers of rural people were displaced, while the rural labour force was further depleted by military conscription, by both UNITA and the government, and many peasant households lost most of their livestock, including traction animals, and other assets to raiding troops. One-third of rural families ended up being headed by women, deprived of male labour for land-clearance. In some parts of the country, peasants had to concentrate, for

---

[10] In the colonial period, for example, large numbers of Ovimbundu from the densely populated *planalto central* worked as migrant labourers on the coffee farms of the north-west. Other, more seasonal forms of agricultural employment provided a source of income for poor peasants in parts of the country.

security, in relatively small, overcrowded areas around the cities, resulting in soil erosion and low yields, while landmines strewn on paths and fields were often an additional constraint on farming in these areas.

In the worst situation of all are those who have been uprooted by the war. As has been noted above, almost 1.4 million people, or just over 10 per cent of the population, were confirmed as displaced in June 1999. Most of these *deslocados* are destitute, having been forced to flee their rural homes, abandoning their livestock and other possessions, and settle in camps or the towns, where they are dependent on international humanitarian assistance or extended family solidarity for their survival.

Poverty should not be defined only in terms of household income. In the wider sense of human deprivation, poverty implies the denial of basic social and economic rights, which in other circumstances might be met by free or subsidized public services as well as by access through the market. In Angola, a crucial dimension of poverty is the breakdown of public services, in such fields as education and health. These services have been in long-term decline since the early 1980s, in terms of both coverage and quality, mainly because of inadequate budgets, the decline of institutional capacity and the devastating effects of the war on service provision in the rural areas.

As a result, Angola's social indicators are among the worst in the world. Based on 1998 data, Angola was ranked 160th out of 174 countries in the 2000 edition of UNDP's human development index, a composite index of longevity (life expectancy), educational attainment and standard of living. As Table 3.1 shows, not only are the Angolan people far from realizing their right to development, but for many of them it is the right to survival which is immediately at stake. Life expectancy has been variously estimated at between 42 years (INE, 1999) and 47 years (UNICEF, 2000), lower than the average of 48 years for Sub-Saharan Africa as a whole. It has been estimated that 17 per cent of children die before reaching the age of one and that more than a quarter die before they are five. Indeed, the under-5 mortality rate, estimated by UNICEF at 292 per 1,000 live births in 1998, is more than two-thirds higher than the average for Sub-Saharan Africa.

This situation reflects the precarious living conditions of much of the population, in terms of access to resources and services, as well as environmental hygiene. The breakdown of health services, inadequate nutrition, contaminated water sources and rapid urbanization in a context of virtual absence of urban planning or investments in urban infrastructure are among the key factors that have increased the risks of disease. Throughout the country, it is common to find health posts that are barely functioning or have simply been abandoned, for lack of drugs or staff.

Symptomatic of this situation is the poor vaccination coverage of children, for which the available data show Angola in a significantly

Table 3.1 Social indicators: comparing Angola with Sub-Saharan Africa

(1996 data for Angola, latest available year for Sub-Saharan Africa)

	Sub-Saharan Africa[a]	Angola[b]
Human Development Index (HDI)[c]	0.464	0.405
HDI ranking (out of 174 countries)[c]	...	160
GDP per capita ($)		438[d]
% of urban population living in:		
• Poverty ($39/month per adult-equivalent)	...	61[e]
• extreme poverty ($14/month per adult-equivalent)	...	12[e]
Life expectancy at birth (years)	48	47[f]
Infant mortality rate (per 1,000 live births)	107	170[g]
Under-5 mortality rate (per 1,000 live births)	173	292[h]
% of children 1 year old fully vaccinated[i]	...	17
% of infants with low birth weight (<2.5 kg)	15	18[j]
% of children under 5 with moderate/severe malnutrition:		
• low weight for height (wasted)	9	6
• low height for age (stunted)	41	53
• low weight for age (underweight)	32	42
% of population with access to safe water:		
• total	50	31
• urban	77	46
• rural	39	22
% of population with access to adequate sanitation:		
• total	45	40
• urban	70	62
• rural	35	22
Net enrolment ratio, 1st 6 classes of basic education:		
• total	55	50
• boys	59	52
• girls	51	48
% of pupils starting class 1 who reach class 5	67	30
Adult literacy rate:		
• male	67[k]	50[k]
• female	50[k]	30[k]

Notes

a/ Unless otherwise indicated, average data for Sub-Saharan Africa are from UNICEF, 2000. b/ Unless otherwise indicated, data for Angola are from INE, 1999. This source is the Multiple Indicator Cluster Survey (MICS), a nationwide household survey conducted in 1996 by the *Instituto Nacional da Estatística* (INE) with the technical and financial support of UNICEF. Conducted in all provinces, in both urban and rural areas and in both government- and UNITA-controlled areas, it is the most representative recent survey of social conditions carried out in Angola. c/ The Human Development Index is a composite index, produced annually by UNDP. The index is based on three indicators: longevity, as measured by life expectancy at birth; educational attainment, as measured by adult literacy and combined primary, secondary and tertiary enrolment ratios; and standard of living, as measured by real GDP per capita in US dollars in purchasing power parity terms. Data for 1998 for Sub-Saharan Africa and Angola are from UNDP, 2000. d/ 1999 estimate, from IMF, 2000. e/ 1995 data, from INE, 1996. f/ UNICEF estimate for 1998; calculations from the 1996 MICS data had given a lower life expectancy of 42 years (INE, 1999). g/ UNICEF estimate for 1998; the infant (under one year) mortality rate calculated from the 1996 MICS data was 166 per 1,000 live births (INE, 1999). h/ UNICEF estimate for 1998; the under-5 mortality rate calculated from the 1996 MICS data was 274 per 1,000 live births (INE, 1999). i/ Percentage of children aged 13–24 months fully vaccinated for DPT, measles, polio and tuberculosis (BCG), according to vaccination cards and history. j/ Average data for 1992–95 from Ministry of Health (MINSA, 1997). k/ Estimates for 1995 from UNDP et al., 1996.

worse situation than most African countries: a nationwide survey in 1996 found that only 17 per cent of children aged 1 were fully vaccinated against tuberculosis, DPT, polio and measles (INE, 1999). According to this source, the main causes of death in young children are malaria (38 per cent of deaths of children aged 1–5), acute diarrhoeal diseases (14 per cent) and measles (10 per cent).

Overshadowing these traditional health problems is the spectre of HIV/AIDS. Over the next few years, this is likely to become the single most serious threat to the health and well-being of Angolans, as it already is in most of Southern Africa. HIV prevalence is not yet as high as in countries such as Botswana, Malawi, Mozambique, Zambia and Zimbabwe, due probably to the fact that Angola has been much less integrated into the region, particularly in terms of transport and migration. Nonetheless, the disease already has a firm foothold and is likely to develop rapidly in the near future. Besides reducing further the already low life expectancy of Angolans, the development of the pandemic risks overwhelming the country's creaking health services, plunging yet more households into poverty and producing a generation of AIDS orphans. It is also likely to have devastating effects on production and become a fundamental constraint on economic recovery and development.

By bringing about the death of many of the country's few qualified professionals in the prime of their life, HIV/AIDS is expected to accentuate the acute shortage of skills in the country. This would compound a problem, which had its origins in the failure of the Portuguese colonial authorities to make significant investments in education until the years immediately preceding independence. The post-independence government placed a high priority on widening access to education and this resulted in an impressive rise in school enrolment in the second half of the 1970s. However, the increase in enrolment was not matched by adequate investments. As Pinda Simão, one of the leading education specialists in the country, and in the late 1990s vice-minister of education, has noted:

> The education explosion, in terms of hugely increased numbers at all levels of regular basic education, was not matched by expansion of the educational infrastructure, nor by improvements in teacher training. The result was a sharp decline in quality (Simão, 1995: 62).

Furthermore, during the 1980s, the spread of the war and resource constraints actually reversed the post-independence increase in enrolment. Large numbers of schools were destroyed or abandoned in the rural areas and, as the population swelled in the cities, urban schools were overwhelmed. To try to cope with this situation, the Ministry of Education introduced a triple-shift system, whereby each classroom was used by three groups of pupils each day. Despite this, total enrolment in the three levels of basic education (the eight grades of *ensino de base*) fell from a peak of 1.52 million in 1980/81 to only 1.03 million in 1995/96 (MED, 1996). Meanwhile, rapid population growth meant that the school-age population continued to increase by around 3 per cent a year, and more and more children therefore ended up not attending school.

As a result, enrolment ratios are significantly lower than the averages for Sub-Saharan Africa. For the first six grades of basic education, for example, the net enrolment ratio (defined as the proportion of the 6–11 year old age-cohort which is enrolled in classes 1–6) was only 50 per cent in 1996, compared with 55 per cent in Sub-Saharan Africa. Pupils drop out in large numbers from class to class, with the result that only 30 per cent of those who begin school succeed in reaching the fifth grade, compared with 67 per cent in Sub-Saharan Africa. Very few reach upper secondary, technical or higher education (UNICEF, 1999).

It is questionable, moreover, how much pupils in Angolan schools really learn. Grossly inadequate budgetary allocations have resulted in severe shortages of qualified teachers, textbooks and other teaching materials. Due mainly to low salaries, even the total number of teachers has declined since the early 1980s, from 43,899 in 1981/82 to 38,896 in 1994/95, according to data from the Ministry of Education (MED, 1996). Although there have been no recent scientific studies of school pupils' learning attainment, it is probable that many of those who do manage to complete the first few years of primary education leave school without achieving functional literacy. As Simão (1995: 63) has put it,

> It would be no exaggeration to say that if present trends continue, Angolan youth will be condemned to illiteracy, with all the implications this will have for the nation's future.

Indeed, adult literacy is well below the average rates for Sub-Saharan Africa. It is estimated that only 50 per cent of men and 30 per cent of women are literate (UNDP et al., 1996). This not only deprives a large part of the population of its basic social and cultural rights, but, by constraining and diminishing human capital, it is one of the principal obstacles to future growth and development. The adult literacy programme, which won international acclaim in the post-independence period, had almost entirely collapsed by the early 1990s. In 1994–96, less than 20,000 adults were enrolled in literacy classes, compared with 190,140 in 1980 (UNICEF, 1999).

The low priority accorded to the social sectors in the General State Budget (OGE), due to the crowding-out effects of defence and security expenditure, deserves to be highlighted as one of the fundamental reasons for the decay of these public services. A rigorous analysis of public expenditure is difficult because of the shortcomings in budget execution data, resulting from the fact that substantial extra-budgetary expenditures are not recorded. Since 1999, however, the IMF has been able to obtain a fuller picture of state expenditure, including unrecorded spending not appearing in the normal budget accounts, and on this basis has provided a more accurate sectoral breakdown of expenditure than has been possible in the past (IMF, 1999a, 2000).

These data, illustrated in Figure 3.3, show that, while the share of defence and public order (the armed forces and police) in executed government expenditure remained well above 30 per cent throughout the period 1994–97, the share of the social sectors (education, health, social security, welfare and housing) has consistently been below 15 per cent and in some years below 10 per cent. These are very low proportions, compared with most African countries. The situation worsened following the resumption of the war at the end of 1998. Defense and public order devoured 41 per cent of the executed budget in 1999, while spending on the social sectors dropped to 9.4 per cent. The latter included education, with 4.8 per cent of actual government expenditure, and health, with a mere 2.8 per cent (IMF, 2000).

Figure 3.3 Share of defence/public order and social sectors in General State Budget, 1993–99 (%)

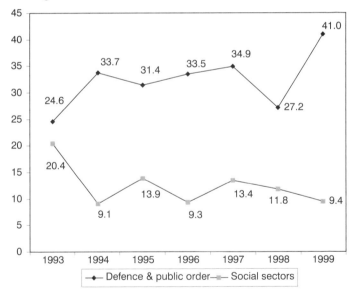

Source: IMF, 1999a, 2000

The formation of a post-colonial elite

The pauperization of the majority of the population has taken place alongside the rise of a wealthy elite, resulting in greater social stratification and inequality. According to the urban poverty study carried out in 1995 (INE, 1996), the monthly expenditure of the wealthiest decile of urban households is twelve times higher than that of the poorest decile of households. This finding indicated a widening of inequality since an earlier study on household incomes and expenditure, limited to Luanda, in 1990, when households of the wealthiest decile spent nine times more than those of the poorest decile (Bender and Hunt, 1991).

The extent of the inequality is not fully captured in such studies, because of the difficulty of obtaining data on the income and expenditure of the wealthiest families and the fact that the latter are but a tiny part of the richest decile. However, the chasm between the richest stratum, collectively dubbed by some Angolans as the '100 families', and the rest of the population is real enough. As one commentator (Boudreau, 1996) has remarked, 'the contrast between very rich and very poor is evident in images encountered daily throughout the country: the sight of malnourished children begging next to brand new Land Rover Discoveries, or destitute amputees leaning against an advertisement for cellular telephones'.

The historian David Birmingham has traced the origins of the present Angolan elite to a fusion of two groups he calls the 'old creoles' and the 'new creoles'. His analysis begins by noting that an indigenous class of black bourgeois families, the 'old creoles', many bearing Portuguese and Dutch names such as Dos Santos and Van Dunem, rose to prominence and wealth in the colony in the nineteenth century. According to Birmingham, they bore with pride the cultural legacy of Europe that gave them their names and their mother tongue, and they looked down on Africans, although they were themselves African and saw themselves as the true sons and daughters of Africa, the 'heirs to the future' (Birmingham, 1995: 91).

The destiny that the old creoles envisaged for themselves in the late nineteenth century was to be thwarted when the republicans seized power in Lisbon in 1910 and introduced half a century of enhanced racism that gave preference to colonial immigrants, to the detriment of culturally assimilated Africans. Resentment among these old *assimilado* families was later to emerge in a political form, through the formation of the MPLA in the late 1950s.[11] In that process, they fused with political

---

[11] In the colonial period, the term *assimilado* loosely meant an African or *mestiço* who could speak and write Portuguese and who had adopted Portuguese cultural values. From the 1920s, it had a more specific legal meaning, referring to those Africans and *mestiços* who were exempted from the status of *indígena* or 'native', and enjoyed the full rights of citizenship. To be recognized as an *assimilado*, a person had to be over 18, speak Portuguese fluently, be self-supporting, adopt Portuguese cultural values and 'be of good character'. Because of the weakness of the education system, there were only about 80,000 *assimilados* by 1960, compared with some 4.5 million *indígenas*. The legal classification was abolished in reforms introduced after the 1961 revolt.

activists from a more recent Portuguese-speaking urban group, the 'new creoles', coloureds (*mestiços*) and *assimilados* who had been educated at mission schools and were likewise competing for jobs with settlers, often less educated than themselves (Birmingham, 1995). Several of the leaders of the MPLA came from this mission-educated *assimilado* and *mestiço* elite. Agostinho Neto, for example, was the son of a Methodist pastor who began his education at a Methodist mission school before continuing on to a state *liceu* in Luanda and university in Portugal. Similar modern elites developed among the Ovimbundu and Bakongo, due to the role in those regions of other Protestant churches, notably the Congregationalists and the Baptists.[12]

Despite the Marxist-Leninist orientation of many of the new creole leaders of the MPLA, the old creole families identified more with the urban Luanda-based MPLA than with the more rural-based movements, UNITA and the FNLA, which appeared 'foreign' and menacing. In short, the creole elite in Luanda saw the MPLA as their best protection against an uncertain future (Messiant, 1992; Zenos, 1996). Moreover, the departure of the Portuguese settlers gave these families new opportunities. As Birmingham has observed, 'the Portuguese-speaking creoles acquired a virtual monopoly of state employment and protected their position not only by running the army and the police but also by preserving often redundant bureaucratic positions and salaries for themselves and their clients' (1995: 93).

Although they also controlled the state enterprises of the command economy, the parallel economy fell largely into the hands of another elite, Bakongo businessmen who had honed their commercial skills in the cutthroat capitalism of Zaire. During the 1980s, these *retornados* began to take over the role previously played by petty Portuguese traders. Birmingham notes (1995: 93)

> ...by the time they returned to Angola they had acquired financial skills which were much needed and very scarce in newly decolonised Angola. They had also developed a political ideology of entrepreneurial capitalism which was in sharp contrast with the ideology of state service which was adopted by Angolans who had remained at home during the colonial war and aspired to step into the shoes of fleeing Portuguese bureaucrats rather than into those of fleeing Portuguese peddlers and merchants.

---

[12] Protestant missions played an especially important role in the formation of a modern educated elite. Martin (1980: 63) has pointed out that, in order not to overlap, the main missions divided up their areas of activity, with the Methodists focusing on the Mbundu, the Congregationalists on the Ovimbundu and the Baptists on the Bakongo. 'These religious loyalties contributed to the tripartite division of Angola by the three main nationalist movements.'

When the FNLA crumbled, following a rapprochement between Mobutu and the Angolan government in 1978–79, many of its former leaders were absorbed into the MPLA state structures and armed forces. Zenos argues that, as in the case of many of the Luanda creole families, this was a survival tactic, rather than the result of a sudden conversion to Marxism.

In the mid-1980s came the first signs of internal questioning of the command economy. The system was a manifest failure. No long-term development plan was ever prepared, despite the pretence at centralized planning, which was reduced (by lack of cadres and the inadequacy of data) to an annual exercise in setting production targets and allocating budgetary resources, foreign exchange and inputs. Due to both the inefficiencies of the system and the disruption caused by the war, production remained far below pre-independence levels in all sectors of the economy, apart from the oil industry where the state pragmatically provided attractive incentives to foreign companies. Meanwhile, the rigidities and distortions created by the arbitrary price controls and an administratively fixed exchange rate generated the development of a huge parallel economy. This grew in scale from the mid-1980s, as shortages became more widespread in the official economy due to the effects of the war and the decline in international creditworthiness and import capacity following the slump in oil prices in 1985–86.

It is reasonable to conjecture that many of those who had joined the MPLA as 'closet capitalists', or who had simply been content in the initial period of MPLA power to take over the roles of the former Portuguese administrators and soldiers, began to see their opportunity to press for economic liberalization. The turning point, in retrospect, appears to have been the second congress of the MPLA-PT in December 1985, which, while not questioning the state's role in the economy as such, acknowledged that the system was not working well and advocated reforms that would give more prominence to market mechanisms.

As Chapter 5 will discuss, the process of change was slow at first. The first economic reform programme, the *Programa de Saneamento Económico e Financeiro* (SEF), was unveiled in August 1987. Few reforms were implemented in practice, although a significant development was the adoption of legislation on the restructuring of state enterprises and the establishment of the *Gabinete do Redimensionamento Empresarial* (GARE), the Office for Enterprise Restructuring, which began the groundwork for later privatization measures.

When more far-reaching and rapid economic reforms began, in 1990–91, they were accompanied by a formal and explicit rejection of Marxism-Leninism, without any change within the top political leadership. The implication is that the leadership itself resolved to embark on a new 'project' for the organization of society and the economy. What is most striking, however, about this transition is that it did not lead to a modern form of capitalism with efficient market mechanisms and a regulatory environment to promote fair competition and protect wider social, environmental and other interests. Instead, the elite families were able, through their political power and influence, to manipulate residual administrative mechanisms to their private benefit.

Since the early 1990s, the opportunities for enrichment by those well-placed in the political system have been enormous, partly, although not only, because of the resources available for redistribution from the state's oil revenues. Munslow (1999: 563) postulates that 'for the political elite with the necessary access, the route to accumulation was fundamentally arbitrage, utilising the dual exchange rate'. As we shall discuss in greater detail in Chapter 5, part of the oil revenue has been made available to the well connected at an artificially low exchange rate, enabling the privileged beneficiaries to make large profits through 'round-tripping' between markets. Often, the recipients have also obtained privileged access to rationed credit from state banks at negative real interest rates. In conditions of high inflation, huge profits could be made from the time lag between the receipt and repayment of the funds, and in some cases the loans have never been repaid. Other opportunities arise from the award of state contracts to businesses owned by the top families, in a system where there are no clear rules for tenders, and from the negotiation of 'under the table' commissions with foreign suppliers of military equipment and other goods and services imported by the government.

The fact that all these funds have come essentially from oil revenues has led some analysts to coin the term 'oil *nomenklatura*' to describe the emergent Angolan bourgeoisie (Ferreira, 1995; Le Billon, 1999). However, diamond mining concessions and diamond trading (both legalized and underground) have also been instrumental in the process of accumulation. There have been additional mechanisms, not directly related to mineral resources, including the acquisition of privatized state assets, including prime real estate, for nominal payments, without prior valuations or competitive bidding, and administrative favouritism in providing business opportunities, such as the allocation of business permits, partnerships with foreign investors and state contracts.

Some of these advantages are mutually reinforcing. For example, profits from arbitrage on foreign-exchange markets are ploughed back into a highly profitable, self-perpetuating cycle of imports and foreign-exchange dealings. Often, the same individuals will have additional business privileges, such as de facto monopolies in certain goods, by virtue of the denial of import licences or business permits to rivals, or the employment of the Economic Police to shut down or thwart rival businesses, citing non-compliance with one or other of the myriad of selectively applied regulations governing business operations inherited from the era of centralized planning. Foreign companies, well aware of the importance of political connections for the winning of contracts and the protection of their investments, tend to reinforce still further the position of these well-placed individuals, by selecting them as business partners or 'advisers'.

The elite families have also been able to gain privileged access to social benefits such as state scholarships for their children to study abroad (in secondary schools as well as at university level), provided by the *Instituto Nacional de Bolsas de Estudos* (National Scholarships Institute) and, until recently, by SONANGOL. The same families are also the main beneficiaries of the *Junta Nacional da Saúde* (National Health Board), a state body which provides for medical evacuation to foreign hospitals. These programmes have received a shockingly high proportion of the limited budgetary resources available for education and health, despite the fact that the national education and health systems are severely under-funded and in a state of crisis. Overseas scholarships accounted for 18 per cent of total education expenditure in 1996, while the *Junta Nacional da Saúde* received 7 per cent of the national health budget in the same year.[13]

In general, the retention of administrative, non-market mechanisms for allocating resources, opportunities and benefits, in the absence of transparent rules and procedures, has encouraged arbitrariness and 'cronyism', while also encouraging rent-seeking behaviour, at the expense of rational resource allocation and wider societal interests. This 'rule-less' system is not only arbitrary, but provides no social protection for the weakest and most vulnerable. In this respect, the abandonment of Marxism-Leninism has left a philosophical or even a moral void, in which there is no longer any sense of social obligation or solidarity. The ethos of 'law of the jungle' capitalism has bred extreme forms of venality in the elite, contributing to a strong sense of moral decay, or a crisis of values in the society.

---

[13] In some years, these figures have been even higher: in 1995, foreign scholarships took 36 per cent of the education budget, while in 1994 the JNS received 15 per cent of health spending (MINFIN, 1995, 1996; UNICEF, 1999).

4

Governance | The Contradictions
of a Stalled Transition

The successive phases of governance in Angola have been closely inter-related with the political, ideological and social evolution described in the preceding chapter. The starting point, after independence, was the superimposition of a Stalinist political model on the already highly centralized and authoritarian political system inherited from Portuguese colonialism. The original aim was to establish a strong state, which could fend off and defeat external and internal enemies, achieve national unity and promote social and economic development through *dirigiste* means. Powerful security forces were built up, with Soviet bloc assistance, and a command economy was established. Soaring oil prices in the late 1970s and then a sustained upward trend in oil production, from the early 1980s, brought about a large increase in the revenue available to the state. However, the 'strong state' was undermined by the lack of popular partic-ipation, a dearth of qualified personnel, the spread of the South African/US backed UNITA insurgency and, from 1986, an unsustainable debt burden.

In the early 1990s, changes in the international context and the urgency of achieving peace with UNITA brought radical changes in governance, including the introduction of a multi-party system, the reduction of the state's role in the economy, partial liberalization of the press and greater space for an active civil society. However, the depth of these changes has been limited by the historical weight of past traditions and methods, the vested interests of the ruling elite and the practical imperatives of state security in conditions of unstable 'quasi-peace' (in 1994–98) and all-out civil war (in 1992–94 and the period since late 1998). The reforms have not been fundamentally reversed, however, leaving governance in an ambiguous state of frozen transition.

As has been described above, vestiges of the old system of adminis-trative allocation of resources have remained, disconnected from their former rationale (central planning or the pursuit of social goals), and have become mechanisms for patronage. Inadequate systems of accountability and lack of transparency facilitate arbitrariness and hinder effective management. At the same time, the state itself has been further weakened by the continued warfare and economic decline, despite unprecedented oil revenues. Budgetary constraints, exacerbated by the war, a heavy debt burden and the virtual evaporation of non-oil revenue, have crippled all branches of the public administration apart from the armed forces and the police, while the war has effectively destroyed local government and public services across large swathes of rural Angola.

The colonial heritage

Like Portugal itself before the 1974 revolution, colonial Angola had a highly centralized administrative system and a repressive political climate. There were no legal opposition parties, the press was tightly controlled, there was no independent judiciary, and dissent was quickly and ruthlessly crushed. Furthermore, the colonial administration was intended fundamentally to serve Portuguese interests, rather than those of the indigenous population. In such a climate, there was no accountability, except to the imperial government in Lisbon, and little transparency, while the top-down administrative culture tended to encourage lack of initiative and excessive red tape.

At independence, Angola inherited the administrative structures and culture of the colonial administration. It had no previous tradition or experience of peaceful, pluralist political competition. Even in the British and French colonies, where independence had been preceded by a brief period of multi-party politics and parliamentary government, later events would show that the democratic tradition had sunk roots that were too shallow to withstand the political, social and economic challenges that would follow independence. In Angola, however, there was no such tradition at all. Worse still, as we have seen earlier, there were intense rivalries among the nationalist movements, resulting in military clashes between them even while they were fighting for independence (Marcum, 1969, 1978). Each of them saw the brief period of coalition government, ushered in by the Alvor Accords of January 1975, ten months prior to independence, as a temporary compromise that would give way to a struggle for total hegemony. Expectations quickly became self-fulfilling.

Another feature of the colonial system that would have far-reaching consequences for post-independence governance was that all modern institutions were staffed overwhelmingly by Portuguese at the technical and managerial levels. Unlike in the British and French colonies, there was no conscious attempt to train and promote Africans to take over senior positions. This reflected, in part, the slow pace of development of the educational system in the colonial period. Although primary school enrolment expanded from the 1960s, 85 per cent of Angolans were still illiterate by the early 1970s and very few had received secondary education. A university was established in 1963, but, as late as 1973, 73 per cent of its students were non-Angolan (Ferreira, 1978; UNICEF, 1999). When Portugal's colonial empire suddenly disintegrated, in a period of just one and a half years following the April 1974 revolution in Lisbon, the large settler population in Angola emigrated *en masse*. This affected all sectors of the economy and undermined most institutions dependent on Portuguese managers, technicians and skilled workers, including in particular the public administration.[1]

The centralized state and political monolithism

During the struggle for independence, the MPLA had been strongly influenced by Marxist-Leninist ideas, due to its links with the Soviet bloc, which provided diplomatic and military support, and underground relations with the Portuguese Communist Party. After independence, the internal and external threats faced by the new regime drove it to construct a strong state, with powerful armed forces and internal security services. At the same time, the abandonment of thousands of small businesses and commercial farms by the departing settlers provided an initial impulse to bring much of the non-oil economy into state ownership. This further encouraged a centralized system of control and decision-making (Tvedten, 1997).

Immediately after gaining power in Luanda, the MPLA proclaimed a one-party state. On Independence Day, Agostinho Neto declared that 'the organs of the state will be under the supreme guidance of the MPLA and the primacy of the movement's structures over those of the state will be ensured'.[2] The leading role of the MPLA was then formally enshrined in the country's first post-independence Constitution, which was ratified by the Central Committee of the MPLA in October 1976. The same Central Committee meeting officially adopted Marxism-Leninism as the MPLA's guiding philosophy (ACR, 1976/77; Somerville, 1986).

However, the establishment of a monolithic political system did not take place overnight. The period accompanying the collapse of the colonial regime and the emergence of an independent state, in 1975–76, had seen a brief interlude of pluralism, popular mobilization and participation – as well as the descent into civil war. Even within the MPLA,

---

[1] It has been estimated (UNDP, 1998) that the civil service lost 80,000 staff. This would seem to be an overestimate, considering the size of the settler population and the fact that many were employed in the private sector or were outside the labour force. However, some non-white civil servants, including in particular many *mestiços*, also left Angola at this time.
[2] Lisbon radio, 11 November 1975.

there were several competing factions, owing to the previous dispersal of the movement's leadership in exile and weak links with its social base at home. During 1975–76, a grass-roots 'people's power' movement developed in the *bairros* of Luanda, under the leadership of far-left groups (ACR, 1976/77). Fierce inter-factional struggles culminated in an unsuccessful coup attempt, led by a former guerrilla commander, Nito Alves, in May 1977, which finally enabled President Neto to eliminate his rivals and achieve uncontested supremacy within the MPLA.

It was only after the bloody events of May 1977 and the subsequent purges in the party, known as 'rectification', that the movement was transformed into a small and disciplined vanguard party, as the MPLA-*Partido do Trabalho* (MPLA-PT), at the first party congress in December 1977 (ACR, 1977/78). Indeed, the 1977 coup attempt may be seen as a watershed in the process of formation of a monolithic political system after independence. One immediate consequence was that it permitted a peaceful transition after President Neto's death in September 1979 to José Eduardo dos Santos, one of Neto's closest collaborators, who was unanimously selected to succeed him by the Central Committee.

The wider consequences of the coup attempt and its aftermath were less beneficial. The mass arrests and executions of dissidents that followed the coup particularly affected the Angolan intelligentsia.[3] The violence of the crackdown instilled a mood of fear that endured until the 1990s, deterring Angolans from dissent and instilling a culture of conformism, dependence on the state and lack of initiative.

Inevitably, this affected the performance of the civil service as well, since many of those killed or purged were working for government ministries. While the public administration was gravely weakened by the settler exodus in 1975 and the events of May 1977, it was called upon to undertake tasks that were far more ambitious than anything attempted during the colonial period. Not only did the new government take action to widen rapidly the hitherto limited access to education and to launch other major social programmes, but, with minimal human resources and inadequate statistical data, it attempted to set up a system of centralized planning. It established a large state sector through extensive nationalization, and attempted, through administrative, non-market methods, to control prices and wages and to allocate foreign exchange and inputs among industries and individual companies.

During these early years, there was no parliament. Instead, the supreme state organ set up at independence was the *Conselho da Revolução*

---

[3] Although the full truth of what happened at that time may never be known, it is probable that a substantial proportion of the limited number of Angolans with a university education were killed or imprisoned. Along with many of his supporters (and some Neto loyalists), Nito Alves was killed in the fighting that broke out in the capital in May 1977. For a detailed account of this episode in Angola's post-colonial history, see ACR, 1977/78.

(Council of the Revolution), a body consisting of nominated members. This was eventually replaced in 1980 by a legislature known as the *Assembleia do Povo* (People's Assembly), which was elected indirectly, in a one-party framework. This body played almost no substantive role, meeting twice a year for sessions lasting no more than a few days in order to rubber-stamp legislation.

While Marxism-Leninism, as practised in its post-Stalinist permutation in the Soviet bloc, provided the ideological framework for the forms of governance established in Angola after independence, it is also quite clear that the attempt to establish a strong state need not have hinged on this particular ideological option. Historical factors in the Angolan case explain why the MPLA-PT took the political route that it did. However, authoritarian systems were established in many African countries on different ideological foundations, albeit usually with less extreme forms of state intervention in the economy.

Indeed, it is important to stress that the UNITA movement practised even more violent forms of political totalitarianism within its own movement and in the areas under its control. Savimbi maintained an iron grip on power and brooked no criticism whatever. UNITA officials who dared to question the leader or fell under his suspicion were executed and, in the late 1980s, there were notorious incidents of entire families of UNITA dissidents, including children, being burned alive on bonfires, accused of witchcraft (Human Rights Watch, 1989; Amnesty International, 1992).

In the MPLA-PT, by contrast, a limited degree of pluralism re-emerged within the party, despite the 'rectification' that followed the events of May 1977. While there were no formalized factions as such, loose groupings competed for influence, particularly after President Neto's death in 1979. During the 1980s, the more doctrinaire Marxists, several of whom were *mestiços*, lost influence. Key members of this group included Lúcio Lara, who was effectively the 'number two' in the regime in the immediate post-independence period and acted as the party's organization secretary until his removal from the Political Bureau in 1985, and Henriques 'Iko' Carreira, the defence minister from 1975 to 1980. A group of more nationalistic black Africans, primarily Kimbundu like the head of state, came to the fore around President dos Santos, and their position was consolidated at the second party congress, held in December 1985.[4]

---

[4] Symptomatic of the internal power struggle between these groups in the early 1980s was the staging of a satirical play which publicly lampooned the 'Afro-nationalists'. The play was audaciously staged at a ceremony marking dos Santos' birthday in August 1982 and resulted in the arrest and detention of its author, Costa de Andrade Ndunduma, until January 1984. The alleged involvement of Lúcio Lara's wife and son in the affair may have hastened the decline of the organization secretary's influence and his removal from the Political Bureau at the second party congress in December 1985.

This development paralleled the emergence of new class interests, discussed in Chapter 3.

The rise of a presidential system

While in formal terms the post-independence Constitution established the primacy of the party and thereby also the pivotal decision-making role of its leading organs (the Central Committee and Political Bureau), the post-independence political system also displayed a strong tendency towards presidentialism from the outset. Under the Constitution, the head of state combined three powerful positions, as president of the party, president of the country and commander-in-chief of the armed forces. He was also effectively the executive head of the government. The fact that Agostinho Neto had acquired an aura and prestige of almost mythical proportions during his long years of exile and leadership of the liberation struggle gave the president great influence in the party, both among the rank and file and in its leadership bodies. Somerville (1986: 92) described Neto's status in the following terms:

> His pre-eminent position introduced the 'presidential' factor into party and national politics. Although decision-making was the prerogative of the congress, the Central Committee and the Political Bureau, Neto was clearly the dominant force and guided the work of leading party and state organs. He had to have the support of his colleagues, but he was very much the first among equals on the Political Bureau.

After Neto's death, this trend towards the concentration of power in the presidency continued, as the regime became overwhelmingly preoccupied with the growing threats from UNITA and South Africa. These security concerns also resulted in growing military influence. The party, meanwhile, had been reduced to a small rump as a result of the purge of membership during the rectification campaign. Between 1975 and 1979, the party's membership fell from 60,000 to 16,500 (ACR, 1979/80; Tvedten, 1997).[5] Most important of all, the external threats provided an opportunity for dos Santos, who still faced some residual factional problems within the party (in particular an underlying current of suspicion from the group around Lúcio Lara), to introduce institutional

---

[5] Membership had recovered to about 30,000 at the time of the second party congress, but, as President dos Santos had noted at a party gathering in January 1985: 'In organisational terms the main problem continues to be the small number of party members compared with our country's population. This has made it impossible for the party to exist, even in the vital and priority sectors of our nation's life' (*Angola Information*, 18 February 1985).

changes that greatly strengthened his position at the expense of the party leadership bodies.

In December 1982, the Central Committee granted the head of state special powers 'in view of the grave situation facing the country'. This was followed, in July 1983, by a decree empowering the president to appoint regional military councils 'in parts of the nation affected by armed acts of aggression, vandalism and banditry'.[6] These councils, which were directly answerable to the president, had sweeping powers concerning economic and political affairs, as well as the conduct of the war, in their respective regions. Through these bodies, as well as the participation of several military officials in government as ministers, vice-ministers and provincial governors, the armed forces came to be closely involved in broader public administration. The FAPLA also had a prominent position in the party, with which it had been intertwined since the days of the liberation struggle against Portugal.[7]

Another related development, in April 1984, was the establishment of a Defence and Security Council, chaired by the President, which effectively became the country's top decision-making body, eclipsing the Political Bureau.[8] This was convenient for dos Santos while he was still contending with Lara, prior to the changes in the Political Bureau at the second party congress at the end of 1985. After that, dos Santos had his own people in both bodies, whose membership then largely overlapped. The President's commanding position by then was reflected in the development of a personality cult, although this did not become as grotesque as that crafted around Savimbi in UNITA territory. The second party congress adopted a thesis entitled *The Role of the Leader in the Revolution*, which eulogized the President in the following glowing terms:

> His prestige, authority and the respect and admiration of militants and the people are becoming increasingly evident, owing to his consistency and honesty in respect of the principles of the revolution and his intelligence and modesty in analysing and solving the party's central problems.[9]

---

[6] *Jornal de Angola*, 31 July 1983.

[7] At the second party congress in 1985, the armed forces accounted for a quarter of the delegates (*Angop*, 2 December 1985).

[8] Chaired by the president and comprising the ministers of defence, state security, interior, planning and provincial co-ordination, as well as the chief of staff of the armed forces, the Defence and Security Council had a very wide mandate to co-ordinate defence and to ensure that sufficient human and material resources were mobilized to win the war (*Angop*, 21 and 30 April 1984). In effect, it became a kind of inner cabinet, supervising the whole government. It carried out this role until it was dissolved in 1991.

[9] *Angop*, 13 December 1985.

By the second half of the 1980s, therefore, power had become increasingly personalized, with its base at Futungo de Belas, the presidential compound on the outskirts of Luanda. Writing at the beginning of the 1990s, one of the foremost analysts of Angolan politics, Christiane Messiant noted that the 'real centres of power...have ceased to be the party itself, its central committee or even its political bureau as such', but have not passed to the government, 'which is still without any real autonomy'. Rather, 'while the military have entered in high numbers into the party-State structures, power has progressively concentrated around the presidency, and the President has been able, although lacking any other social base than the party-State, to impose himself by playing between the various party-State factions' (Messiant, 1992: 21).

Given the size and influence of the armed forces and the military's predisposition to seize power in so many other African countries, it might seem strange that the FAPLA never posed a direct threat to dos Santos during the 1980s. The common threat posed by UNITA and South Africa may provide part of the explanation. The efficient security services, developed with East German assistance, were doubtless another dissuasive factor. Even more important, the presence of large numbers of Cuban troops in the country until 1991 provided a security shield, not just against UNITA and the South Africans, but against potential internal plotters as well.[10]

The democratic reforms of 1991–92

The emergence of new class interests and the triumph of the Afro-nationalists around dos Santos eventually opened the way for the jettisoning of Marxism-Leninism as the regime's official ideology. At the same time, the end of the Cold War, the demise of the strategic alliance with the USSR, a desire for closer relations with the West and the growing urgency of a settlement with UNITA created new imperatives for political liberalization. By its very nature, accommodation with a rival party implied shifting to a more pluralist political system, unless the two parties fused into one. Given their history of intense competition and mutual distrust, however, a merger was not a plausible option.

After the party's formal abandonment of Marxism-Leninism at its third congress in December 1990, a constitutional revision law (law 12/91) was enacted in May 1991, coinciding with the Bicesse Accords. This proclaimed a democratic state based on the rule of law and respect for human rights, and introduced a multi-party political system. The consti-

---

[10] Cuban forces had helped to protect the Neto regime against the Nito Alves group in May 1977.

tutional revision was accompanied, in the same month, by new laws on associations (law 14/91), political parties (law 15/91), the right of assembly (law 16/91), the press (law 25/91) and the right to strike (law 23/91). Further laws in April 1992 established a new electoral system, permitted the establishment of private radio stations, set up a National Press Council (*Conselho Nacional da Comunicação Social*) and eased the requirements for registering political parties, and a second constitutional revision law in September 1992 made additional changes, including provisions for decentralization and elected local government. It also changed the country's name from People's Republic of Angola to the less ideologically charged Republic of Angola.

In this new climate, numerous new parties came into being, along with scores of national non-governmental organizations, community groups and professional associations. Trade unions became independent of the state for the first time, and some small private news weeklies and FM radio stations emerged. Most important of all, the country held its first-ever multi-party presidential and parliamentary elections in September 1992.

However, the transition to a more pluralist, participatory system of governance quickly came under threat. The resumption of the civil war after the elections posed a serious challenge to democratic politics. The war in 1992–94, and later the ambiguous state of 'neither war nor peace', meant that the second round of the presidential elections, required by dos Santos' failure to win an absolute majority of votes in the first round, could not take place. Initially postponed, the second round was officially cancelled in February 1999. The deputies of the second largest party, UNITA, did not take their seats in the National Assembly until almost five years after their election, in 1997. Then, only a year and a half later, the resumption of the war compromised the development of an effective system of parliamentary accountability. Some other key dimensions of democratization, in particular decentralization, were shelved. By the end of the 1990s, a more restrictive, repressive political climate was developing, although the reforms of 1991–92 were not fundamentally reversed.

Presidential power and survival strategies

An important feature of the constitutional changes in 1991–92 is that they confirmed the concentration of power in the presidency, establishing in effect a presidential system of government. In constitutional terms, this was partly due to the formal ending of the 'leading role' of the party and thus its primacy over the executive organs of the state. As we have seen, however, this primacy was little more than theoretical by the late 1980s. The 'vanguard party' had already been relegated to a relatively minor role in the real processes of decision-making, although it was still an important vehicle of social legitimation for the regime.

Under the new Constitution, the government (Council of Ministers) became ambiguously accountable to both the head of state and the National Assembly. In practice, however, the President called the shots, since he was constitutionally empowered to appoint and remove governments and their ministers. The MPLA had in any case a large majority in parliament and, on account of the continued bipolarization of politics resulting from the struggle with UNITA, its parliamentary bench did not break ranks with the president.

At times there have been figurehead prime ministers and at others (including since January 1999) the President has dispensed with the office of prime minister altogether. Throughout, he has chaired the meetings of the Council of Ministers, acting as the effective head of government. He also remains commander-in-chief of the armed forces and appoints the provincial governors, who exercise authority on his behalf in the 18 provinces.

The executive role of the President means that there is a high degree of presidential intervention in the day-to-day management of state affairs. Presidential advisers often have greater influence than ministers, leading to a situation where ministers are unable to assert their authority. Along with shifts in the President's own views on policy issues and frequent changes in ministers, this has resulted in a certain instability in policy-making, particularly with respect to economic reforms.

Dos Santos' ability to retain this dominant position, despite the protracted economic crisis, the pauperization of the population and the failure to restore a lasting peace, appears quite remarkable. In part, the explanation lies in the strength of the army, which, apart from a brief period in late 1992 and during 1993, was able to withstand the direct military challenge from UNITA and, by 1999, was beginning to gain the upper hand. Behind this strength lies the enormous disparity in resources between the two sides, due mainly to the growth in the government's oil revenues.

However, military might does not fully explain dos Santos' ability to retain power during the 1990s. The President has also been able to sustain a certain popularity, especially in the MPLA's traditional core urban/Kimbundu constituency, to fend off urban protests against the decline in living standards, to out-manoeuvre and co-opt potential rivals within the MPLA and in the small independent parties which have emerged since 1991 and, above all, to detract the powerful armed forces from the temptation of coup-plotting.

These achievements are all the more remarkable for a politician who is by nature withdrawn and low-key. He is not a charismatic figure, in the manner of a Nelson Mandela or, closer to home, his arch-enemy Savimbi.

His speeches are pedantic and dull. Moreover, possibly because his health is not good, he has become a recluse since the electoral campaigning days of 1992. For seven years after the elections, until a visit to the southern province of Cunene in 1999, dos Santos never once set foot in the provinces. He remained closeted in Futungo de Belas, rarely venturing out, except to make foreign visits.

To some extent, dos Santos has succeeded by default. He won the 1992 elections (strictly speaking, the first round) largely because of UNITA's continued bellicosity. For all his charisma, Savimbi employed a menacing rhetoric which frightened most of the Angolan population – particularly the non-Ovimbundu and those living in the cities. This sustained the bipolarization of Angolan politics, rallying to the MPLA many of those who, discontented with economic mismanagement and corruption, might otherwise have been tempted to vote for the new 'third way' opposition parties. By contrast with Savimbi, dos Santos employed a slick advertising campaign, designed by a Brazilian public relations company, to project himself and the MPLA as champions of peace, reconciliation and democracy. He demonstrated that, despite his poor public speaking skills, he was a more astute politician, who knew how to connect with the people and their aspirations.

UNITA's failure to grasp that its long-term future lay in the political arena, particularly in the urban areas, was even more evident during the post-Lusaka period, in 1994–98. Although the UNITA deputies provided a modest focus of opposition during a brief period in 1997–98 between their return to the National Assembly and the resumption of war, Savimbi himself remained holed up in his rural heartland in the Central Highlands. By declining to return to Luanda, he was unable to exploit the discontent swelling in the cities at the soaring cost of living, particularly during the economic crisis in 1996 (see Chapter 5), and once again proved his inability to adapt to civilian politics.

Apart from profiting from the political mistakes of Savimbi, dos Santos has astutely cultivated his political base and built alliances, through forms of legalized patronage, or what Messiant has called 'clientelist redistribution' (Messiant, 1992). The privatization of small businesses and property was one of the main methods employed, particularly during the 1991–92 electoral period. The beneficiaries went far beyond the elite to include tens of thousands of urban families who obtained legal title to previously state-owned apartments for token payments. Although the privatization programme ground virtually to a halt from the mid-1990s, after complaints of lack of transparency, the privatization of urban property continued, creating a class which believes that its property rights derive from the current regime (and might be at risk if a rural/Ovimbundu UNITA moved into the cities after taking power). Certain economic policies, such as the large subsidies for fuel, water and electricity, have also been intended to conserve the loyalty of the MPLA's traditional urban social base.[11]

It is important, however, not to overstate the social impact of 'clientelist redistribution'. In the case of the privatization of urban property, its limits have been quite clear. The beneficiaries were the segment of the urban population who lived in the 'concrete city', mainly consisting of apartment blocks built for the waves of Portuguese settlers in the 1960s and early 1970s and then occupied by Africans after the settler exodus in 1975. The majority of the urban population, made up of the more recent urban migrants living in the informal shantytowns around Luanda and other cities, did not benefit. The same was true for the subsidies on electricity and water. These mainly benefited the 'concrete' city-dwellers, rather than the inhabitants of the *musseques*, most of whom do not have electricity and, because they are not linked to the public mains, have to buy their water at free market prices from private vendors.[12]

Another method employed to reconstitute, or stem the erosion of, the regime's traditional social base has been to blame the people's problems on the war, and thus by extension UNITA. The war has served as an alibi for economic mismanagement, allowing the regime to wash its hands of many problems that in truth are of its own making. In addition, the regime has deliberately sought to deflect urban discontent by whipping up xenophobia. In August 1996, when annual inflation exceeded 12,000 per cent and there was intense public discontent at the collapse in living standards, the government blamed the 'speculative' activities of foreign businessmen and launched a campaign, distastefully named Operation Cancer, to round up and deport West African and Asian immigrants.

Over the past decade, thousands of Lebanese businessmen and petty traders from Senegal and Mali have entered the country by bribing corrupt officials. Prominent in the import trade, retailing and currency dealing (sometimes linked to the diamond trade), they are an easy group to scapegoat. During Operation Cancer, which was launched in the wake of the *Nova Vida* programme (see Chapter 5), great publicity was given on

---

[11] Due to delays in adjusting administratively fixed prices and tariffs and the rapid depreciation of the currency, the cost in dollar terms of petrol, water and electricity fell to absurdly low levels. Petrol, for example, cost 4 US cents a litre until a large price hike in February 2000.

[12] An urban poverty study in Luanda in 1995 found that 47 per cent of households obtained water from cistern trucks or tanks, while 43 per cent were supplied from the mains (INE, 1996). Although some of the water obtained from tanks may originate from the water mains, it is sold at free market prices. Thus, less than half the population of Luanda benefits from subsidized water tariffs, which during the 1990s have virtually been free. Due to the growth of the urban population and the scarcity of water supplied from the mains, the free market price, paid by the poorest income groups, soared. In December 1996, the free market price of water ($89 per cubic metre at the parallel exchange rate) was 721,153 times higher than the official water tariff (0.0001 US cents per cubic metre). For a detailed analysis of the urban market for water, see DW, 1995, and UNICEF, 1999.

television to their detention and departure on special flights. In all, about 2,000 immigrants were expelled. The consequent closure of their businesses probably did more damage than good to the economy by further limiting competition, but aspiring Angolan businessmen stood to benefit from the government's action. The campaign was applauded by many urban Angolans and helped to restore the government's popularity at a time when it had fallen to a particularly low ebb. Since then, the anti-foreigner card has been played again: more immigrants were rounded up and foreign businesses closed down in 1999, when the government launched Operation Cancer II.

At the same time, President dos Santos has sought to bolster his own personal reputation by distancing himself from the failures of his government. Although he nominates the ministers and chairs the Council of Ministers, he has on frequent occasions publicly lambasted his ministers for failures for which he ultimately bears responsibility. The hyper-inflationary conditions that developed in May 1996, for example, prompted the president to shield himself from the growing public anger by making a well-publicized visit to a Luanda supermarket, where he expressed his 'astonishment' at the high prices, and then firing his prime minister, Marcolino Moco, replacing the entire team of economic ministers and denouncing their reform-oriented policies. This populist posture was accompanied by attempts to mobilize mass support – significantly not through the MPLA, but instead a new, rather implausibly named body called the National Spontaneous Movement (*Movimento Nacional Espontâneo*).

The events of May 1996 also showed how the regime is prepared to revert to overt forms of repression when the chips are down. Despite the constitutional guarantees of freedom of association, heavily armed anti-riot police were deployed in the streets of Luanda to deter would-be protesters from engaging in demonstrations or strikes.[13] At the same time, an antiquated law from the repressive armoury of the one-party state, the 1978 law on state security (law 7/78), was dusted off to arrest and charge a German Catholic priest, who had dared to distribute leaflets protesting about the high cost of living in a Luanda market. The trial of Padre Barbas, as the priest was known because of his long white beard, was a warning to potential political opponents that attempts to exploit the economic crisis by appealing directly to the masses were off-limits. As we shall see below, the same law has subsequently been rolled out to curb or punish journalists who have displayed excessive independence. These developments have shown that the pluralist democracy established in 1991 is a democracy with clear limits beyond which opponents and critics run

[13] Fear of the *ninjas*, as the paramilitary PIR are popularly known, has been engrained in the public mind since their involvement in the bloody pogrom of UNITA supporters in the capital in October 1992.

serious risks. To keep tabs on potential opponents, the regime has maintained a highly effective internal security apparatus, a body now known
as the *Serviço de Informação*, which reports to the Minister of the Interior.
The intelligence services also monitor the activities of members of the
armed forces. Equally important, the development of the *Polícia de
Intervencão Rápida* (PIR-Rapid Intervention Police) during the 1990s as a
well-equipped paramilitary force independent of the FAA, under the
aegis of the Ministry of the Interior, has created a deterrent to potential
coup-plotters, in some ways compensating for the departure of the Cuban
troops, who performed this deterrent role in the late 1970s and the 1980s.

While clientelist redistribution has had only limited impact in making
up for the loss of purchasing power of the urban population and thus
heading off the risk of a social explosion, much more successful has been
the patronage directed to the *nomenklatura* of politicians, military and
police officers, magistrates, businessmen and senior civil servants.
Patronage, in the form of diamond concessions, the granting of land titles
and other economic favours, has helped to buy the loyalty of military
officers and thwart the risk of a coup d'état.

Along with the risks associated with crossing into the domain of the politically impermissible, the discreet bestowal of favours has also been the
favoured strategy for taming the civilian opposition and limiting the 'risks'
of democracy. One of the most important tools is the financing of political
parties. All the small parties established after the 1991 reforms have
depended almost entirely on state subsidies, which can be turned on and off
as and when the president wishes. Furthermore, numerous new parties
were artificially sponsored by the state, to divide the opposition while
creating an impression of pluralist diversity. Another form of leverage
comes from the fact that virtually all members of the political establishment
(ministers and vice-ministers, provincial governors, senior military and
police officers, presidential advisers, party leaders, deputies in the National
Assembly, senior civil servants with the rank of *director nacional* or above,
magistrates and others) receive annual 'Christmas bonuses', which in some
years have run as high as $30,000, dwarfing their annual salaries.

Oil wealth provides the presidency with enormous resources to buy off
opponents and build alliances, while the lack or non-enforcement of
transparent rules and procedures for the allocation of resources (whether
diamond concessions, state contracts, privatization of state assets, land
titles or business licences) gives the head of state an array of mechanisms
with which to dispense favours. These mechanisms, and the huge scale
on which they are practised, give an important financial dimension to the
highly personalized type of presidential state that developed under dos
Santos during the 1990s.

A new and particularly poignant manifestation of this type of personalized power and private dispensation of state patronage was the creation

of the Eduardo dos Santos Foundation (FESA) in March 1996 as a result of a quasi-private initiative of the head of state.[14] Portrayed as a philanthropic non-profit venture, modelled on the private foundations of the developed world, FESA officially aims to complement the actions of the government by promoting 'the citizens' social welfare and economic development'.[15] According to its prospectus, it provides financing in such areas as education and training, research, community programmes ('mainly intended for displaced people and victims of the war'), cultural programmes and sports (FESA, 1997). Oil companies and other businesses have felt obliged to contribute funds to FESA, to maintain good relations with the authorities, while part of the signature bonuses received by the state upon the award of oil blocks (see Chapter 6) has also been channelled to FESA. Some FESA funds also appear to come from the government budget (Messiant, 1999).

It is ironic that the President should promote his own private philanthropic venture on behalf of honourable social causes when his own government, which he has presided over for more than two decades, has so lamentably failed to prevent over the country's economic decline and the descent of ever greater swathes of the population into penury. The funding made available by FESA is, however, far too small to compensate for the inadequacy of the government's own budgetary allocations for vulnerable groups or for social and economic development. It is difficult to resist the conclusion that the real rationale for the Foundation is to promote the public reputation of the head of state so that he can gain personal credit for actions that should really be financed and implemented through government institutions and programmes. Apart from carrying the President's name and thus creating an aura of presidential concern and generosity (apparently at variance with the real origin of the funds), FESA provides a new avenue for patronage, drawing into its circle NGOs and others who seek to tap its funds.[16] In Messiant's words, FESA crowns the 'process of privatisation of the state'.

---

[14] 'Quasi' is a necessary qualification, as the foundation was later approved by the Council of Ministers, in October 1996 (FESA, 1997).

[15] In some respects, however, the Foundation appears to be working at cross-purposes with the government. A graphic example is FESA's intention to help establish a new private university, the *Universidade Nova de Angola* (UNANG), while the country's single public university, *Universidade Agostinho Neto* (UAN), is under-funded and struggling to survive.

[16] FESA also engages in overt glorification of its 'founder' by organizing week-long seminars and celebrations each year to mark the President's birthday. On one of these occasions, in August 1997, it went so far as to propose his candidature for the Nobel peace prize.

Parliamentary accountability and the party system

Presidential power has been all the stronger in a context where the parliament's ability to provide real checks and balances remains weak. One of the main reasons for this is that UNITA, as the major opposition party, did not take its seats in the new National Assembly from 1992 to 1997 and then was able to provide a credible parliamentary opposition only for a short time before the drift back to war in 1998.

The absence of the 70 elected UNITA deputies in 1992–97 left only 21 non-MPLA deputies, splintered among ten minor parties, in an Assembly dominated by its 129 MPLA deputies. A real parliamentary process did finally begin to take shape when the UNITA deputies took up their seats in April 1997, at the time of the formation of the GURN. For the first time, there were serious parliamentary debates about important policy issues, and state television and radio broadcast these debates live, arousing considerable public interest. This was an important step forward for the development of a pluralist political culture, as well as the process of making government accountable to an elected parliament.

However, the Assembly's effectiveness was still limited by weaknesses in parliamentary procedures, inadequate resources and poor access to information. Deputies have no right to initiate legislation, which can only be submitted by the executive branch of government. Although nine parliamentary commissions were set up, their role in the legislative process and their powers of inquiry were not clearly defined.[17] The research resources available to the commissions and to individual deputies remained extremely limited, and the culture of secrecy and confidentiality in the public administration made it difficult for deputies to obtain adequate data. Deputies also have a very weak sense of representing or being accountable to constituents, largely because of the way in which they are elected on national and provincial party lists. A survey in mid-1998 found that 54 per cent of deputies had never visited their provincial constituencies since their election in 1992.[18]

It might be argued that a more fundamental problem is the financial dependence of opposition parties and most deputies on the state. None of the opposition parliamentary groups, except to a limited extent that of UNITA during a brief period in 1997–98, had significant sources of

---

[17] The nine commissions are for: (1) constitutional and legal affairs; (2) defence, security and internal order; (3) foreign relations, international co-operation and Angolan communities abroad; (4) local govenment; (5) the economy and finance; (6) education, science and technology, culture, religious affairs, sport and the media; (7) health, environment, social affairs, employment and war veterans; (8) the family, youth, children and advancement of women; and (9) human rights and citizens' petitions, demands and suggestions.

[18] Information provided by the Angolan office of the United States Agency for International Development (USAID) on a survey conducted by the International Republican Institute.

income apart from the subsidies provided by the government. Most deputies personally depend on their parliamentary salaries and benefits, which are paid from the government budget, and so are disinclined to challenge the government too overtly on the most serious issues.

The slide back to war during 1998 cast a new cloud over the National Assembly. In March, the government terminated the live coverage of parliamentary proceedings, claiming it was too expensive. Increasingly, the fate of the National Assembly became intertwined with the attempts by the government to weaken UNITA, as it became more and more obvious in mid-1998 that the movement would continue to refuse to honour its obligations under the Lusaka Protocol. As the war clouds gathered, the government tried to engineer a split among UNITA's political cadres, by enticing and cajoling the movement's members of parliament and other UNITA officials in Luanda to break ranks and denounce Savimbi as an unreconstructed militarist. In doing so, the government was able to exploit the growing unease of many of the Luanda-based UNITA parliamentarians and officials about Savimbi's intentions. Many had come to appreciate living in Luanda, where they had been reasonably well housed and subsidized by the government, and were appalled by the prospect of having to return to the bush or exile for a cause that, by then, seemed fated to ultimate failure.

The government did not, however, allow this process of disaffection within UNITA's ranks to develop unaided. Anxious to bring the brewing crisis within UNITA to a head before the outbreak of full-scale hostilities, it became directly involved in generating a split within the movement, using coercion and threats and thereby unintentionally damaging the credibility of the UNITA dissidents, who came to be seen as pawns of the regime. The context of war preparations in which the struggle took place, along with the methods used, inevitably made the National Assembly one of the principal casualties of this battle for the loyalty of UNITA's Luanda-based officials and parliamentarians.

The crisis erupted at the beginning of September 1998, when a dissident faction of UNITA, calling itself UNITA-*Renovada* (UNITA-R), broke ranks with Savimbi. It was led by Eugénio Manuvakola, a former secretary-general of UNITA and the official who had signed the Lusaka Protocol on behalf of Savimbi, and Jorge Valentim, another long-standing UNITA cadre who, like Manuvakola, had been deeply involved in the negotiations in Lusaka and had later become a minister in the GURN. The government immediately threw its weight behind the breakaway group, by branding Savimbi a 'war criminal' and announcing that it recognized the *Renovada* group as the true UNITA and its sole interlocutor, including in the UN-chaired Joint Commission. On 1 September, the government suspended UNITA's four ministers and seven vice-ministers in the GURN and, the following day, police surrounded the headquarters of UNITA in

Luanda, preventing Savimbi loyalists from entering the building, and handed it over to the leaders of UNITA-R.

The crude manipulation of this split by the government alienated many UNITA parliamentarians and officials, despite their unease about Savimbi's course of action. They knew that the breakaway faction would have no influence in the zones controlled by UNITA, where it would be dismissed as a group of government stooges, and that it therefore would not help ward off the threat of war. Consequently, many of UNITA's 70 members of parliament and other Luanda-based officials disassociated themselves from the *Renovada* group. When the President of the National Assembly, Roberto de Almeida, recognized a member of UNITA-R as leader of UNITA's parliamentary bench in place of Abel Chivukuvuku, who had refused to align with the breakaway faction, 53 UNITA deputies signed a declaration on 26 September reaffirming that Chivukuvuku was the leader of their parliamentary group.

Through a crude mix of carrot and stick tactics, the government quickly tamed the UNITA parliamentary bench. It threatened to strip UNITA parliamentarians of their parliamentary privileges and salaries, unless they threw in their lot with UNITA-R. The police raided a number of homes, seized cars and deactivated the cellular phones of several UNITA officials (HRW, 1999). There was a palpable atmosphere of fear and tension, which was dramatized by a shooting incident on 2 October, when Chivukuvuku's vehicle was fired on by unknown assailants outside his home.[19] Some UNITA deputies who had been absent from Luanda at the time of the split and then failed to return were suspended from parliament and replaced by UNITA-R supporters. There was no need to hold by-elections, as Angola's party slate system allows for vacancies to be filled by substitutes on the party list from the previous elections. In January 1999, five UNITA deputies were arrested for alleged complicity with UNITA's military campaign and lost their parliamentary immunity (UN, 1999c). Although one was later freed, the four others were charged in May with rebellion. Most of the UNITA deputies, including Chivukuvuku, ended up steering a middle course, distancing themselves both from Savimbi and from UNITA-R, while keeping a low profile to avoid personal danger. In this climate, the National Assembly could no longer play an effective role as a check on the executive and much of the progress made in developing the parliamentary system in 1997–98 was undone.

The prolonged postponement of new parliamentary elections, although understandable given the insecurity in the country and then the return to full-scale war, has posed a further serious danger for democratic accountability. Under the Constitution, the National Assembly is supposed to have a four-year term of office. New elections were therefore due by

---

[19] His wife and bodyguard were in the vehicle but were not hurt.

September 1996. However, the mandate of the Assembly elected in September 1992 was extended for a minimum of two years in October 1996, due to the delays in the peace process. By mid-2000, the parliament was almost eight years old. New elections were promised for 2001.

Provincial and local government

Democratization at the local and provincial levels, and administrative decentralization, have been further casualties of the failure to sustain and consolidate the peace process begun in 1991–92. The constitutional revision law of September 1992 had envisaged the introduction of elected local government, and had stated that the modalities would be spelt out in a new law, but since then this law has never been submitted to the National Assembly.[20] Throughout the period from late 1992 to the present, the issue of democratization at local level has effectively been shelved, while the government has sought to re-establish state administration in the numerous localities under UNITA control.

Angola therefore retains a system of sub-national government which is based entirely on the nomination of officials from above. This system is a pyramid with three tiers of administration corresponding to the three geographical levels of administrative division: the 18 provinces, 163 *municípios* and 532 *comunas*.[21]

The provinces have provincial governments, headed by governors, who are appointed by the head of state and are considered his representatives at the provincial level. They are generally assisted by two or three vice-governors, one of whom is specifically responsible for defence. There is no provincial assembly or council of any kind, whereas under the former one-party system there had been at least some degree of representation through Provincial Popular Assemblies. In that respect, the lack of follow-up to the 1992 constitutional revision law has made provincial government more remote from the people than it already was.

The militarization of many war-torn inland provinces, along with their isolation from the outside world and the weakness of civil society organizations in these areas, has made it possible for most governors to exercise absolute and unchallenged authority in the areas they rule. Meanwhile,

---

[20] The constitutional revision law stated (Articles 145–7) that local government would be based on two different types of structures: *autarquias locais*, which would have elected representative organs; and local administrative bodies, which would not be responsible to the latter, but would be 'decentralized local administrative units of the central power' (República de Angola, 1994).

[21] Despite their name, *municípios* are not urban units, but geographical districts within provinces. Each province is sub-divided into *municípios* and each *município* into several *comunas*.

the central government, due to difficulties of communication and lack of resources, has to a considerable extent left the governors to their own devices, although they are ultimately removable by the President. Likewise, although many of the ministries have provincial (and in some cases even municipal) 'delegations', in most cases they too are abandoned, receiving little or no resources or guidance from their central headquarters in Luanda. In practice, the governor usually exerts much more influence over these bodies. Increasingly, the provincial governments have also established their own directorates, shifting the locus of responsibility formally away from the central ministries. Ironically, therefore, the centralized, top-down system of government has spawned a high degree of provincial decentralization – but a decentralization by default, without any accompanying provisions for democratic representation, accountability or fiscal decentralization.

It is not surprising in these conditions that some provincial governors have abused their power, turning their provinces or the parts of them under their effective jurisdiction into private fiefdoms. Some governors have used their administrative authority and powers of coercion to create private monopolies (by keeping out or closing down rival businesses), to award public contracts to companies under their control (by ignoring or manipulating procurement regulations) and to acquire local properties.

The pyramidal system of administration continues downwards from the provincial governments to the municipal administrations, and beneath them to the communal administrations. Their heads, the municipal and communal administrators, are appointed by the provincial governors. Again, there are no councils or any other type of representative body to control their actions or voice local concerns.

It must be stressed that, over much of rural Angola, these lower-tier institutions have not existed in any real sense for many years, because of the war. Local administrators and public officials have fled many rural areas, although UNITA established alternative structures to assert its control over local populations.

In the light of this situation, the restoration of state administration in UNITA-controlled areas was one of the principal political components of the Lusaka Protocol. State institutions were to be re-established in 335 localities previously under UNITA control, but this process of administrative normalization did not begin until more than two years after the Lusaka Protocol, in April 1997. By May 1998, state administration had been restored in 272 localities, meaning in most cases that a municipal or communal administrator had been appointed and sent in with a unit of police. However, the subsequent breakdown of the peace process meant that the extension of state administration effectively halted from mid-1998 and then went into reverse. By the end of 1998, most of the areas where government officials returned in 1997–98 had reverted to UNITA control, a situation which continued until the government's military successes at the end of 1999.

Establishment of an effective representative system of local and provincial government would require action at several levels. First, the politico-military division of the country would have to be ended, permitting the re-establishment of a nation-wide unified system of sub-national government and public administration. The second task would be to draft and enact the long-awaited legislation on local government, providing for elected bodies at provincial and municipal levels that would oversee the provision of local services and make these bodies accountable to their populations. Third, measures would be required to provide capacity-building support to these institutions, including training and incentives for the return of personnel to previously war-affected areas, to reverse the exodus of recent years.

Fourth, but by no means last, reforms in the taxation and budgetary systems would be required, to provide for fiscal decentralization and for a system of increased and more fairly distributed transfers from the General State Budget (OGE) to the provinces and local governments. At present, provincial governments and municipal administrations have almost no rights to collect or retain taxes, and thus are dependent more or less entirely on budgetary transfers from the centre. Given the general budgetary constraints facing the state, these transfers have been derisory in recent years, with the provinces receiving only 17 per cent of executed budgeted expenditure in 1996 (MINFIN, 1997).

The armed forces and police

Because of the security threats facing the government, substantial resources have been invested in building up the armed forces and police, which are consequently the primary and arguably the only real manifestation of a 'strong state'. The *Forças Armadas de Angola* (FAA) are backed up by the National Police, which includes a substantial para-military component, the *Polícia de Intervenção Rápida* (PIR), popularly known as the *ninjas*. Alongside the FAA, these police units have played a prominent part in the military struggle against UNITA.

As of late 1998, the troop strength of the FAA was officially 90,000. This number may have increased somewhat as a result of the reintroduction of compulsory conscription in 1999, following the resumption of the war, although there were also substantial losses in manpower from desertions and deaths. Diplomatic sources in Luanda in mid-1999 suggested that the number of troops had not risen much, if at all, above 90,000. Other sources give figures up to 110,000 troops (HRW, 1999). There are no available figures for paramilitary forces, apart from the PIR, which has about 7,000 men. However, the fact that the wage-bill of the police is higher than that of the armed forces, according to the budget reports of the Ministry of Finance, suggests that the number of police is extremely high.

Even taking the lower figure of 90,000 troops for the FAA, and excluding the *ninjas* and other paramilitary forces, Angola still has the largest armed forces in Southern Africa, apart from South Africa where the armed forces number about 130,000, but for a population three and a half times larger than that of Angola. Figure 4.1, which compares Angola with other countries belonging to the Southern African Development Community and with Nigeria, shows that Angola has a higher ratio of troops to population than any of these countries, without taking into account the tens of thousands of additional troops in the UNITA army. While there are 2.5 soldiers for every primary school teacher in Angola, there is less than one in all the other countries, apart from Mozambique.

Nonetheless, even this manifestation of the 'strong state' must be qualified. The inability of the state to provide adequate security has resulted in the proliferation of private security companies, many of which, it is ironic to note, are owned by FAA generals. The private security industry

Figure 4.1 The militarization of Angolan society

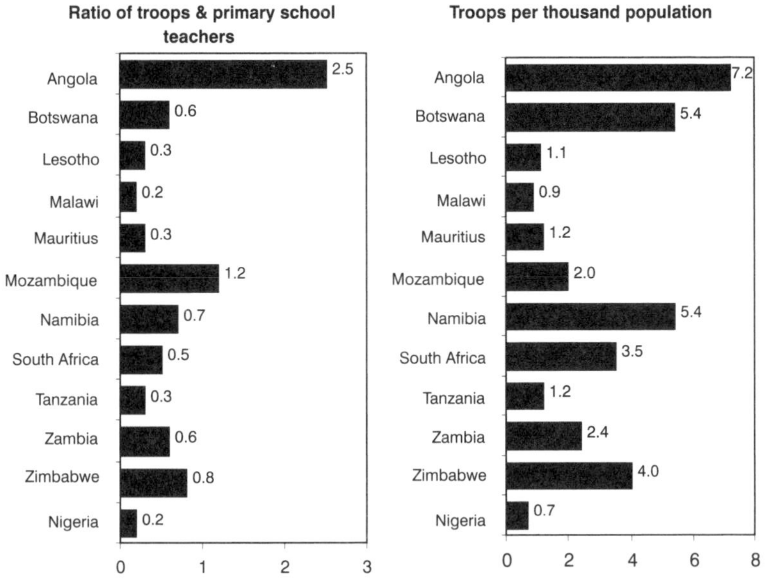

	Ratio of troops & primary school teachers	Troops per thousand population
Angola	2.5	7.2
Botswana	0.6	5.4
Lesotho	0.3	1.1
Malawi	0.2	0.9
Mauritius	0.3	1.2
Mozambique	1.2	2.0
Namibia	0.7	5.4
South Africa	0.5	3.5
Tanzania	0.3	1.2
Zambia	0.6	2.4
Zimbabwe	0.8	4.0
Nigeria	0.2	0.7

Sources: Angolan data from government (for troops), from IOM, 1996 (for population) and from Ministry of Education (for school teachers); data on other countries from International Institute for Strategic studies (for troops), from UNDP, 1999b for population, and from UNDP et al., 1996, for school teachers.

is one of the few booming non-oil sectors of the economy and a prime example of the involvement of senior state officials in private business.

The FAA, of course, have vastly greater financial resources at their disposal than does UNITA. They are given priority in budget allocations and in access to the country's foreign exchange earnings from oil. While UNITA's diamond revenue has been substantial, the limited data available suggest that, on average during 1995–97, the government's expenditure on defence and public order was at least three times higher. This ratio widened dramatically after 1998, as a result of UNITA's loss of control over the main diamond-mining areas and very high government spending on defence and security, which in 1999 amounted to 22 per cent of GDP (IMF, 2000).[22]

The key problems for the FAA are poor morale, discipline and leadership. These debilitating weaknesses result from low pay, arrears in wage payments, the lack of a motivating 'cause' and the preoccupation of much of the officer corps with business activities. The senior generals' extensive interests in the diamond industry, private security companies, air transport companies and other businesses divert their time and commitment from their professional military duties. This decadence in the FAA, which became increasingly evident during the years of peace or quasi-peace in 1994–98, may help to explain why, despite their vastly superior financial resources, the FAA performed so poorly in the initial offensives against the UNITA strongholds in the Central Highlands following the resumption of the war in December 1998.

Public administration

While the regime's main priority has been to build up and maintain strong security forces, the rest of the state administration has been allowed to wither. Public administration already suffered from a high degree of centralization and bureaucracy under the colonial regime. Its effectiveness was severely eroded by the haemorrhage of qualified personnel in 1975–77, while the 'leading role' assumed by the MPLA-PT after independence made it even more difficult to develop a professional civil

---

[22] Information provided by industry sources suggests that total unofficial diamond sales from Angola on the 'outside market' averaged about $575 million a year in 1995–97. Part of these sales was probably accounted for by independent *garimpeiros* (illegal miners and smugglers) not acting on behalf of UNITA. In addition, a significant proportion of the value of diamonds sold by UNITA is likely to be taken by middlemen, because of the high risks involved in this trade. Even assuming that UNITA's net revenue was two-thirds of the gross value of unofficial sales (i.e. about $380 m. a year), this compares with an average of $1,241 m. a year spent by the government on defence and public order in 1995–97, according to IMF estimates of government expenditure (IMF, 1999a). In 1998, there was a sharp decline in diamond sales from UNITA-controlled areas, to an estimated $200 m., because of the restoration of government control of the main diamond-mining areas in December 1997 and the exhaustion of some alluvial deposits previously being mined by UNITA.

service based on principles of public service, transparency and promotion through merit. Since then, the leading role has passed to the presidency, leaving the civil service (and government ministers) exposed to the vagaries of presidential intervention, including the subversion of administrative norms, notably in the management of government finances.

As part of the reforms introduced in the 1990s, the first steps were taken to reform the public administration. An Inter-Ministerial Commission for Administrative Reform was set up in February 1994 and a Programme of Institutional Reform and Administrative Modernization (PRIMA) was launched, with the support of the United Nations Development Programme (UNDP). However, not only have old bureaucratic habits been slow to die, but the quest for improved administrative effectiveness was undermined by the uncontrolled growth of civil service employment and the steep real decline in civil service salaries caused by rapid inflation and budgetary constraints in the early 1990s.

The low level of civil service salaries, along with the increased demand from the private sector for skilled personnel resulting from liberalization of the economy and the growth of the oil industry, has aggravated the severe shortages of qualified personnel in the public administration, while also encouraging moonlighting and corrupt practices by public employees. Furthermore, there have been inadequate systems to ensure transparency, whether in the management of public finances, or in such fields as procurement, the allocation of foreign exchange and import licences and the privatization of state companies. The resulting arbitrariness and abuses have contributed to the tarnishing of the image of the administration, which is widely seen as serving entrenched special interests rather than the public good. A UNDP study has summed up the situation by stating that the Angolan public administration is suffering a 'crisis of values, principles and ethical standards of behaviour' (UNDP, 1998).

The administrative culture still retains many of the characteristics of the hierarchical, centralized system promoted by the colonial and post-colonial regimes. The slow progress towards administrative or fiscal decentralization to the provinces and *municípios*, discussed above, is an example of this. Within ministries, there is little delegation of responsibility, and a tendency for subordinates to avoid taking initiatives, for fear of being seen to challenge the authority of superiors. This has perpetuated the climate of lethargy, resulting in long delays in bureaucratic processes and lack of follow-up of policies and programmes. There is also a weak sense of public duty or service among officials, including in front-line service delivery institutions, such as the National Health Service. This problem has been made much worse in the 1990s by the generalization of the practice of public officials demanding bribes or tips (*gasosas*, literally 'soft drinks') for the provision of services.

Meanwhile, administrative efficiency has been further undermined by the long-term growth in the size of the civil service, which has accumulated numerous overlapping and redundant institutions, and the low level of skills. The proliferation of ministries (and divisions and departments within them) reached a peak with the formation of the GURN in April 1997. Driven by the political need to incorporate virtually all former opposition parties (with seats in parliament), as well as UNITA, the GURN had about 90 ministerial and vice-ministerial posts. In addition, donors have contributed to the proliferation of institutions, by encouraging the establishment of special project units (with special salary regimes justified by the need to provide incentives for effective project execution), duplicating existing bodies within the ministries.

These trends have been accompanied by a growing payroll, which has reflected the tendency to give primacy to the role of the civil service as a source of employment, at the expense of salary levels and efficiency. This expansion has continued, despite a decision by the government in 1991 to freeze the recruitment of public employees with the exception of health workers and teachers. Between 1990 and 1998, total civil service employment rose by 49 per cent from 131,178 to 195,786 (MINTAPSS, 1990; MAPESS, 1999a). Including the armed forces and police, for which there are no comprehensive data, the total size of the government payroll may well be close to 350,000. Although this is only about 5 per cent of the economically active population, it is almost 30 per cent higher than employment in the formal private sector, estimated at 273,500 in 1998.

Data from an exercise to reclassify all civil servants, completed in March 1998, confirm the low level of education of most government employees (MAPESS, 1999a). Only 3 per cent of government employees have received a university education and only 16 per cent have received education at upper secondary or technical level (*ensino médio*). Almost 17 per cent have had less than four years of primary education. The main growth in the civil service has been among administrative and auxiliary staff, which accounted for 73 per cent of personnel in 1998, compared with slightly less than half in 1990.[23]

There has also been a marked tendency towards increased concentration of public employees in the capital and a few other provincial capitals on or close to the coast, because of the insecurity in the hinterland and the successive waves of population displacement. Although 84 per cent of government employees were employed in provincial or local government in 1998, 32 per cent were concentrated in Luanda, 10 per cent in the southern coastal province of Benguela and 9

---

[23] For data on the composition of the public administration and on civil service salaries, see Tables A-1 to A-5 on pp. 175–77.

per cent in the south-western province of Huíla. The other 49 per cent were scattered across the remaining 15 provinces.

Beginning in December 1999, the government planned to reduce civil service employment by 40,000 posts through early retirement or attrition over a three-year period. It remains to be seen whether it will honour this commitment, which is politically sensitive, since it risks pushing yet more urban families into extreme poverty unless special measures are taken to assist those leaving the civil service, most of whom would be likely to have few marketable skills. Nonetheless, civil service reform is essential for achieving real improvements in pay and productivity. The growth in the size of the civil service, along with the large number of ghost workers on the payroll, has been one of the main contributory causes of the low level of civil service salaries, which has undermined morale and performance in the public sector. However, civil service restructuring is only part of the solution. Resources for civil service salaries have also been crowded out by the huge personnel costs of the military and paramilitary forces and by the general budgetary constraints on the government.

During the first half of the 1990s, periodic salary adjustments failed to keep pace with the high rate of inflation, which reached hyper-inflationary levels in 1995–96, resulting in a steep fall in real wages. In the second half of the 1990s, there was some recovery in wage levels, although they are still at very low levels, while efforts to impose fiscal restraint have caused long delays in payments, often for several months at a time, further eroding the commitment of civil servants to their official duties.

Converting data on salaries at the parallel exchange rate, which is applicable to most households' purchases, it may be seen that a university educated professional (*técnico superior*), who earned $269 a month in December 1991, was earning just $8 by December 1995 (Figure 4.2). His/her average salary recovered slightly in 1996–97 but was only $66 in December 1998. Mid-level professionals with an upper secondary or technical college education (*técnicos médios*) were earning on average $38 in December 1998 compared with $136 in December 1991. It should be noted that non-salary benefits add little to the gross value of civil servants' earnings, except at the very highest levels (*directores* and *chefes*).

Because of the steep decline in salary levels in the first half of the 1990s, the share of personnel in the total government budget fell sharply, from 37 per cent in 1992 to 15 per cent in 1994, as Figure 4.3 shows. Since then, it has risen again slightly, reaching 23 per cent in 1998.[24] These

---

[24] It should be noted that these proportions would probably be lower if unrecorded government expenditure was included, since extra-budgetary expenditure is thought not to include a significant salary element.

Figure 4.2 Average salaries of civil servants with university or technical college qualifications, 1991–98
(US dollars per month at parallel exchange rate)

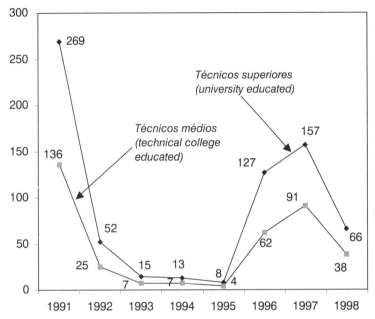

Sources: MAPESS, INE

figures, however, are for the government's total expenditure on personnel, including the armed forces and police. Owing to the size of the security forces, civil service salaries and benefits now make up only about half of the total expenditure on personnel (52 per cent in 1998). Consequently, civil service salaries and benefits accounted for only 8 per cent of total recorded government expenditure at their lowest point, in 1996–97, rising to 12 per cent in 1998.

Households can no longer rely on civil servants' salaries for their survival. In March 1995, when salaries were almost at their lowest point, with a director earning $11 a month and the minimum monthly wage at less than $1, The National Statistics Institute calculated that the minimum basket of goods and services for the survival of an urban household of eight persons was $187. During the 1990s, therefore, households have had to diversify their sources of income, mainly through activities in the growing informal market, increasing the number of household members participating in the labour market and/or individuals engaging in more than one form of employment. In the public administration and public services, this has resulted in high levels of absenteeism, while government employees supplement their incomes through private

Figure 4.3 Share of salaries in executed government expenditure

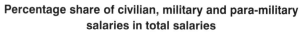

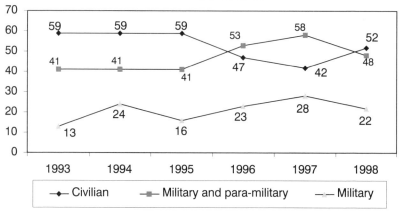

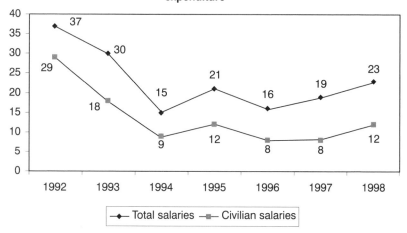

Source: Ministry of Finance

activities. For example, most, if not all, doctors and many other health sector workers unofficially devote a part of their working week to parallel employment in private health clinics, while many teachers in government schools also teach part-time in private schools. These practices have become widespread as a result of the legalization of private health and education services, implemented in 1991 as part of the liberalizing reforms, and the lack of effective controls to prevent private clinics and schools using resources (personnel, equipment, drugs and other materials) diverted from the government sector.

It has been argued (UNDP, 1998) that morale and commitment in the public administration are also adversely affected by discriminatory practices that benefit a few officials at the top. These benefits have included access to foreign exchange at heavily subsidized official exchange rates, to bank credits at negative real interest rates, and to special shops with subsidized prices, and opportunities for travel abroad with high per diem rates. Meanwhile, the practice by which some donors have established special project units within ministries, with much higher salary scales than those prevailing in the civil service, has created additional distortions that undermine still further the morale of civil servants left to survive on low government salaries.

Corruption and lack of transparency

Low salaries are one of the main driving forces of petty corruption, which has become endemic throughout the public administration, particularly in services with a high degree of contact with the general public, such as the police, health services and education. In a survey of civil servants, conducted by the Ministry of Public Administration, Employment and Social Security (MAPESS) and the National Statistics Institute (INE) in 1998, 67.5 per cent of those in professional posts (*quadros técnicos*) and 74 per cent in administrative posts admitted that they would be prepared to accept a 'gift', or *gasosa*, to perform a service (cited in UNDP, 1998).

Teachers, for example, sometimes charge informal fees to enroll pupils in government schools, which are supposed to be free, or to pass pupils in examinations. Indeed, a nationwide survey in 1996 found that 47 per cent of all school-children had to make some kind of payment, in cash or in kind, to attend school, although this is prohibited by the Ministry of Education (INE, 1999). Similar practices are common in the National Health Service, where health workers often charge informal fees for the provision of services. Due to poor management and security, the National Health Service also loses substantial resources from the diversion of equipment, drugs and other materials to private clinics, pharmacies and markets.

Employees of other institutions in contact with the public exploit their positions of authority to extort money for the issuance of documents, such as driving licences, vehicle registration documents and trading licences, which can take months, if not longer, to obtain without a *gasosa*. The obverse of this state of affairs is the harassment of the public by various branches of the police, who supplement their incomes through the imposition of private fines on motorists, traders and others found without the necessary array of documents. For example, the *Polícia de Trânsito* (traffic police) mount innumerable roadblocks in their zeal to catch motorists without valid documents and extract private fines from them. In the same spirit, the *Polícia Económica*, a force set up originally to combat 'economic sabotage', specializes in extorting payments from businesses that try to circumvent the complex bureaucratic procedures needed to maintain their operations.

There is very little documented information about higher-level corruption, although there is a more or less universal presumption among Angolans that it is deeply entrenched in a system of public administration characterized by arbitrariness and lack of transparency. The corrupt image of the regime was reflected in the popular street saying during the 1992 elections that 'the MPLA steals, UNITA kills' (Maier, 1996). One reason that there is so little documented information on this, apart from occasional unproven allegations and insinuations in the private media, is that almost no corruption cases have ever been brought to court. Nonetheless, the problem is acknowledged at the highest levels and, in 1996, the National Assembly adopted legislation establishing a specific body to tackle it, the *Alta Autoridade contra a Corrupção* (law 10/96 of 5 April 1996, reproduced in MAPESS, 1997).

This body is described as an independent organ, functioning under the aegis of the National Assembly, with a mandate to inquire into suspected acts of corruption or fraud within the civil service, armed forces, police, state companies and other public bodies, and to refer alleged cases of criminal behaviour to the Attorney-General's Office *(Procuradoria Geral da República)*. The legislation has remained a dead letter in practice, as the National Assembly has never appointed the president and vice-presidents of the *Alta Autoridade*. The fact that these officials are selected by the National Assembly (for a four-year term) and must command a two-thirds majority of deputies suggests that, if it did exist, this body might not act in a truly independent manner.

It is widely suspected that commissions on government contracts, especially those negotiated for arms contracts (Messiant, 1999), are a prime mechanism of large-scale fraud. Such commissions would be facilitated by the fact that the Angolan government has no operative rules and procedures for procurement.

The lack of transparency in government finances, highlighted by the fact that a large proportion of government revenue and expenditure is not recorded in the official budget accounts (see Chapter 5), makes it especially difficult to detect cases of outright fraud. Furthermore, there is no independent body to audit government accounts. This is supposed to be done by a judicial organ known as the *Tribunal de Contas* (Court of

Accounts), established by law 5/96 in April 1996. According to its mandate, the *Tribunal de Contas* is supposed to audit the executed state budget, for which purpose it has the right to solicit information from any public body, and to submit a report to the National Assembly prior to the annual budget debate. However, as in the case of the *Alta Autoridade contra a Corrupção*, law 5/96 has never been implemented. The president and magistrates of the *Tribunal de Contas* have still not been appointed and this judicial body has therefore never functioned.

Fraud or the theft of public resources is only one extreme way in which state officials might use their positions of power for private enrichment at the expense of society. Possibly more important is the incentive to bribery in a system which places innumerable bureaucratic hurdles in the way of any type of economic activity, while also having minimal transparency and weak, corrupted police and judicial systems. Inadequate transparency and the absence or non-enforcement of rules, procedures and criteria for many types of administrative decisions make it possible for well-connected families or individuals to obtain privileged access to various kinds of resources, opportunities and benefits, at the expense of wider societal interests.

The rule of law and human rights

The constitutional revision laws in 1991 and 1992 provided for the independence of the justice system and, as we have seen, enshrined in law a set of basic rights and freedoms of the citizen. In practice, however, the long history of human rights abuses during the war, along with the repressive practices and methods inherited from the colonial era and the subsequent period of one-party rule, have entrenched habits and reflexes that are antithetical to human rights and the rule of law. As in other domains, the return to war created an inauspicious context in which to overcome that legacy and move forward to build a culture of respect for rights. Furthermore, as in the public administration, chronic weaknesses in the police and the justice system have undermined these institutions' ability to perform their most elementary functions.

During the war, there have been harrowing human rights abuses on a massive scale by both sides. These violations of international humanitarian law, which have been documented in a series of in-depth reports by Human Rights Watch (HRW, 1989, 1994, 1996 and 1999), have ranged from village massacres to rape and other sexual crimes against women, abductions and the stripping of villagers' assets by marauding armies.[25]

---

[25] Along with poor leadership and discipline, the fact that troops are often paid in arrears or not at all has helped to instill a culture of pillage in the FAA. UNITA troops, who are not paid at all, also have to loot to survive.

Very little has ever been done on either side of the conflict to bring the perpetrators of these war crimes to justice. Indeed, even during the inter-regnum of peace in 1991–92 and in 1994–98, upholding human rights was a low priority for the parties to the conflict, who benefited from general amnesties. There have been six successive amnesties in Angola since 1981. Human rights were also given scant attention by the UN and the troika, which feared that holding those guilty of atrocities to account would rock the fragile process of reconciliation.[26] Unfortunately, this approach has simply helped to instill a culture of impunity. Political and military leaders on both sides have little concern for human rights and appear to believe that, as in the past, they will simply be exonerated for crimes through new amnesties in the event of a new peace agreement.

Some of the abuses have nothing to do with the war. For example, there has been great concern, especially among NGOs working with children, about the abuses, including arbitrary detention and rape, committed by the police against street children in Luanda (CIES, 1997).[27]

Despite the liberalization in 1991–92, some of the repressive security laws inherited from the colonial regime or the one-party system have remained on the statute book, although they are clearly inconsistent with the rights and freedoms enshrined in the 1992 Constitution. The failure to set up a Constitutional Court, although this was provided for in the 1992 Constitutional revision law, has made it impossible to challenge the constitutionality of these laws. As we have seen, the government has at times employed the 1978 Law on Crimes against State Security (law 7/78), which dates back to the repressive period that followed the May 1977 coup attempt, to silence political opponents and critical journalists.

Just as significant is the non-application of laws, without any real possi-bility of challenge in court, when it suits the government to ignore them.

---

[26] In a comprehensive report on the breakdown of the Lusaka Protocol, entitled *Angola Unravels*, Human Rights Watch has documented how UNAVEM and later MONUA gave low priority to addressing human rights issues, despite having a Human Rights Division. 'The UN's Human Rights Division was ineffective because it had chosen not to report abuses in the public domain....This was consistent with UN Special Representative Beye's belief that exposing human rights abuses could undermine the peace process and his public welcoming of an amnesty....The UN approach to human rights issues in the period November 1994 to May 1998 did little to create awareness of human rights issues or accountability for even the gravest abuses. It achieved even less in advancing a culture of respect for human rights' (HRW, 1999). Human Rights Watch noted that, with the peace process in crisis in mid-1998, the UN finally adopted a more forthright approach, but within a few months the country was back at war, making it far more difficult to promote and protect human rights. After the return to full-scale war, MONUA's mandate expired in February 1999. Significantly, however, the UN decided to retain a strong human rights unit in the country, transforming the Human Rights Division into the UN Human Rights Office in Angola (UNHROA).

[27] In May 1997, a group of street children with the support of NGOs communicated their complaints of harassment and ill-treatment directly to the Ministry of Justice (*Folha 8*, 20 May 1997; *Agora*, 24 May 1997). This prompted the National Police to set up a committee to inves-tigate the treatment of street children (*Jornal de Angola*, 12 June 1997).

One example among many has been the recruitment of under-age soldiers, in violation of the military service law, which lays down a minimum age of 18 for voluntary recruitment and 21 for obligatory conscription. Following the resumption of the war in 1998, the government reverted to its old methods of arbitrary forced conscription by sending squads of police to schools, markets and other locations frequented by young people, to round up those appearing old and fit enough to fight and dispatch them to other parts of the country where they could not escape.

Years of civil conflict, deepening poverty and institutional decay have bred conditions for widepread criminality. Hundreds of thousands, possibly millions, of Angolans carry weapons. During the post-Bicesse period in 1991–92, large numbers of government soldiers deserted, taking their weapons with them, instead of waiting for their orderly demobilization. In addition, huge numbers of AK-47 automatic rifles were distributed to civilians in Luanda in October–November 1992, to help the government crush UNITA during the 'battle of Luanda'. In the rural areas, both the government and UNITA armed 'civil defence' units in the villages, to supplement and support their regular forces. In a context of social upheaval, economic collapse and breakdown of law and order, banditry became widespread. In the south-western province of Benguela, cattle rustling developed into a serious problem. In Luanda, car hijackings became common, usually targeting four-wheel drive vehicles, which would then be delivered to the diamond-mining areas of Lunda Norte and Lunda Sul, where they were in high demand among the miners and traders. These diamond provinces acquired the reputation of an Angolan 'wild west', where there was no law other than that of the gangsters and rival armies battling for diamond wealth.

More often than not, the poorly disciplined, underpaid police were part of the problem, rather than the solution. A large number of violent crimes, including robbery, vehicle hijackings, assault and kidnapping, rape and murder, were committed by members of the police and military, both in and out of uniform (HRW, 1999). As has been noted above, government security forces have also engaged in widespread pillage of civilian property during military operations.

Obtaining redress for these crimes, whether committed by the security forces or by common criminals, is almost impossible through the justice system. The fact that the security forces are themselves deeply involved in criminal activity means that the police will often not investigate crimes at all. This problem is compounded by the fact that the police body responsible for pursuing criminal investigations, the *Direcção Nacional de Investigação Criminal* (DNIC), is starved of resources and manned by inadequately trained, poorly paid officers.

Furthermore, there is no tradition of a strong independent judiciary. Several key institutions exist only on paper. At the summit of the system, there is supposed to be a Constitutional Court, but, as has been noted above, this court has never been set up. This mirrors the situation of the *Tribunal de Contas* and the *Alta Autoridade contra a Corrupção*. Yet another example is the Ombudsman's Office, which was likewise enshrined in the constitutional revision law of 1992, but still does not exist in practice, thereby limiting citizens' ability to seek redress for wrongs suffered as a result of state actions.

The justice system, as it is currently constituted, consists of a Supreme Court, which is the highest court in the country and the ultimate court of appeal, and provincial and municipal courts. There are 19 provincial courts, one for each of the provinces, except Benguela, which has two such courts. A very small number of *municípios* (23 out of 157 at the last count) have municipal courts. The courts are overseen by the Ministry of Justice, while state prosecution services are provided by the *Procuradoria Geral da República* (Attorney General's Office) and its provincial and municipal structures. As in the case of the courts, very few state prosecutors, even in the case of those serving as *procuradores municipais*, operate outside the provincial capitals.

Because of the war and inadequate financial resources, the formal justice system is not operating in most parts of the country outside the major cities and a few coastal enclaves, although there are traditional customary systems of justice and conflict resolution administered by the local *sobas* (chiefs and headmen). Where the system does operate to some extent, it largely fails to uphold the rule of law or provide fair and equal access to justice because of the low salaries, corrupt practices and inadequate training of judges, state prosecutors and police, the lack of legal aid and inadequate material resources. The low levels of training are illustrated by the fact that only about a quarter of the approximately 200 state prosecutors hold a university law degree. Many are continuing to study while working in the state prosecution services. A similar situation pertains with respect to the judges (UNHROA, 1999).

As in the civil service, low salaries are one of the root causes of the decline in institutional capacity. It is not surprising that there are few credible, qualified personnel in the state judicial system when, according to data from 1997, provincial and municipal judges and prosecutors earn between $75 and $150 a month.[28] Trained lawyers can earn vastly more as private attorneys or as legal advisers in private companies. In addition, legal personnel have to work in conditions where the most basic resources, such as office equipment and even paper, are often lacking. In the provinces, they rarely have access to legal documents, such as volumes of laws and past judgements and works of jurisprudence.

---

[28] In 2000, the government introduced a new salary system for magistrates, raising their salaries to about $1,000 a month.

By providing a fertile breeding ground for corrupt practices and abuses, low salaries have also undermined in a more insidious way the performance of the justice system, as well as police bodies such as the DNIC, which plays an important role in preparing cases for trial. A UN study has spoken of *gasosas* permeating the system. Many Angolans believe that justice is not meted out equally, but depends on individuals' status or wealth, resulting in impunity for crimes committed by the powerful (UNHROA, 1999).

The low levels of material resources and commitment to duty also contribute, along with ineffective channels of communication between the DNIC, the Attorney General's Office and the Ministry of Justice, to long delays in bringing cases to court, resulting in one of the most widespread human rights abuses – periods of pre-trial detention that often greatly exceed the legal limit of 135 days. Together, these problems have resulted in low public confidence in the legal system, encouraging reliance on private, parallel forms of justice or retribution, which tend to exacerbate the arbitrariness and violence in Angolan society.

Civil society

The democratic reforms of 1991–92 lifted the previous restrictions on independent non-governmental organizations (NGOs) as well as, with some exceptions, the private media. The trade unions, which had previously been linked to the ruling party, became more independent. As a result, a more vibrant, active civil society came into being for the first time since the post-independence crackdown on independent organizations that had accompanied the consolidation of the MPLA's hold on state power in 1976–77. The independent associations, NGOs, trade unions and media organizations that emerged in the early 1990s remained quite weak, however, and their growth and development were hindered by the return to war, the politico-military division of the country and actions taken by the government to prevent these organizations, in particular the unions and the press, from posing a threat to its hold on power.

Legally, one of the most important reforms in 1991 was the adoption of the law on associations (law 14/91). This made it possible for civic and professional associations, church-based organizations and other national NGOs not linked to the ruling party to be registered and undertake activities.[29] Previously, even charitable work on behalf of displaced persons and other needy groups was largely limited to agencies of the government or the ruling party, although some church-based groups, such as the Catholic

---

[29] The national NGOs have a co-ordinating body, the *Forum das Organizações Não Governamentais Angolanas* (FONGA).

Church's Caritas organization, were allowed to run relief programmes.[30] Prior to 1991, almost no international NGOs were allowed into the country and donors' programmes were based almost entirely on bilateral co-operation agreements, with aid channelled through government ministries. The involvement of the International Red Cross (ICRC) and UN agencies in large-scale humanitarian assistance, which had begun in the mid-1980s, was the main breach in what had otherwise amounted to a virtual government monopoly of humanitarian and developmental activity.

The new space created for NGOs in 1991 happened at a time when donors were increasingly seeing NGOs as vehicles for channelling foreign aid (the so-called 'new policy agenda' for donor assistance). This international trend was reinforced in Angola by most donors' lack of confidence in official Angolan institutions, due to the weak capacity of government ministries, the government's failure to take the lead in co-ordinating humanitarian relief or rehabilitation and the low budgetary priorities accorded to the social sectors. As a result, much of the aid to Angola from the donor community, whether for emergency relief or for rehabilitation and development, came to be channelled through NGOs. The majority of NGOs have engaged in what can best be described as 'service delivery': due to the decline in social provision by the state, particularly in health and education, and its failure to respond in any meaningful way to the humanitarian crisis, the vacuum was filled during the 1990s by NGOs acting as contractors to donors and UN agencies (Christoplos, 1997).

As the humanitarian emergency deepened in 1993, following the resumption of the war, the UN established in Luanda a Humanitarian Assistance Co-ordination Unit (UCAH), which not only co-ordinated the relief efforts of the UN agencies but also, in the absence of government leadership in this field, provided a minimal framework for the humanitarian actions of international and national NGOs. UCAH was responsible for preparing annual humanitarian appeals, which helped to mobilize emergency assistance from the international community, particularly for food aid, assistance for the displaced, de-mining and, during the Lusaka peace process, assistance for the UNITA quartering areas administered by the UN. The biggest programme of all was run by the UN World Food Programme (WFP), which during the mid-1990s was administering a larger food aid programme in Angola than anywhere else in the world. Other large food aid programmes were run by the European Union (EU) and the United States Agency for International Development (USAID).

While many of the humanitarian programmes were led and co-ordinated by UCAH and the UN agencies, they worked through NGOs for programme

---

[30] One non-church NGO, *Acção Angolana para o Desenvolvimento* (AAD), had been allowed to establish itself in 1989, sponsored by patrons from within the MPLA-PT.

delivery. To implement their food aid programmes, agencies such as WFP, the EU and USAID signed contracts with NGOs (mainly the large international NGOs) for local food distribution in different parts of the country. The NGOs have been the privileged partners of the donor agencies because of the lack of government institutions with the commitment and capacity to carry out food distribution and other humanitarian assistance. Much the same happened with respect to health services. During the 1990s, primary health care services virtually collapsed, due to the war and underfunding. Hospitals and health posts were destroyed or abandoned, or functioned with minimal services, often without any medicines or equipment. In many parts of the country, virtually the only medical services available were provided by international NGOs, funded by donors. Even de-mining was being carried out mainly by NGOs.[31]

The government agency nominally responsible for humanitarian activities is the Ministry of Social Assistance and Reintegration (MINARS). However, it played second fiddle to the UN system in designing, co-ordinating and implementing humanitarian programmes, because of its weak institutional capacity (Sanches, 1996). It was hamstrung by a lack of interest and commitment at the highest levels of government. Similar problems faced the ministries responsible for health, education, water and other basic social services. The government failed to allocate more than token budgetary resources to humanitarian assistance, which was effectively abandoned to the international agencies and NGOs, and, as Chapter 3 has shown, even the allocations for education and health were extremely low by comparative African standards.

This abdication of responsibility on the part of the government extended into the post-war rehabilitation programme that was designed and launched, with the assistance of the United Nations Development Programme, after the Lusaka Protocol. Known as the Community Rehabilitation Programme (CRP) and presented to an international donors conference in Brussels in September 1995, attended by both President dos Santos and Jonas Savimbi, this was supposed to help the population recover from the devastation wrought by the war. Communities were to be assisted in reviving agriculture, fisheries and other productive activities, while health posts and schools were to be rebuilt or repaired, basic social services revived and critical local infrastructure, such as roads and water supply systems, restored. It was expected that this would contribute to broader economic recovery, reduce poverty and food insecurity and help communities reintegrate returning IDPs, refugees and demobilized

---

[31] Despite substantial assistance from the UN, the government's own agency for dealing with the landmine problem, the National Institute for the Removal of Explosive Obstacles and Ordnance (INAROEE), was plagued by poor leadership and lack of government funding. It was largely overshadowed by international de-mining NGOs, such as Norwegian People's Aid, which cleared far larger areas of mines in the late 1990s.

soldiers, thereby consolidating the peace (RA, 1995). The donors saw the CRP as a crucial part of the post-war process of peace-building and pledged $810 million for its implementation (UNDP, 1995). The government, however, squandered this extraordinary opportunity. It failed to provide effective leadership or co-ordination and, within a year, the CRP had withered away, forgotten. Despite this, donors did disburse aid for rehabilitation during the post-Lusaka period of fragile peace, but it was provided in an ad-hoc unco-ordinated way, outside the framework of any coherent strategy or plan for post-war recovery. Once again, nearly all the aid was disbursed through NGOs.[32]

It is hardly surprising that many ordinary Angolans began to see the NGOs and their donor patrons, rather than the state, as the main provider of basic social services, humanitarian relief and resources for rehabilitation. One commentator has remarked that:

> In the eyes of the people, the NGOs and the UN are assuming the legitimacy of the state. If an NGO rehabilitates a health post, it is they who are expected to pay the staff and stock it, not the government. (Christoplos, 1997)

The willingness of donors and NGOs to take on these responsibilities let the government off the hook; it could continue to divert the substantial public revenues from oil to other uses. Nonetheless, the situation was more and more of an embarrassment to the government. It began losing legitimacy, not just in the eyes of the international community, but before its own people. The population was likewise becoming increasingly less dependent on the state. Although national NGOs were relatively minor actors, compared with the international NGOs, they too looked to donors, rather than the government, for funding. These developments were worrying to the regime, which reacted by hindering the activities of international NGOs, notably by denying visas to international personnel, and trying to draw national NGOs into the circuits of state patronage.[33] By 1998–99, there were growing indications that the government was also

---

[32] Of the $41 m. disbursed for the CRP in the first year after the Brussels round table conference (September 1995–August 1996), only 8 per cent went to government ministries. The remaining funds were disbursed to NGOs and UN agencies (MINPLAN, 1996).

[33] On 20 April 1999, the government announced that it planned to regulate the 'anarchic' activities of certain NGOs. A MINARS official stated: 'those who come to help the Angolan people must do so within parameters established by the government' (*Lusa*, 20 April 1999, cited in HRW, 1999). In 1998–99, the government drafted legislation to circumscribe the rights of NGOs, by requiring them to obtain the formal approval of government bodies for their programmes and limiting the number of expatriates they could employ. This draft law was not adopted by the Council of Ministers or submitted to the National Assembly, possibly because, with the return of the war and another major humanitarian crisis, the state was more dependent than ever on donor-funded NGOs for the delivery of emergency relief and other social programmes.

exploring ways of forcing donors to channel a larger share of funds through government structures.[34]

To achieve these objectives, the regime realized that it would have to do more to live up to its own responsibilities towards the poor, displaced and disadvantaged. In July 1999, it launched the National Emergency Programme for Humanitarian Assistance (PNEAH), with a secretariat in the Ministry of Planning and $55 million of government funding, and set up an inter-ministerial committee to oversee the programme. This was still small, compared with the level of international humanitarian assistance, but it indicated that the government was no longer prepared to leave the field entirely to international donors, UN agencies and NGOs. The PNEAH complemented the earlier initiative of the FESA, which was also intended in part to claw back some of the credit for humanitarian assistance from the international community and bring national NGOs into the orbit of the state, although in FESA's case the credit was to be transferred to the head of state individually rather than to mainstream government institutions. A third initiative, launched in 2000, was the establishment of an Economic and Social Development Fund, to be funded by signature bonuses, the up-front exploration payments made by oil companies for exploration rights.

This attempt to reassert the influence of the state vis-à-vis the NGOs is a contradictory phenomenon. On the one hand, it is positive that the government should take belated steps to play a more active role in humanitarian assistance and in promoting economic and social development. On the other, the weak national NGOs could become sucked into a game of competing for state patronage, thereby making them unlikely to criticize government policies and actions.

Most of the national NGOs remain weak, in terms of management, logistical capacity, diversification of sources of funding and practical experience of designing and implementing community-level programmes.[35] In the absence of a philanthropic culture and tradition, they have no significant private sources of local funding and, until now, have been more or less entirely dependent on foreign donors. Precisely because of their institutional weakness and lack of experience, however, it has been international rather than national NGOs that have received the vast majority of donor assistance. While the main motive for many of the founders of national NGOs (usually civil servants or former civil servants) was to

---

[34] This desire to reorient donor assistance intersected with concerns among civil servants in the financially starved ministries that they were being marginalized by better-resourced NGOs. It also played on a certain public distaste for the relative opulence of international 'aid workers'. In addition, some hostility to NGOs seems to have come from private business interests, as some NGO services unintentionally compete with businesses such as private health clinics.

[35] There are very few exceptions to this pattern, the most notable being *Acção para o Desenvolvimento Rural e Ambiente* (ADRA).

exploit a new source of income generation to compensate for the collapse of state salaries, most have been competing for the crumbs from the donor table.[36]

It is also important to underline the fact that, as 'service providers', these NGOs are not representative bodies. They deliver services to communities or segments of the population, rather than represent them in any structured, organic sense. There are, as yet, only limited signs of the emergence of genuinely representative grassroots associations. The development of such community-based organizations (CBOs) has been held back by the sense of helplessness felt by ordinary people in a context of war, displacement and poverty and by the weakness of the tradition of self-organization, which was not encouraged either by the colonial regime or by the one-party state.

This general state of affairs is not completely uniform. In some rural areas, there are local farmers' associations which have evolved as quasi-autonomous village organizations from the branches of the now almost defunct *União Nacional dos Camponeses de Angola* (UNACA).[37] Other incipient signs of community organization may be found in bodies such as the parents' committees set up by some schools and the local committees organized by NGOs for the management of community water schemes (Hodges and Pacheco, 1999; Hodges and Viegas, 1998; DW, 1997; SCF-UK and ADRA, 1997). Since the early 1990s, another notable development has been the formation of numerous associations of residents and 'friends' of individual localities.

Another type of representative association which has emerged in Angola during the 1990s is the professional association. Bodies have come into being to represent groups such as journalists, lawyers, doctors and economists, as well as business organizations representing the commercial interests of the private sector. Some of these associations have begun to sponsor public discussion of important policy issues in their areas of professional concern, as have some thematic associations with an explicit advocacy mandate.[38]

The trade unions are among the potentially most influential corporate bodies but, like the other components of civil society, they still remain quite weak. Until 1991, they had been tied to the ruling party through the

---

[36] A survey of 124 NGOs operating in the country in 1996, of which 64 were national and 60 international, found that the international NGOs accounted for 93 per cent of their combined expenditure of $157 m. (MINARS and UNDP, 1997). The average annual budget of the international NGOs ($2.4 m.) was more than 14 times that of the national NGOs (less than $170,000).

[37] UNACA was launched in 1990, bringing together the co-operatives and peasants' associations set up after independence.

[38] The latter category includes groups like the *Campanha Angolana para o Baneamento das Minas* (Angolan Campaign for the Banning of Landmines) and the *Juventude Ecológica de Angola* (Angolan Ecological Youth).

União Nacional dos Trabalhadores de Angola (UNTA) and were effectively a mechanism for the transmission of government instructions and propaganda to the formal sector workforce. The 1991 reforms freed the unions from state tutelage and also permitted new unions independent of UNITA and the MPLA to come into being. The right to strike was formally recognized by law 23/91. As a result of these changes, independent-minded unions began to champion workers' rights, particularly in the public sector, where the steep decline in real wages during the 1990s stirred deep discontent. The teachers' union, *Sindicato Nacional dos Professores* (SINPROF), became the most active, organizing a series of strikes to press for higher wages, the payment of salary arrears and improvements in education.

Nonetheless, the development of independent trade unionism has been held back by repression and intimidation and, perhaps even more important, by the nature of the labour force. When faced by strikes or the threat of strikes, usually by the teachers or other public sector workers, the government has tended to deploy heavily armed para-military police, such as the *ninjas*, as a deterrent. This has been quite effective in instilling fear and discouraging union militancy. Strikes have also invariably been subject to reporting black-outs in the state-controlled media. Another key reason for the weakness of the unions is the fact that so little of the labour force works in the formal sector of the economy, in institutions or enterprises where there is a critical mass of workers to unionize. Overall, well under 500,000 people out of an adult population of approximately 6–7 million are employed in the formal sector. Significantly, it has only been in public services such as education and health, where there is a large concentration of workers, that the stronger independent unions have emerged. Although these unions have engaged in some quite lengthy and determined strikes, they have not been joined by workers in other sectors of the economy.

The media

During the single-party period, all the mass media in the government-controlled areas were owned by the state. Private media were prohibited by law. Likewise, in the UNITA areas, there was, and still is, no press freedom, the media being restricted to an anti-government radio station run by the movement, called *A Voz da Resistência do Galo Negro* (VORGAN), or the 'Voice of the Resistance of the Black Cockerel'.[39]

---

[39] The cockerel is a symbol of UNITA, appearing in black in the centre of its red, green and black flag.

As in other spheres of life, the democratic reforms of 1991–92 brought positive changes in the government-controlled areas. A new press law in May 1991 (law 25/91) permitted the publication of independent newspapers and magazines, and this was followed in April 1992 by legislation allowing the establishment of private FM radio stations (law 16/92). A third law, also enacted in April 1992 (law 7/92), created a press council, the *Conselho Nacional de Comunicação Social*, which included representatives of the government, the main political parties, the churches, the judiciary and the press itself, and had a mandate to uphold press freedom and a code of conduct. The membership of the council was widened in January 1996 (law 1/96) to include all political parties with seats in the National Assembly. As a result of these legal changes, several small privately owned news journals came into being, although none was published daily, while private FM radio stations were set up in some of the larger cities. The state-owned media also became more pluralist, reporting at times on the activities of opposition parties and providing a forum for debate. Nonetheless, the scope and impact of these reforms remained quite limited. Various legal restrictions have remained in place, while the press council has ceased to function in practice.

Angola has a relatively low density of radio and television ownership, compared with most African countries. According to the results of a nationwide survey in 1996, 33 per cent of households own a radio set (51 per cent in urban areas and 22 per cent in rural areas) and only 9 per cent (all in urban areas) own a television (INE, 1999).[40] Lack of electricity and low incomes limit wider television ownership. However, both radio and television audiences are much larger than these figures suggest, due to access to neighbours' sets, and even television is therefore a critically important means of communication in urban areas.

It was doubtless on account of the much greater audience of radio and television that the main legal restrictions were on these branches of the media, rather than the printed press, which is read by only a few tens of thousands of Angolans, at the most. Under law 16/92, private radio stations were not allowed to broadcast on short or medium wave, giving the state-owned *Rádio Nacional de Angola* (RNA) a monopoly in the rural areas and smaller towns. RNA has 49 stations nationwide. Its impact is all the greater because it broadcasts in 15 languages, including all the main African languages spoken in Angola – a pragmatic policy which reveals a markedly more positive attitude to the country's national languages than is evident in other domains of public life, such as the education system.

---

[40] More advanced African countries, such as South Africa and Mauritius, have about five times as many radio sets per population. In South Africa, there are 123 television sets per 1,000 population, compared with 19 per 1,000 population in Angola. Comparative figures for Nigeria and Zimbabwe are 55 and 29 television sets per 1,000 population. See UNDP, 1999b.

The state has also retained a legal monopoly on television broadcasting. *Televisão Pública de Angola* (TPA) broadcasts from studios in Luanda, Benguela, Cabinda and Lubango, and has transmitters in each of the provincial capitals.

After law 16/92, four private FM radio stations were established: *Luanda Antena Comercial* (LAC), *Rádio Cabinda Comercial*, *Rádio Morena* in Benguela and *Rádio 2000* in Lubango. It has been argued that these radio stations were set up with discreet financial support from within the MPLA in order to assist the ruling party during its electoral campaign in 1992 and that their broadcasts rarely criticize the government (HRW, 1999). This lack of independence is probably over-stated, as on several occasions some of these radio stations have attempted to broadcast material that was unwelcome to the government.[41] The independent media were further strengthened in 1997 by the re-establishment of *Rádio Ecclésia*, a Catholic radio station expropriated by the state in 1977. However, as we shall see below, the government used a mix of subtle financial inducement and direct harassment, particularly after the country began sliding back to war in 1998, to encourage self-censorship in the private radio stations.

A major concern of the government has been to stop VORGAN broadcasting anti-government propaganda. VORGAN has been able to reach most of the country on short wave from transmitters in rebel-controlled territory. Under the Lusaka Protocol, VORGAN was supposed to be converted into a commercial FM radio station, to be called *Rádio Despertar*. For three years after the Lusaka Protocol, however, VORGAN continued to broadcast, pouring out a torrent of propaganda that was hardly conducive to advancing the peace process or promoting national reconciliation. Eventually, under intense international pressure, it went off the air for a brief period in 1998, but *Rádio Despertar* was never set up and, as the peace process unravelled, VORGAN resumed its clandestine broadcasts at the end of the year.

As in other parts of Africa, many Angolans turn to international radio stations for non-partisan news coverage of developments in their country. Foreign short-wave radio broadcasts in Portuguese, such as the Portuguese services of the BBC and Voice of America (VOA), have long been an important source of information for Angolans.[42] The government has not allowed these foreign broadcasters to retransmit directly from

---

[41] Notably by flouting government instructions not to broadcast interviews with UNITA officials following the resumption of the war at the end of 1998.

[42] A survey conducted in 1996 for the BBC by the Angolan company *Austral* found that 6 per cent of adults listened to the BBC and 5 per cent to the Voice of America at least once a week. Access to foreign television broadcasts or news through the Internet is limited, however, to a tiny minority of wealthy urban Angolans and expatriates who can afford satellite dishes, computers and telephones.

within the country, either through RNA or the private FM radio stations, and in April 1997 the authorities in Lubango prevented *Rádio 2000* from retransmitting VOA programmes.

Economic and social factors, such as the high level of illiteracy, the lack of a newspaper-reading culture, limited infrastructure and high costs, have held back the development of private newspapers and magazines. This has resulted in a de facto monopoly of the daily printed press by the state-owned *Jornal de Angola*. The private printed press is limited to semi-artisanal weeklies, bi-weeklies and monthlies, which were estimated in 1996 to have a combined circulation of less than 22,000 (Mogalakwe and Lima, 1996). Even the *Jornal de Angola*'s daily print run was only 4,000, with distribution limited almost entirely to the capital. Indeed, Angola has one of the lowest daily newspaper print runs in the world: about one copy per 3,125 inhabitants.

The economic survival of the independent press is also at risk from government lawsuits brought against newspapers and journalists for alleged libel and defamation. More insidiously, the regime has been adept at co-opting journalists by offering financial inducements for favourable articles or broadcasts. Ultimately, the owners, editors and journalists of private media organizations know that there are limits to press freedom that they cross at their peril. To some extent this has been a side-effect of the failure to establish a real and sustainable peace. However, the war does not entirely account for the dangers facing the independent press. The murder of Ricardo Mello, the editor of a leading private newsletter, *Imparcial Fax*, by unknown gunmen in Luanda on 18 January 1995, was widely believed to be related to that publication's role in exposing allegations of corruption scandals. *Imparcial Fax* ceased publication after Mello's death. Another journalist, António Casimiro, the Cabindan correspondent of TPA, was assassinated in Cabinda on 30 October 1996. Although two inquiries were opened into the killing, their findings have never been made public (HRW, 1999).

Journalists working in the provinces face especially difficult conditions. Apart from the fact that no Angolan journalists apart from UNITA propagandists are allowed (by either side) to operate freely in UNITA-controlled areas, independent journalists are barely tolerated by the petty autocrats who run the provincial governments. Several journalists based in the provinces have been banned from working or have lost their jobs as a result of reports found displeasing by provincial governors. Harassment and intimidation of journalists have worsened markedly since the return to war in late 1998. The government was embarrassed and irritated by media reports of the setbacks suffered by the FAA in the early stages of the new war and by negative coverage of the reintroduction of military conscription, and tried to stop the press from reporting or broadcasting interviews with UNITA officials. To apply pressure on the media to stay within the official limits on reporting, about 20 journalists, most of whom worked for privately owned radio stations and newspapers, were briefly detained in 1999.[43] Most were investigated in connection with alleged 'crimes against state security' and then freed after learning a salutary lesson.

These incidents were interspersed with directives and warnings to the media from the information minister, Hendrik Vaal Neto. On 21 January 1999, the minister warned the independent media that their operating licences would be revoked if they continued to report in a negative manner on conscription. He issued a second warning on 1 June 1999, threatening unspecified measures to curb 'anti-patriotic' reporting in the private press.[44] This aroused speculation that the wartime conditions were being used as a pretext for closing down newspapers or silencing journalists who had been too daring in their coverage not only of the war but of other sensitive issues such as corruption. These suspicions were reinforced by the arrest, detention and sentencing of Rafael Marques, one of Angola's most outspoken independent journalists. Marques was arrested in October 1999 and later charged with defaming the head of state, in violation of provisions in the Law on Crimes against State Security (law 7/78), because he had called President dos Santos a 'dictator' in an article in the independent weekly *Agora* and in an interview broadcast by *Rádio Ecclésia*.[45] After 41 days in jail, he was released on bail, before being brought to trial in March 2000, along with the publisher of *Agora*, Aguiar dos Santos. Found guilty in a trial that, according to international human rights organizations, was marred by irregularities, both Marques and Aguiar dos Santos were found guilty on 31 March and sentenced respectively to six and two months imprisonment and hefty fines.[46] The case triggered an unusually strong reaction from the diplomatic community and international human rights bodies and earned President dos Santos the dubious distinction of being included in May 2000 on the annual list of the world's 'ten worst enemies of the press' published by the US-based Committee for the Protection of Journalists.

Human Rights Watch has remarked that the attacks against the right to freedom of expression have undermined the defence of other rights, while also delaying peace and reconciliation by obstructing access to

---

[43] These included journalists from *Rádio Morena*, *Rádio Ecclésia* and *Folha 8* and several free-lance journalists, some of whom were reporting for foreign media. For details, see AI, 1999, and HRW, 1999.

[44] *Agora*, 5 June 1999.

[45] In the article published in *Agora* on 3 July 1999, Marques had accused President dos Santos of being responsible for 'the destruction of the country…(and) for the promotion of incompetence, embezzlement and corruption as political and social values', as well as being a dictator.

[46] Appeals against the sentences were subsequently submitted to the Supreme Court.

information and free debate (HRW, 1999). The attacks on press freedom and the overall weakness of the media in general also make it more difficult to develop an environment in which the government is held to account for its actions, including in such critical domains as its management of public resources. The defence of media rights and the development of financially sound, professionally competent and pluralistic media will therefore remain one of the fundamental building blocks for improved governance in Angola.

5
Economic Crisis & the Limits of Reform

Few African countries have such a favourable natural resource endowment as Angola. Indeed, the country's potential for rapid growth was amply demonstrated during the latter part of the colonial period, although there were great inequalities in the distribution of wealth and access to resources. Since the end of the colonial period, however, almost all sectors of the economy, apart from the oil industry, have stagnated or declined. In most cases, there was a large fall in production resulting from the disruptive shocks that accompanied independence and the outbreak of war, followed by a long period of stagnation, with alternating periods of modest recovery and renewed decline, reflecting shifts in the politico-military situation or in international oil prices. This has left Angola over-whelmingly dependent on oil revenue, which has been used to finance imports, mainly armaments and consumer goods.

The war has not been solely responsible for Angola's poor economic performance. A second factor has been the shortage of skilled human resources since the sudden settler exodus in 1975, and a third has been poor economic management. The ultimately unsuccessful attempt to establish a system of centralized planning, based on a large state sector and extensive administrative price-setting and resource allocation, was followed by a period of economic reform, intended to bring about a transition to a market economy. However, the reforms have not been followed through consis-tently, leaving Angola with many vestiges of the old system. This has been accompanied by weak macroeconomic management, resulting in large budgetary and balance-of-payments deficits (despite the country's substantial oil revenues), high rates of inflation, heavy external indebt-edness and loss of creditworthiness in international financial markets.

The resource endowment and economic potential

If human progress depended on natural resources alone, Angola's people would be among the most fortunate in Africa. The country has an unusually rich and diverse endowment of natural resources, including large oil deposits, numerous other minerals, soil and climatic conditions propitious for the cultivation of a wide range of crops and for the raising of livestock, rich fishing waters and extensive hydroelectric power potential. Well harnessed, these resources could make Angola one of Africa's most prosperous countries, with social indicators far ahead of the continental averages, instead of far below as at present.

According to the oil minister, Botelho Vasconcelos, Angola's proven oil deposits doubled in 1994–99 to some 10 billion barrels, as a result of the large deepwater oil discoveries in the late 1990s.[1] With production in 2000 close to 800,000 b/d, reserves would last for almost 35 years. Given the high rate of exploration success, however, it is probable that proven reserves will rise further in the years to come.

The country has numerous other mineral resources, including some of the most valuable diamond deposits in the world. These include both alluvial (surface) and kimberlite (underground) deposits, and although to date only alluvial deposits have been mined, the kimberlites are thought to hold the major promise for the future. Prior to independence, Angola was also a medium-sized producer of iron ore (the fourth main export in the early 1970s, after oil, coffee and diamonds), as well as marble and granite. Other known mineral resources include gold, manganese, copper, lead, zinc, tin, wolfram, vanadium, titanium, chromium, phosphates, beryl, quartz, kaolin and gypsum, although there has so far been limited prospecting and few of the known deposits have been fully assessed.

In addition to these non-renewable mineral resources, Angola has extensive renewable natural resources, particularly in agriculture and fishing. A wide range of climatic zones and soil types makes it possible to cultivate numerous different crops. With a total land area of approximately 1.25 million square kilometres, the country has between 5 and 8 million hectares of arable land, much of which is currently not cultivated. In terms of topography, a narrow low-lying coastal plain rises through an escarpment to a high plateau (*planalto*), which covers about four-fifths of the country. Rainfall is highest along the escarpment and the higher, western parts of the *planalto*. These longitudinal zones are dissected by successive latitudinal zones, running from the hot and humid north to the drier south – the south-western coastal area being true desert.

In the colonial period, Angola was self-sufficient in most food crops and exported a surplus of maize, the main food crop in the south and

---

[1] *Financial Times*, 7 January 2000.

centre of the country. Cassava is the main staple in the north. Numerous cash crops were cultivated, both by settler farmers and small-scale peasants, for whom cash crops provided a source of income to supplement subsistence food production.

The most important export crop was coffee, which grows well in the higher altitudes on the western borders of the *planalto*, particularly in Uíge and Kwanza Sul. This was the main export until it was overtaken by oil in 1973. In the early 1970s, coffee was being grown by about 2,500 large commercial farmers and some 250,000 peasant families. Almost 600,000 ha were planted with coffee, making Angola the fourth largest producer in the world after Brazil, Colombia and Côte d'Ivoire, with output of more than 200,000 tons a year.

Angola was also the third largest producer of sisal, after Brazil and Tanzania, in the early 1970s. Cotton was grown in the provinces of Malange, Kwanza Sul and Bengo, supplying both a domestic textile industry and export markets. There are excellent conditions for cultivating sugar cane in the coastal areas, where large cane plantations were established in Benguela and Bengo. Other cash crops have traditionally included tobacco, grown in Malange in the colonial period, oil palms, which flourish in the hot humid north, and citrus fruits, in the south. Most of the manufacturing industry set up prior to independence processed agricultural commodities.

The semi-arid rangelands of the south-west, which are free from the tsetse fly, are excellent for raising cattle, the main source of wealth for the pastoralist peoples of that region. A commercial livestock and meat-packing industry developed there in the colonial period.

In addition, the waters off the southern coast (Namibe and Benguela provinces) have some of the best fishing resources in Africa – comparable in importance to the Senegal-Mauritania coast – although over-fishing appears to have reduced stocks, as in many other parts of the world. The cold waters of the Benguela current, which flow northwards from the Namibian coast, meet warm tropical waters off the southern Angolan coast, creating conditions favourable to plankton. In addition to artisanal fishing, a large industrial fishing sector developed in the southern coastal ports of Benguela, Moçâmedes (now Namibe) and Tômbwa before independence.

Finally, mention should be made of the country's energy resources. Besides oil and deposits of both associated and non-associated gas, Angola is endowed with large hydroelectric resources on its many rivers. With a potential estimated at 7,710 mw compared with installed capacity of under 600 mw and present available capacity of less than 300 mw, hydroelectricity provides an opportunity for low-cost power for industrial development.

Decline of the non-oil sectors of the economy

In conditions of peace and with sound economic policies and management capacity, there can be little doubt that this resource endowment would enable Angola to achieve high rates of growth and make major gains in human development. The reality has been quite different. The economy has been in prolonged recession, outside the enclave oil sector, ever since the chaotic transition to independence in 1975. The outbreak of war, the sudden loss of most of the country's skilled manpower and the abandonment of thousands of commercial farms and small businesses, including the entire rural trading system, threw the economy into a crisis from which it has never recovered. There are acute shortages of qualified personnel in all sectors of the economy and in the ministries responsible for economic management and policy-making. Infrastructure has been destroyed, or has simply decayed for want of investment. Many of the state companies set up after the settler exodus and nationalizations in 1975–77 failed to maintain operations, and the rudimentary attempt at centralized planning led to serious resource misallocations and inefficiency, producing bottlenecks in the supply of industries and the emergence of large parallel markets.

Meanwhile, the war ravaged sectors like agriculture, agro-processing and domestic trade, and created a situation where there was no longer a unified national market but, rather, a coastal enclave economy, cut off from the rest of the country, using oil revenue to import virtually all goods and services. Some of the government-controlled pockets in the hinterland are linked to the coastal towns only by costly air transport, while most of the rural areas have receded into a very basic form of subsistence economy, more or less completely cut off from markets. In Le Billon's words (1999: 9):

> The dualistic nature of the colonial economy was exacerbated by the decolonisation process and turned into a caricature of itself by the war: the enclave of Luanda sustained by oil-financed imports, versus a hinterland underdeveloped by warfare and economic isolation....Cut off from the main urban centres and export markets on the coast by the departure of Portuguese traders, the destruction of transport infrastructure, and pervading insecurity, the agricultural sector in the hinterland has turned into a wasteland. In turn, the main cities are overcrowded and mostly sustained by imports.

With domestic production in almost all sectors except oil at historically very low levels, and a heavy debt burden limiting import capacity despite the rise in oil earnings, the supply of goods has been unable to match demand, which has been buoyed by the continued monetization of large deficits in government finances. This has caused severe macro-economic disequilibria, provoking large balance-of-payments deficits and high rates of inflation. Large extra-budgetary operations have confounded attempts to restore fiscal balance. Although economic reforms began in the late 1980s, progress in implementing them has been patchy and sporadic, held up in some cases by vested interests that stand to lose privileges obtained from non-transparent administrative methods of resource allocation.

Overall, during the 1990s, the failure to revive the non-oil sectors of the economy may be summarized as having five inter-related causes. The first has been the state of insecurity – not just during the periods of outright war but also during the interludes of quasi-peace, due to the continuing obstacles to the free movement of persons and goods and the low levels of confidence in the durability of the peace process.[2] The second, as mentioned above, has been the extreme shortage of skills. A third factor has been the macroeconomic instability and uncertainty. Fourth, economic recovery has been compromised by the maintenance of distor-tionary policies, in particular the administrative management of foreign-exchange and credit allocation, despite the reforms aimed at moving away from centralized planning to a more market-oriented system of economic management.

A fifth and final factor has been the severe and prolonged deterioration in physical infrastructure and services, which greatly increases the costs of business activities in most sectors of the economy. This includes the lack of reliable sources of electricity or water, the deterioration (and mining) of the roads, the breakdown of railway services and the weakness of banking institutions and financial services. Due to low budgetary outlays and tariffs set well below operating costs, utility companies responsible for electricity and water have been unable to maintain or repair supply systems, or to make necessary investments. Transportation costs have remained high, partly because of the security risks, but also due to the levying of illegal transit fees by police and army posts on the highways, the poor state of repair of road surfaces, the inefficiency and lack of security in the country's ports, and cumbersome customs procedures.[3]

A brief review of the agricultural, manufacturing and mining sectors will show the extent of the economic decline outside the oil industry since the mid-1970s. In the absence of long-term sectoral production indices, Table 5.1 provides data on the output of a few representative products. 　　　　　　　　　　　　　　　　　·

---

[2] Whether on the part of foreign investors or of displaced peasants judging the advisability of returning to their home areas to restart farming.

[3] According to one source (World Bank, 1996), shipping costs are very high, with operators' liabilities and insurance premiums reaching 60 per cent. The rates of damage and/or loss of cargo are among the highest in Africa.

Table 5.1   Production of selected commodities, 1973–97

	Unit	1973	1993	1994	1995	1996	1997
Agriculture & fisheries							
Maize	1,000 tons	854	274	201	211	398	370
Coffee (exports)	1,000 tons	213	2	5	2	3	3
Fish (landed in							
Angolan ports)	1,000 tons	467	129	135	137	170	...
Mining							
Crude oil	1,000 b/d	172[a]	504	550	617	689	713
Diamonds							
(official sales)	1,000 carats	1,940	295	537	628	917	1,212
Iron ore	Million tons	6	0	0	0	0	0
Manufacturing							
Beer	Million litres	120	27	28	39	72	...
Cloth	Million sq metres	18	5	3	2	3	...
Cement	1,000 tons	768	135	251	186	204	...
Refined petroleum							
products	1,000 tons	743	1,522	1,710	1,760	1,776	1,776

a/ 1974.
Sources: IMF, 1999a; INE; Hodges, 1993.

First, in the agricultural sector, Angola has shifted from being a net food exporter to a country heavily dependent on international food aid, averaging about 200,000 tons a year in the 1990s. In the early 1970s, Angola had exported annually more than 100,000 tons of maize, but by the 1990s it was producing on average only about half its cereal needs, the balance being made up roughly equally by commercial imports and food aid (FAO and WFP, 1997). Food production was adversely affected by the collapse of the colonial market system in 1975 (due to the mass departure of the *comerciantes do mato*), the disruption of urban-rural trade by the war, the large decline in the rural proportion of the population (due to the exodus to the towns), the state's post-independence focus on promoting unviable state farms and trading companies rather than peasant producers and private traders, and a pricing system (for agricultural commodities until the mid-1980s and for foreign exchange until the late 1990s) which discriminated against rural producers in favour of imports and urban consumers.

In the case of cash crops, the most dramatic development has been the collapse of coffee production. The decline began in 1975 with the abandonment of coffee estates by the departing settlers and the departure of the largely Ovimbundu migrant work-force from the coffee-growing provinces of the north-west. The loss of manpower also affected peasant producers, who had accounted for about one half of coffee output. The abandoned estates were nationalized, but the decline was accentuated by the ineffectiveness of the state coffee companies, the disruption of cultivation and marketing as the war spread into the coffee-growing areas in the 1980s, and the harmful effects of an overvalued currency on incentives to produce. Coffee exports in 1993–97 were on average about 1 per cent of their level in the early 1970s.[4]

Cultivation of most other former cash crops, including sisal, sugar cane, cotton and tobacco, has more or less completely halted, again due to the flight of commercial farmers in 1975, the failure of subsequent state companies and the wartime disruption of production by peasant farmers, who were significant producers of some cash crops, in particular cotton.

In the case of fisheries, there has been a large fall in the quantity of fish landed in Angolan ports, from 467,300 tons in 1973 to around 170,000 tons in 1996, despite extensive rehabilitation of the fish processing plants and investments in the fishing fleet in the southern coastal towns. Among the causal factors have been over-fishing by foreign fleets, both licensed and unlicensed, and the inability of the government to control fishing in its territorial waters.

In the manufacturing sector, which was growing at an average real rate of 11 per cent a year in 1960–73, there was a steep fall in production after independence, as a result of the abandonment of settler-owned businesses and the poor performance of the state companies set up after their nationalization. Another factor was the loss of domestic sources of supply of agricultural raw materials, as many of the manufacturing plants were originally set up before independence to process locally produced agricultural commodities.

Although some state manufacturing companies were privatized in the 1990s, they were often transferred to their new owners as political favours and were then poorly managed. They also faced many difficulties. Most inherited antiquated plant and machinery but found it impossible to obtain long-term credit from the rudimentary Angolan banking system to finance investments. The war continued to limit or entirely prevent the local sourcing of inputs and the national marketing of production, while raising the costs of domestic transport. In addition, production costs were inflated by the country's poor infrastructure, as, for example, when manufacturers had to invest in generators to substitute for the unreliable electricity supply from the grid. In effect, domestic producers were caught in a vice, as the overvalued exchange rate meanwhile made it difficult to compete with artificially cheap imports. For many of the same reasons, as well as the bureaucratic hurdles faced by investors the virtual impossibility of enforcing commercial contracts through the judicial system and the added disincentives of political uncertainty and macroeconomic instability, there has been little foreign investment in manufacturing or, indeed, in any sector outside oil and diamonds. Petroleum refining has been the only branch of manufacturing industry to expand. Overall, the

---

[4] See Table A-19 on p. 185.

share of manufacturing in GDP has fallen from 16 per cent in 1973 to 6 per cent in 1998.

In the mining sector, one of the main casualties of the outbreak of war in 1975 was the halt of iron ore production. Based at Cassinga, in Huíla province, this had been the fourth main export, with the ore exported to the coast by railway to the port of Moçâmedes. Iron ore mining has never resumed. The insecurity across the country has made it almost impossible, with a few limited exceptions, for mining companies to engage in prospecting. Diamonds have remained the second main export, but as Chapter 7 will discuss in detail, UNITA and illegal mining operations took over much of the industry in the 1990s. There is large-scale smuggling of diamonds, including from government-controlled areas, and the government earns very little fiscal revenue from the industry.

Human capital

Along with the continuing war, the poor state of the country's infra-structure, macroeconomic instability and the weaknesses in the institutional and policy framework, the low level of development of human capital is one of the main underlying constraints on economic recovery and development. A problem whose origins go back to the lack of investment in training Africans in the colonial period and the sudden exodus of skilled personnel at independence, the situation has worsened since the early 1980s because of the deterioration of the education and health systems. The result is low productivity throughout the economy – and continued costly dependence on expatriates.

Chapter 3 has already highlighted some of the problems that underlie the low educational and health status of the population. High morbidity, including, in particular, the high prevalence of malaria and the spread of the HIV/AIDS pandemic, greatly diminish productivity. Although at an earlier stage of development than in the rest of Southern Africa, HIV/AIDS will have its most dramatic impact among young adults, eroding still further the small pool of skilled human resources and so undermining the prospects for post-war economic recovery and development. Even without the impact of HIV/AIDS, the weakness of the education system, discussed in Chapter 3, has resulted in an acute shortage of skills which is one of the most serious constraints on the economy.

The decay and destruction of infrastructure

Another serious constraint facing most sectors of the economy is the destruction and decay of physical infrastructure. Not only have railway lines, bridges, power plants, transmission lines and water systems been destroyed or damaged during the war, but others have simply decayed because of the lack of maintenance, repairs and modernization. Investment in the extension of infrastructure has been minimal, due to low budgetary allocations and the lack of effective cost-recovery mechanisms. As a result, operating costs are high in most sectors of the economy.

Numerous roads have been mined, de-mined during interludes of peace and then re-mined, while becoming virtually impassable in some places because of the lack of upkeep of road surfaces and the destruction of bridges. Almost no new roads have been built in the past 25 years.[5]

None of the country's three railway systems is working properly. Running eastwards from ports on the coast (Luanda, Lobito and Namibe), these railways were originally intended to provide access to important agricultural and mining areas inland, while the Benguela railway linked the Atlantic port of Lobito with the mining regions of south-eastern Zaire (RDC) and northern Zambia. Rolling stock, track and other equipment have decayed – or, in the case of wooden sleepers, been torn up from the track and burnt as firewood. International traffic on the Benguela railway stopped in 1975 and has never been resumed (except for a brief period in 1978–79), and by the 1990s the railway was operating only on a small coastal stretch of line between the cities of Lobito and Benguela.

In the energy sector, sabotage and inadequate maintenance have put roughly half of the installed electricity generating capacity out of operation. Some provincial capitals have been without electricity for ten or more years, or have only limited periods of power supply for a few hours during the day. Ironically, this is one sector where there has been high investment, but it has been directed to a single large project, the construction of a 520 mw dam at Capanda, on the River Kwanza, while few resources have gone to investments in rehabilitating or extending the existing power plants and distribution systems. The Capanda dam will almost double the country's installed generating capacity, but it has so far taken almost 15 years to build, partly because of long periods of UNITA occupation of the dam site. It has been criticized as a high-cost folly that has drained resources away from maintenance and rehabilitation of the existing power plants, transmission lines and distribution networks, which would have a much higher return (World Bank, 1987).

Apart from the Capanda dam, public investment in physical infrastructure has consistently been crowded out by defence and security expenditure, public debt service and recurrent expenditures, as well as

---

[5] Angola reached independence with a fairly extensive road network (built by the Portuguese largely for military reasons), totalling about 75,000 km, of which about 16,000 km had an asphalt or hard gravel surface.

weak capacity to prepare and appraise projects for the Public Investment Programme (PIP). The budget execution reports of the Ministry of Finance indicate that investment projects received only 9 per cent of recorded government expenditure in 1997 and just 3 per cent in 1998 (MINFIN, 1998, 1999).

Another limiting factor, particularly in sectors such as energy and water, has been the weakness of cost-recovery mechanisms. Tariffs have been kept so unrealistically low that they cover only a small proportion of operating costs, leaving the utility companies dependent on unpredictable government subsidies. The lack of effective cost-recovery mechanisms has been the main cause of the decay of urban water, sanitation and electricity supply systems in areas not directly affected by the war.[6]

Macroeconomic instability

Severe macroeconomic disequilibria first emerged in the mid-1980s and at first were directly related to the external shock of a steep fall in international oil prices, in 1985–86. Previously in surplus because of rising oil exports and net capital inflows, the overall balance of payments shifted into deficit. Although the fall in prices was quickly offset by the rise in the volume of oil exports, the balance-of-payments strains became increasingly more serious from the late 1980s, with even the current account moving into deficit from 1988, due in part to rising interest obligations on the external debt.

From 1986, the government had begun to face difficulties in meeting its external debt-service obligations, resulting in the build-up of arrears and the loss of creditworthiness in international financial markets and among official export credit agencies. Although the expanding oil industry ensured continuing large net inflows of direct foreign investment, this was more than offset by the high level of amortization of loans. Rising repayment obligations were outstripping new lending by the end of the 1980s, due to the loss of creditworthiness and the political changes in the Soviet bloc, which had been the main source of official lending.

The balance-of-payments deficits continued through the 1990s and were financed primarily by accumulating ever larger arrears, although some debt was rescheduled or written off (mainly by the Russian Federation in 1996). Unable to finance imports in any other way (except

---

[6] In December 1996, the water tariff in Luanda was less than one-tenth of a US cent per 10 cubic metres, while the parallel-market price of water sold to those living in areas not served by the mains (roughly half the Luanda population) was 721,153 times higher. Measures to raise electricity and water tariffs to commercial levels were eventually taken in the framework of IMF-supported reforms in 2000.

by paying cash), the government was obliged to contract oil-guaranteed loans on highly disadvantageous terms, tying up most of the oil available to it through SONANGOL for debt servicing. Foreign reserves fell to very low levels, particularly after the collapse in oil prices in 1998, when the average price of Angolan oil dropped to $12 a barrel. Key macroeconomic indicators are provided in Table 5.2.[7]

Table 5.2   Macroeconomic indicators, 1994–99

	1994	1995	1996	1997	1998	Est. 1999
GDP ($ billion)	4.1	5.0	6.5	7.7	6.4	5.6
Real GDP growth (%)	1.4	10.3	10.0	6.2	3.2	2.7
Oil sector	9.2	12.0	10.4	4.7	3.5	4.1
Non–oil sector	–3.8	8.1	9.4	8.4	2.9	1.8
GDP per capita ($ m.)	341	439	554	634	518	438
Exports fob ($ m.)	3,017	3,723	5,169	5,007	3,543	5,344
Imports fob ($ m.)	1,454	1,852	2,040	2,477	2,079	3,267
BOP current account ($ m.)	–564	–994	–249	–869	–2,023	–1,797
BOP current account as % of GDP	–13.9	–19.7	–3.8	–11.3	–31.4	–32.1
BOP overall balance ($ m.)	–1,132	–1,218	–346	–810	–1,372	–240
Gross international reserves ($ m.)	190	369	558	392	201	481
Equivalent in months of imports[a]	1.2	1.0	1.3	1.0	0.4	0.9
Public external debt ($ m.)	10,818	11,675	8,499	8,570	8,782	9,591
Public external debt as % of exports	342	304	156	164	240	175
Public debt service/exports ratio[b] (%)	56	47	34	15	24	17
Public sector external arrears ($ m.)	...	5,641	2,528	3,086	3,822	4,441
Overall budget deficit as % of GDP[c]	20.1	37.5	15.8	17.8	15.1	13.1
Inflation[d] (%)	972	3,784	1,651	148	135	329
Exchange rates[e] (thousand Kzr per $)						
Official exchange rate	0.15	2.74	127.8	229.1	392.6	...
Parallel exchange rate	0.32	6.17	165.1	303.1	612.3	...
Spread (%)	110	125	29	32	56	...

a/ In months of next year's merchandise imports. b/ Total debt-service obligations as % of exports of goods and non-factor services. c/ On commitment basis. d/ Luanda consumer price index, year to December. e/ Annual averages; the new kwanza (NKz) was replaced by the readjusted kwanza (Kzr) in 1995, at Kzr1 = NKz1,000; exchange-rate data prior to 1995 have been converted to Kzr; the new Kwanza was replaced by Kwanza (kz) in December 1999, at Kz1 = Kzr 1m.

Sources: IMF (1999a, 1999c, 2000), derived from government data and IMF staff estimates.

---

[7] More detailed economic data are in Tables A-12 – A-22 on pages 181–188.

The difficulties in the external payments situation ultimately reflect the crisis in the domestic economy. Although the external shocks resulting at times from sudden large falls in the oil price complicate the challenges of macroeconomic management, the overall trend in oil export earnings has been upward, because of the rise in the volume of production. The fundamental problem has been the decline in non-oil production, discussed above, which has reduced the supply of domestically produced goods and non-oil exports while making the country exaggeratedly dependent on imports.

As Figure 5.1 shows, the period of renewed warfare in 1993–94 had a particularly devastating impact on the non-oil sectors. In 1993, non-oil GDP fell in real terms by a staggering 31 per cent, contributing to a real fall in total GDP of 24 per cent. After a further, but smaller, real fall in non-oil GDP in 1994, there was a recovery in 1995–97, driven in particular by improved conditions for agricultural production and urban-rural trade following the Lusaka Protocol. However, even by the end of the 1990s, non-oil GDP was still more than 10 per cent less than it had been in 1992. After the return to war at the end of 1998, economic recovery outside the oil sector was set back again, but significantly there was no repeat of the dramatic fall in GDP experienced in the previous period of war.

Figure 5.1: Real trend in non-oil GDP, 1992–99
(index 1992=100; actual 1992–98, estimated 1999)

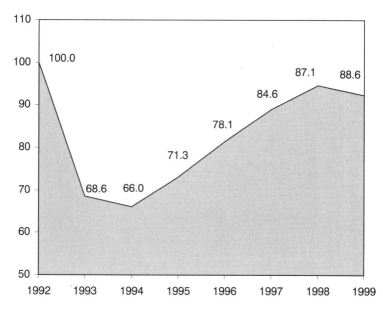

Sources: IMF, 1999a, 1999c, 2000

The slump in domestic production outside the oil sector has contributed to the low level of non-oil fiscal receipts, which had fallen to 11 per cent of total government revenue by 1996. Other factors have contributed to the low levels of non-oil tax revenue. Excessive controls and regulations have encouraged businesses to operate in the informal sector, thereby eroding the tax base. The precarious finances of state companies resulted in many of them being unable to pay taxes and becoming dependent on government subsidies. The tax system is antiquated, with many redundant and unproductive taxes and a proliferation of exemptions. Last but by no means least, the ineffective tax administration leaves ample scope for tax evasion through bribery and fraud (World Bank, 1993). An additional factor has been the impact of inflation on tax payments denominated in national currency, given the time-lags in payments.

On average, over the period 1995–99, non-oil fiscal revenue was equivalent to only 6 per cent of GDP (IMF, 1999a, 2000). The government is therefore overwhelmingly dependent on fiscal receipts from the oil sector and highly vulnerable to sudden falls in oil prices, as happened in 1998–99. Furthermore, the maintenance of an overvalued exchange rate greatly reduced the local currency value of oil earnings until the abolition of the fixed official rate in May 1999.

On the expenditure side, government deficits have been exacerbated by very high levels of defence and security expenditure, large transfers for subsidies, notably for petroleum products, and the expansion of the civil service payroll. Budget management has been rendered extraordinarily difficult by the fact that a large proportion of both expenditure and revenue is off-budget, one of the main complaints of successive IMF missions. On average, the overall deficit in government finances was equivalent to 18 per cent of GDP during the period from 1995 to 1999 (IMF, 1999a, 1999c, 2000).

With limited access to external financing, and in the absence of tradeable instruments such as Treasury bills or government bonds, these deficits have simply been monetized, causing a rapid growth of money supply and, in a context of depressed supply of goods and services, high rates of inflation. These imbalances generated hyper-inflationary conditions in the mid-1990s, with annualized inflation peaking at 12,035 per cent in July 1996 before stabilizing somewhat as a result of the imposition of tighter fiscal controls, but at the cost of a substantial build-up of domestic arrears. Although inflation was brought down to 107 per cent in the year to December 1998, it accelerated again thereafter, reaching an annualized rate of 329 per cent by December 1999 and 438 per cent by May 2000 (IMF, 2000).

Due to the high import dependence of the Angolan economy, inflation has by and large accompanied the depreciation of the national currency, although movements in the administratively set official exchange rate tended to lag behind the fall in the currency on the parallel market, until the abolition of the official rate in May 1999.

The chequered history of economic reform

Economic reforms began in 1987 with the launching of the *Programa de Saneamento Económico e Financeiro* (SEF, or Programme of Economic and Financial Clean-Up), partly in response to the problems created by the fall in oil prices in 1985–86. As in other African countries undergoing adjustment, the reforms have had two main thrusts: first, the restoration of macroeconomic stability, and second, institutional and structural reforms aimed at improving the efficiency of the economy and stimulating growth. In the Angolan case, the second dimension has been more comparable in some respects to the reforms in the transitional economies of the former Soviet bloc than in some other African countries, because of the scale of previous state intervention in the economy. Angola has been involved in a complex transition from a state-run economic system to one based on the market.

Although radical changes have taken place since the announcement of the SEF, it is striking in retrospect to see how the reform process has been punctuated by frequent changes in direction, resulting in alternating periods of reform, policy reversal and drift. Table 5.3 presents in summary form the successive economic programmes between 1987 and 2000.

During this thirteen-year period, there were no less than nine different economic programmes, some lasting barely a year – and in one case only a few weeks. Seven could be described as being broadly reformist in nature, although with varying degrees of implementation, and two, the *Programa de Emergência do Governo* (Government Emergency Programme) in 1993–94 and the *Programa Nova Vida* (New Life Programme) in 1996–97, were clearly anti-reformist, reversing previously implemented reforms. In a series of papers on macroeconomic policy in Angola, economists from Gothenburg University (Aguilar & Zejan, 1991, 1992; Aguilar & Stenman, 1994, 1996) have traced the evolution of some of these programmes, showing a pattern in which initial bursts of reforming energy have resulted in the partial implementation of the proposed measures, usually without adequate policy co-ordination, followed by setbacks (often resulting from the lack of consistency in the measures), political intervention from above to halt the reforms and then a period of drift or, as in March 1993 and June 1996, the partial reversal of the reforms.

In the early period (1987–90), little was done beyond making declarations of intent. The first reforms to be implemented followed the announcement of the *Programa de Acção do Governo* (PAG, or Government Action Programme) in August 1990. Several structural measures dismantled much of the former system of administrative price-setting. Most prices were liberalized (by abolishing official price controls for hundreds of products), wages (which had previously been paid partly in kind) were fully monetized, the former ration card system was abolished, privatization of state enterprises was launched, with the sale of several hundred small businesses and farms, reform of the banking system began and the first steps were taken to devalue the currency, with a view to closing the gap between the official and parallel market exchange rates.

Macroeconomic stabilization efforts focused on a bold move to try to rein in money supply through a change in currency, the famous *troca de moeda* in September 1990, when the kwanza was replaced by the new kwanza. The changeover was accompanied by the freezing of 95 per cent of the value of bank accounts, a measure intended to reduce liquidity through shock therapy and curb the inflationary tendencies in the economy. This impulsive measure failed to take into account both the drastic side-effects of the medicine (a collapse in confidence in the banks which endures to this day) and the fact that the rapid monetary growth was a symptom of a more deep-rooted problem, the monetization of government deficits. The draconian monetary measures had to be abandoned after a few months. The start of devaluation, which could have contributed to fiscal stabilization, was postponed until six months after the *troca de moeda*, and no progress was made in tackling the budget deficit.

Overall, the experience of the PAG highlighted one of the basic weaknesses of the reform programmes in Angola: the lack of synchronization of policy measures. More specifically, these programmes (with the partial exception of the *Nova Vida* programme) failed to address the large deficit in government finances, consequently undermining the effectiveness of other measures. Successive devaluations, for example, were generally not accompanied by fiscal restraint and so simply contributed to an inflationary spiral. The weakness of fiscal management is closely inter-related with the problem of extra-budgetary operations, which prevents effective transparency and accountability in government finances and thus makes it extraordinarily difficult to implement or monitor a coherent fiscal policy.

In short, the lack of a holistic approach has been one of the main limitations of attempts at economic reform. Reviewing the experience of economic reform efforts in Angola, the World Bank made the following pertinent observations in August 1996 (World Bank, 1996):

> Most typically, partial reforms are implemented and replaced by others as they fail to bring inflation under control. This sequence of

Table 5.3: Economic programmes, 1987–2000

Programme with date launched	Main features
Programa de Saneamento Económico e Financeiro (SEF) August 1987	A follow-up to the 2nd congress of the MPLA-PT in December 1985, the SEF was intended to begin the transition from central planning to a market-based economy, but little was done in practice.
Programa de Recuperação da Economia (PER) January 1989	This was supposed to be the first stage of implementation of the SEF. Again, however, few measures were actually implemented, apart from the establishment of offices to promote foreign investment and prepare for restructuring of state companies, and entry into the IMF and World Bank (1989).
Programa de Acção do Governo (PAG) August 1990	This was the first major attempt to introduce economic reforms in practice. A change in the currency (from the kwanza to new kwanza) in September 1990 was accompanied by shock monetary measures, including the freezing of 95 per cent of the value of bank accounts, which dealt a fatal blow to public confidence in the banks. The restrictive monetary policy was then abandoned during 1991, while continued monetization of large budget deficits fuelled inflationary pressures. Meanwhile, currency devaluation began in March 1991, while most official price controls were swept away in 1991–92, wages were fully monetized in late 1991, and many small businesses were privatized in 1991–92. Reform of the banking system began in 1991.
Programa de Estabilização da Economia (PEE) January 1993	Intended to push forward with economic reforms, this short-lived programme gave priority to introducing an auction system for allocating foreign exchange and setting the exchange rate. The first auction, in February 1993, resulted in a steep fall in the official value of the new kwanza, causing a political backlash and the dismissal of the finance minister and governor of the BNA.
Programa de Emergência do Governo (PEG) March 1993	Under the leadership of a more conservative economic team, the government reversed the reforms by abandoning the auction system and revaluing the new kwanza upwards. Coinciding with the return to war, the PEG marked a return to more administrative methods of economic management. However, economic pressures eventually forced the government to begin a series of devaluations and allow a limited open market.
Programa Económico e Social para 1994 (PES 94) April 1994	The PES 94 signalled a return to reform, focusing on devaluation, fiscal stabilization and a restrictive monetary policy. The gap between the official and parallel exchange rates narrowed sharply, but a continued large fiscal deficit stoked inflation.
Programa Económico e Social para1995–96 (PES 95–96) April 1995	This was a re-edition of PES 94. Through regular 'fixing sessions' with the banks, a managed float of the currency resulted in near-convergence of the exchange rates by mid-1995, when a new currency (the kwanza *reajustado*) was introduced. For the first time,negotiations with the IMF reached agreement on the start of a staff-monitored IMF programme in July 1995, although still without IMF financing. However, the programme went seriously off-course and was terminated in December 1995. The managed float of the kwanza had been terminated, widening the gap between the official and parallel exchange rates. Continued monetization of a large fiscal deficit produced hyper-inflationary conditions. The IMF expressed particular concern at the lack of transparency in government finances and the weak political consensus in favour of reform.

Table 5.3: Economic programmes, 1987–2000 *Continued*

Programme with date launched	Main features
Programa Nova Vida June 1996	With the country in the grip of hyper-inflationary conditions (monthly inflation reached 84 per cent in May 1996), the PES was abandoned and replaced by the *Nova Vida* (New Life) programme, which, under a more conservative economic team, restored many past administrative controls, including a fixed exchange rate, rigid import licensing procedures and price controls. These measures were accompanied by tighter fiscal and monetary policies, which helped to reduce inflation, but at the cost of a large increase in public domestic debt through the accumulation of arrears.
Programa de Estabilização e Recuperação Económica de Médio Prazo 1998–2000 January 1998	This marked a return to previous liberalizing measures. Progress was made in closing the exchange-rate gap through staged devaluations. A new agreement was negotiated with the IMF in mid-1998, but was never signed, while the policy of step-by-step devaluation halted. Meanwhile, the steep fall in oil prices, coinciding with the slide back to war, amplified the fiscal deficit and the debt-service burden, while eroding international reserves and making the fixed exchange rate untenable. These developments led, in February 1999, to another change in the economic team and more far-reaching reforms. In May 1999, the official exchange rate was allowed to float freely, merging with the parallel market rate, and interest rates were liberalized. A third currency reform restored the kwanza in December 1999 and, in April 2000, the government finally signed an agreement with the IMF for a new staff-monitored programme, promising to ensure greater transparency in government finances.

events characterizes Angola's recent economic policy which followed a piece-meal approach in the sense that measures such as exchange rate devaluation were implemented but never as part of a comprehensive macroeconomic program. The key missing ingredient was a comprehensive budget policy aimed at reducing the size of the fiscal deficit and changing the way it is financed. This is the basic reason why Angola's reform attempts have so far failed.

The follow-up programme to the PAG, the *Programa de Estabilização da Economia* (PEE, or Economic Stabilization Programme), launched in January 1993, was intended to deepen the reforms begun under the PAG, notably by introducing an auction system to allocate foreign exchange and set the exchange rate. The short life of this programme (a mere two months) highlighted two other characteristics of economic policy-making: the tendency for high-level political interventions to halt reforms perceived to be going too far, and the tendency for wartime situations to encourage a return to more administrative methods of economic management. The PEE coincided with the return to full-scale war after the September 1992 elections.

The PEE's introduction of foreign-exchange auctions resulted in a steep fall in the official exchange rate, causing an immediate political backlash. The authors of this innovation, the finance minister, Salomão Xirimbimbi, and the governor of the *Banco Nacional de Angola*, Sebastião Lavrador, were summarily dismissed and replaced by a more conservative economic team, headed by Emanuel Carneiro, who was finance minister from March 1993 to March 1994. Carneiro masterminded the *Programa de Emergência do Governo* (PEG), which was presented as a 'war economy' programme, requiring a move away from market mechanisms and the revival of some of the centralized planning methods of the past. One of its first measures, unique in the economic history of Angola in the 1990s, was an *increase* in the official value of the new kwanza, to reverse partially the large devaluation which had occurred through Xirimbimbi's auction system.

However, even during the PEG, economic realities eventually forced new devaluations and, a year after its launch, there was another swing back to reforming mode, with the unveiling of the *Programa Económico e Social* (PES) for 1994. Together with its successor, the PES for 1995–96, this was perhaps the most coherent attempt yet at macroeconomic stabilization. It focused on devaluation (or exchange-rate convergence between the official and parallel markets), fiscal stabilization and monetary restraint. Once again, a new currency, the readjusted kwanza, was introduced, at one-thousandth of the value of the new kwanza. A system of 'fixing sessions', involving the central bank and the commercial banks, was devised to manage a downwards float of the exchange rate and, by June 1995, convergence of the official and parallel exchange rates had almost been achieved. The IMF was sufficiently encouraged to reach agreement with the government in July 1995 on a 'staff-monitored programme', a shadow programme in which IMF staff would monitor progress towards meeting a number of benchmarks (policy measures and macroeconomic targets) without the commitment of IMF resources.

But, once again, political intervention from above halted the measures agreed with the IMF. The gap between official and parallel exchange rates widened again and the lack of action to tackle the fiscal deficit led to a surge in inflation, which reached an annual rate of 3,784 per cent in December 1995. The IMF abandoned its staff-monitored programme the same month and for the next half year there was a sense of aimless drift as macroeconomic conditions spiralled out of control. This period saw the country lurching into hyper-inflation, peaking at an annual rate of 12,035 per cent in July 1996.

Rising social tension in the cities brought about another sharp reversal in policy in June 1996, with the adoption of the *Nova Vida* programme. The government reverted to a wide range of administrative mechanisms, including the re-imposition of some price controls, the revival of government involvement in imports of strategic consumer goods, and tighter import licensing procedures, in an attempt to ensure the supply of food to the urban population, stabilize prices and head off social unrest. While these measures implied a reversal of previous liberalizing reforms, an attempt was also made to instill greater discipline in government finances – the weak link in all previous reform initiatives. The overall budget deficit was brought down from a record 27 per cent of GDP in 1995 to 16 per cent in 1996, and annual inflation fell to 1,651 per cent in December 1996 and 148 per cent in December 1997. However, this was achieved partly through a substantial build-up of domestic arrears, storing up problems for the future.[8]

Some of the more restrictive administrative measures of the *Nova Vida* programme were eased in 1997–98, and in January 1998 a new reformist programme was launched. For the first time, this had a medium-term horizon, covering three years. Like the PES in 1994–96, it focused on restoring macroeconomic stability through fiscal and monetary restraint and convergence of the official and parallel exchange rates. But, again like the PES, implementation was uneven, with sudden shifts in specific policies, particularly on the exchange rate, resulting once again in sudden reversals in relations with the IMF. A new staff-monitored programme was negotiated with the Fund in mid-1998 but was not signed, because of presidential objections.

In February 1999, however, a change of economic ministers heralded the radicalization of reform measures (GURN, 1999). In May 1999, the government abolished the official exchange rate entirely, by allowing the rate to be determined freely in an inter-bank market. This was accompanied by other reforms which had long been urged by the IMF. Interest rates were liberalized, to restore positive real interest rates and so promote savings and improved efficiency in the distribution of credit. The government also took the first steps towards reform of the commercial banking and insurance sectors, which have historically been dominated by state-owned institutions, and stated that it would prepare some large state companies for privatization.

For the third time in less than a decade, the currency was changed in December 1999, its name reverting to the kwanza (neither 'new' nor 'readjusted'), with one kwanza equivalent to a million of the outgoing readjusted kwanzas. As in the past, the success of the currency change would ultimately depend on whether the government could curb inflation, then running at 329 per cent, through improved fiscal management. With a

---

[8] Government domestic debt to private and parastatal companies was estimated in 1998 to total between $750 m. and $1 billion (UNDP, 1998). Rapid exchange rate depreciation in the first half of 1999, following the fall in oil prices, pointed to a new surge in inflation, since prices and exchange rates are closely inter-related in a country with such a high degree of import dependence.

view to reducing the large budget deficit, the government began tax reforms, to increase non-oil fiscal revenue, and removed the subsidies on fuel. Petrol prices rose by 1,450 per cent in February 2000. Subsidies on water and electricity were also to be phased out, starting with a rise of more than 1,000 per cent in electricity tariffs in March–April 2000.

These steps, along with commitments by the government to improve the transparency of government finances through diagnostic studies of the petroleum and diamond industries, an external audit of the central bank and steps to halt extra-budgetary expenditures, gave sufficient encouragement to the IMF for it to sign an agreement with the Angolan government on 3 April 2000 for a new staff-monitored programme, to run until December 2000. Again, there was no commitment of IMF resources, but, if the programme went well, it was understood that it would be followed by a full-scale adjustment programme backed by IMF lending.

Causes of inconsistency in economic policy

Several factors would seem to explain the inconsistency in economic policy over the past decade. The first is the weakness of economic management capacity, relative to the scale of the tasks to be carried out. This must to some extent explain such shortcomings as the inadequate co-ordination or synchronization of policy measures and the difficulties experienced in converting declared policies into action. It is not just that there is only a small number of qualified economists available for core economic management tasks in the Ministry of Planning, Ministry of Finance and central bank (BNA). Perhaps even more important, their morale has been eroded by low pay and the constant reversals in policy. In addition, the data available for macroeconomic management are deficient, particularly in such key areas as government finances and public debt, because of the substantial unrecorded off-budget operations and the failure to record all debt contracts. These problems are inter-related with a more fundamental political problem, the weak commitment at the highest level to some key reform measures, resulting in periodic intervention from the presidency to undermine or reverse reforms.

In a report on the breakdown of the IMF staff-monitored programme in December 1995, an IMF technical team highlighted these root problems with remarkable frankness (IMF, 1995). It reported that it was:

> ... extremely concerned about the present fragility and vulnerability of the key institutions responsible for economic and financial policies – the Ministry of Finance and the *Banco Nacional de Angola*. ... The mission is also aware that the effort required is gigantic, due largely to the accumulation of inadequate practices

perpetuated, indeed aggravated, in the last few years, the absence of financial discipline at all levels, the small number of qualified technical and professional staff at every level and, last but not least, the significant erosion of the commitment of professional staff and workers in view of the stress caused until recently by the intensification of the armed conflict and the decline in purchasing power resulting from runaway inflation. However, the mission is of the opinion that, apart from the latter factors, there is still considerable interference and pressure at a political level in the conduct and management of the economy and public finances, and of the central bank. This constant interference and pressure, along with the absence of a consensus on the direction of the policies to adopt, has made it exceedingly difficult to undertake consistent, sustainable economic and financial policies.

The report noted that, although the Ministry of Finance and the *Banco Nacional de Angola* had made an effort to meet some of the requirements of the monitored programme,

...these efforts were overtaken and to a large extent annulled by contrary decisions taken at the highest levels of the Government.

This political factor has resulted also in frequent changes in the economic management team responsible for designing and implementing the successive programmes. As Table 5.4 shows, there were eight changes of finance minister between 1990 and 1999. There have been five central bank governors. At times this instability has looked like a game of musical chairs, with the same personalities sometimes reappearing, occupying different posts or returning to posts they had previously occupied. Major changes in economic philosophy, marking shifts between reformist and conservative economic programmes, and occurring usually at times of intensified economic crisis, have invariably involved a complete change in the economic team, accompanied by stinging public criticisms of the outgoing team by the head of state. In May 1996, the crisis that ushered in the *Nova Vida* programme also saw the President criticizing and dismissing his figurehead Prime Minister, Marcolino Moco.

There has also been a tendency for the primary responsibility for economic policy-making to shift back and forth between the planning and finance ministers. During the centralized planning period, up until the end of the 1980s, the Ministry of Planning had unambiguous primacy, laid down in law by virtue of the role of the annual plan as the framework document for all economic and financial programmes and policies, including the annual government budget and foreign exchange budget (Hoygaard, 1995). Law 2/82 established the legal foundations of the

Table 5.4: The instability in economic leadership and policies, 1990–99

Dates	Finance minister	Planning minister	BNA governor	Lead minister	Nature of policies
Jun 1990–Sep 1991	Aguinaldo Jaime	None[a]	Sebastião Lavrador	Finance	Reformist
Sep 1991–Dec 1992	Emanuel Carneiro	None[a]	Sebastião Lavrador	Finance	Anti–reformist
Dec 1992–Feb 1993	Salomão Xirimbimbi	None[a]	Sebastião Lavrador	Finance	Reformist
Mar 1993–Mar 1994	Emanuel Carneiro	None[a]	Generoso de Almeida (to 4/95)	Finance	Anti–reformist
Mar 1994–Jan 1995	Álvaro Craveiro	None[a]	Generoso de Almeida (to 4/95)	Planning	Reformist
Jan 1995–Jun 1996	Augusto Tomás	José Pedro de Morais	(from 4/95) António Furtado	Finance	Reformist
Jun 1996–Feb 1999	Mário Monteiro	Emanuel Carneiro	Sebastião Lavrador	Planning	Anti–reformist
Since Feb 1999	Joaquim David	Ana Dias Lourenço	Aguinaldo Jaime	Finance	Reformist

[a]No minister but a secretary of state for planning

centralized planning system, making all ministries, state secretariats and provincial governments responsible for 'full execution of the tasks, objectives and goals of the plan'. The system was led by the Ministry of Planning, established the same year (decree 8/82) from the previous National Planning Commission, set up shortly after independence. The Ministry of Planning lost its supremacy in 1988, by virtue of law 12/88, following a review of the institutional functions of economic management that began after the second congress of the MPLA-PT in 1985 and accompanied the first steps towards a market-based economy. The Ministry of Planning was downgraded to a Secretariat of State for Planning (SEPLAN) in 1988, while the Ministry of Finance assumed greater prominence and autonomy.

During the periods of reform in 1990–93 (PAG and PEE) and counter-reform in 1993–94 (PEG), the Ministry of Finance was in the lead. In 1994, however, SEPLAN was revamped as the Ministry of Planning and Economic Co-ordination, assuming responsibility for overall leadership of the PES in 1994. In 1995, the pendulum swung back to the Ministry of Finance, then renamed the Ministry of Economy and Finance, which masterminded the PES 95–96, only to revert to the Ministry of Planning with the launching of the *Nova Vida* programme in June 1996. In February 1999, the Ministry of Finance once again became the lead economic ministry, under Joaquim David.

This instability in leadership and institutional responsibilities has been closely related to the shifts and changes in economic programmes. Ultimately, however, it is well understood by all those involved in the economic policy-making process that the key decisions on economic issues are not taken by the ministers, or by the governor of the BNA, but by the head of state, who has his own economic adviser at Futungo de Belas, the presidential compound outside Luanda. The President's own shifting views about the scope and pace of reform have led to the political 'interference' referred to by the IMF, resulting in the signals to ministers switching frequently from green to red and vice versa, as well as the frequent changes in ministers. Although the ministers seem to have had only short-lived intervals of real control over policy-making or implementation, they and sometimes the prime ministers have been the fall-guys for each successive programme failure.

Ultimately, one can only speculate about the real motives for the shifts in policies, programmes and ministers, and for the inconsistent nature of programme implementation. Varying mixes of economic/financial and political/military pressures seem to play a role, along with the pressures of interest groups, the exigencies of patronage systems and the President's inclination to resort to dismissing his economic ministers and denouncing the programmes or policies associated with them in order to shield himself from a public backlash against the mismanagement of the economy. There also seems to be a strong element of reactive crisis management.

Periods of war might be expected to encourage more administrative, as opposed to market-based, approaches to economic management and to encourage less transparency, particularly in the management of government finances, because of the perceived need to circumvent budget execution procedures and procurement rules to obtain urgently needed military equipment. This may explain why there was a shift away from market mechanisms to more administrative forms of economic management when the PEG was launched in March 1993, at a time of extreme military pressure on the government, following the resumption of the war at the end of 1992. It is almost certainly one of the contributory causes of the continued opaqueness in government finances.

In other cases, social tension and the regime's fear of losing political hegemony over the urban population have clearly been the spur for launching or scuttling programmes and policies. This was most evident in May-June 1996, on the eve of *Nova Vida*, when hyperinflation was reaching tornado-like proportions, raising the spectre of demonstrations and strikes. The re-imposition of controls on prices and profit margins, along with the administrative allocation of foreign exchange and import licences, was accompanied by the menacing presence of the Rapid Intervention Police on the streets of Luanda.

At other times, acute economic and financial pressures have dictated policy shifts. For example, the steep fall in oil prices and the collapse in foreign reserves which occurred at the end of 1998 and beginning of 1999, coinciding with the return to war and the need to spend yet more resources on arms procurement, led directly to the change in the economic management team in February 1999. Gross international reserves were so low by the end of 1998 ($201 million or enough to cover only two weeks' imports)[9] that it had become impossible to sustain the fixed official exchange rate. In May 1999, the new governor of the BNA, Aguinaldo Jaime, told parliament that the country was facing one of its 'worst ever crises' and that reserves were 'on the verge of exhaustion'.[10]

The new team was authorized by the head of state to embark on far-reaching economic reform measures, with the aim of shoring up reserves, reaching an agreement with the IMF and obtaining new concessional financing and debt relief. As we have seen, these measures and commitments by the government led to an agreement with the IMF on a new staff-monitored programme in April 2000.

Ironically, the negotiations which led up to this agreement took place at a time when many other donors were scaling back their development assistance, or limiting aid to humanitarian relief channelled through NGOs, out of frustration at the slow pace of reform and concern about entrenched official corruption. The World Bank, for example, decided not to post a replacement when its representative in Angola left in 1999.[11] It also decided to make no new loans to Angola. The UK closed the aid section of its embassy in 1998 and, by 2000, Sweden, the Netherlands and Belgium were all declining to sign new co-operation agreements.

Nonetheless, for only the second time in its history, and a little over four years after the collapse of the earlier short-lived IMF agreement in December 1995, Angola once again embarked on a staff-monitored programme.[12] As in 1995, the decisive issue, which was likely to make or break the agreement, was the question of transparency in public finances. As the next section discusses in further detail, this has been the litmus test of commitment to fundamental reform in economic management, since it goes to the heart of how the country's resources are managed.

Extra-budgetary operations

As has been noted above, military or security imperatives may be one of the causal factors encouraging non-transparency in government finances, one of the core outstanding issues of reform, which is vital both for

---

[9] Despite the subsequent recovery in oil prices, gross international reserves had fallen even lower, to provide only one week's import cover, by September 1999 (IMF, 1999c).

[10] *Reuters*, 6 May 1999.

[11] After the IMF agreement, the Bank was under strong pressure from both the IMF and the Angolan government to re-engage with Angola, notably by providing support for the implementation of the staff-monitored programme.

[12] The staff-monitored programme was due to run until December 2000.

improved fiscal management and for good governance in general. Whether military considerations are the whole explanation for the large extra-budgetary operations is far from clear. Institutional weaknesses may result in the bypassing of formally established budget execution procedures, and lack of transparency could also serve as a convenient cover for fraud and diversion of funds. Here, it is important simply to note the scale of extra-budgetary operations and the concern that this has aroused in the international financial institutions. During the past decade, this issue has been the most important point of contention between the IMF and the Angolan government.

The Fund was forthright about its concerns on this matter when it suspended the staff-monitored programme in December 1995 (IMF, 1995):

> The lack of transparency and recording of financial transactions related to petroleum, both in the BNA and in the Treasury accounts, makes it exceedingly difficult to obtain data on the state of public finances and the accounts of the BNA...
>
> The fiscal implications of the absence of a mechanism ensuring the recording of accounts for government operations related to oil transactions, are perfectly clear in the data uncovered, which show that about 40 per cent of estimated expenditure up till September was carried out bypassing the Treasury, largely financed by petroleum revenues that were also outside the Treasury's purview and as such were likewise not reflected in the budget execution accounts. Besides the so-called petroleum transactions, there was also a high level of expenditures which did not follow the established procedures for executing State expenditures. The mission estimates that the total expenditure outside the normal procedures for Treasury operations amounts to about 64 per cent of total expenditure up to September.

Payments were being made by the BNA without payment orders approved by the Ministry of Finance in accordance with the procedures of the *Sistema Integrado de Gestão Financeira do Estado* (SIGFE, or Integrated State Financial Management System).[13] However, the situation was enormously complicated by the large, complex cross-debts between the government and SONANGOL, related to arrears in the payment of subsidies to SONANGOL for petroleum products sold on the domestic

---

[13] In theory, this system lays down clear procedures for financial programming and the authorization of expenditures. Payment orders (*ordens de saque*) are supposed to be approved by the National Treasury Directorate in the Ministry of Finance, within the framework of the approved budget (OGE) and quarterly expenditure ceilings established by the Ministry's National Budget Directorate. Once it has received authorization of the payment order, the government budget unit (*gestor orçamental*) can obtain the transfer of funds from the unified Treasury account (*conta única do Tesouro*) at the BNA to its own sub-account.

market and the role of SONANGOL in contracting and servicing foreign debt guaranteed by oil on behalf of the state. These problems will be discussed further in Chapter 6.

Some corrective measures were subsequently implemented, including the establishment of a 'petroleum account' at the BNA, which was intended to achieve transparency in all the financial dealings related to petroleum involving the BNA, the Treasury and SONANGOL. However, in June 1997, another IMF mission reported that the situation regarding the transparency of government finances had deteriorated (IMF, 1997):

> Coordination between the Treasury and the NBA [*Banco Nacional de Angola*] has deteriorated since mid-1996 resulting in the NBA not honouring payment orders properly authorized by the Treasury, while carrying out other payments for the account of the government without payment orders....During 1996, lack of coordination between the NBA and the Treasury greatly contributed to the accumulation of domestic arrears....Finally, there is the need to document all outstanding oil-related external credits to SONANGOL, the NBA, or the state...

As has been noted above, the acute external payments crisis that emerged in 1998–99, as a result of the collapse of international oil prices, obliged the government to address these issues because it needed to come to terms with the IMF if it was to alleviate its external financial constraints by gaining access to concessional sources of finance and debt rescheduling.

The IMF has made estimates of the scale of extra-budgetary expenditure on defence and security (see Figure 5.2), showing that this accounted for as much as 26 per cent of total government expenditure in 1996. Although this proportion fell in 1997–98 (to 18 and 14 per cent respectively), approximately half of defence and security expenditure was unrecorded in both years (IMF, 2000).

At the time of writing (mid-2000), it remained to be seen whether the measures promised by the government to reach agreement with the IMF in April 2000 would bring about a real change in the management of public finances, or whether, as during the previous staff-monitored programme in 1995, they would eventually be derailed by political imperatives, vested interests and, with rising oil revenues, the easing of the external financial pressures which had spurred the accommodation with the IMF. The issues involved go to the heart of economic governance. The existence of a large parallel system of government finances outside the framework of the approved budget, bypassing the established rules and procedures for managing expenditures, fiscal receipts and public debt, is one of the most fundamental problems of public resource management. Not only does it confound attempts to instil rigour in

Figure 5.2: Share of defence & public order in government expenditure, 1993–99 (%)

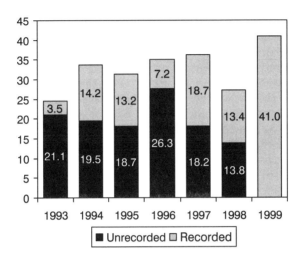

Source: IMF, 1999a, 2000

financial programming, which is central to the challenge of restoring macroeconomic equilibrium, but it makes it impossible to achieve real accountability in financial matters, whether to the National Assembly or, if it is eventually set up, to the *Tribunal de Contas*.

Impact of interest groups and patronage on economic reform

Another explanatory factor regarding the pace and scope of reform has been the influence of groups with vested interests in the maintenance of non-transparent systems and administrative mechanisms for the allocation of resources and the award of contracts, concessions and other economic opportunities. Several spheres of economic policy highlight the importance of these vested interests and how their satisfaction has been a pivotal part of the system of state patronage. Here, we examine, for illustrative purposes, three of the most important mechanisms: exchange-rate policy, credit policy and privatization.

Privileged access to foreign exchange at the administratively set official exchange rate has been one of the principal mechanisms for enrichment by the politically connected elite and has amounted in fact to a transfer of resources, mainly derived from oil revenues, from the state to the individual beneficiaries. Because the official exchange rate was set administratively, well below the market equilibrium rate, the foreign currency sold at this artifical rate had to be rationed. However, there was no rational, transparent way of doing this. In practice, the political authorities simply informed the banks which individuals should receive the foreign exchange on offer.

The scope for arbitrage, or 'round-tripping' between markets, by those with privileged access to foreign exchange at the official rate, has been enormous, because of the wide gap between the official and parallel market rates. The divergence between the two rates had begun during the period of centralized planning, reaching extreme levels in the late 1980s. It narrowed as a result of the successive devaluations after 1991. Overall, during the period 1991–98, there was an average ratio of 2.9 to one between the parallel and official exchange rates. Although the spread between the two rates was much reduced, the government's inconsistent actions (periodic devaluations followed by periods of real exchange-rate appreciation) resulted in the maintenance of a significant, albeit fluctuating, exchange rate spread in 1996–98, shown in Figure 5.3.

The advantages of the system for those lucky enough to receive this cheap foreign currency have been well described by Munslow (1999: 563):

Figure 5.3: Percentage spread between official and parallel exchange rates, July 1996–December 1998

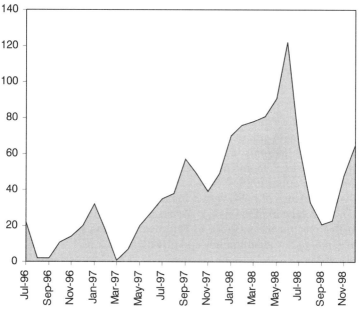

Source: BNA

Dollars could be purchased from the Central Bank at low official kwanza rates of exchange, only for the dollars to then be sold on the parallel market to purchase many more kwanza for an inflated but more realistic dollar equivalent. The increased bundle could then be used to buy yet more dollars and so the licence to make money was complete, but only for the few.

The continued overvaluation of the national currency contributed to import dependence, further benefiting those engaged in the import trade, and made it more difficult to reduce the budget deficit, which was exaggerated by the undervaluing of oil revenues in national currency. Given the obvious macroeconomic costs, it is a plausible hypothesis that well-placed interest groups benefiting from access to foreign exchange at the official rate periodically blocked the implementation of measures to achieve exchange-rate convergence.[14] In a report on the failure of the IMF staff-monitored programme in 1995, when the exchange-rate gap exceeded 100 per cent instead of the programme's target of 15 per cent, the Fund stated that it was 'especially concerned by evidence that the exchange rate policy which has actually been implemented benefits in practice well-connected persons and/or businessmen at the cost of substantial financial losses for the central bank' (IMF, 1995). As has been noted above, it was only in May 1999, at a time of virtual exhaustion of the international reserves and urgent efforts to reach agreement with the IMF, following the decline in oil prices, that the government finally decided to abolish the official rate, by allowing the exchange rate to be determined by demand and supply, through an inter-bank foreign exchange market.

Credit policy provides a second example of how the politically connected elite had a vested interest in holding up reform. The system of administratively fixed interest rates, set well below the rate of inflation, and administrative allocation of credit benefited those with the right political connections. State-owned banks, which dominate the commercial banking sector, allocated credit on the basis of administrative directives received from the central bank or higher political authorities. The system had serious macroeconomic costs, since it resulted in the misallocation of credit and, by maintaining negative real interest rates,

---

[14] The World Bank has described this system and its negative effects as follows (World Bank, 1996). 'Angola's system of foreign exchange management has created an unequal playing field whereby only the few who have access to foreign exchange at the official rate enjoy a considerable advantage over all others (at the expense of the Government, which could sell the foreign exchange at a higher price...). Besides transferring resources to the private sector, the importation of 'priority goods' at the official exchange rate results in an unfair competition with goods produced domestically that often have a large content of intermediate goods imported using non-subsidised foreign exchange.'

discouraged savings. Since bank credits have generally been available only for short periods and almost never for more than two years, the credit system has also created a strong bias towards short-term import operations at the expense of longer-term productive investments. Combined with the opportunities for arbitrage between foreign-exchange markets, it has strongly reinforced the incentives for rent-seeking behaviour. This was well described by the World Bank in the following terms in 1996:

> The credit allocations mirror those of foreign exchange through the official market and are often tied to foreign exchange trading operations. While in theory the sale of foreign exchange would involve the payments of counterpart funds in Kwanza, some clients obtain bank credit (at negative real interest rates) to pay the already subsidized foreign exchange. Because the amount of foreign exchange sold through this market is small and the rents appropriated through its allocation are large, there is fierce competition for these funds.

Furthermore, the bad lending practices of one of the state banks, the *Caixa de Crédito Agro-Pecuária e Pescas* (CAP), which gained the reputation of being a 'slush-fund' for the well-connected and for ailing state companies, resulted in that bank accumulating a large stock of non-performing loans.[15] The weakness of the legal system has made it impossible to recover bad debts, even where creditors formally have collateral. The CAP's lending practices generated concern about the enforcement of prudential regulations and the soundness of the banking system, undermining attempts to rebuild public confidence in the banks, which was shattered by the experience of the *troca de moeda* in 1990. This was another area where the government finally announced corrective measures in May 1999, liberalizing interest rates and suspending the board of the CAP. Later in the year, the CAP was liquidated, but it is unlikely that its bad loans will ever be recovered.

A third example is provided by the privatization programme, which began in the late 1980s. Under two laws adopted in 1988 and 1991 (law 10/88 on economic activities and law 9/91 on state companies), the government set out principles and procedures for the restructuring and partial privatization of the hitherto large state sector. In the absence of an organized capital market, such as a stock exchange, the legislation provided for the sale of companies through public bidding, limited bidding and, in the case of small companies, direct negotiations with

---

[15] In a report in November 1996, the IMF described the CAP as an 'affiliate' of the BNA and expressed concern that its lending 'represents an expansion of credit by the central bank, with potentially inflationary effects, results in quasi-fiscal losses for the State which are non-transparent and difficult to control, and produces inefficient subsidies for those benefiting from this financing' (IMF, 1996).

interested buyers. The main focus was on privatizing small businesses, which were reserved for Angolan rather than foreign investors. It is noteworthy that the privatization of small state companies took place without proper valuations or competitive bidding. As a result, army officers and other high-ranking officials were able to acquire farms and other businesses as political favours, often for nominal sums or for no payment at all. Most small state-owned companies were sold. Overall, by the end of 1996, the number of state companies had fallen from 545 to 254. In all, 202 companies had been privatized, 73 had been liquidated and 16 had come under private management through management contracts.

A notable feature of the privatization programme was the divestment of hundreds of former state farms. These farms had belonged to white commercial farmers in the colonial period and had been nationalized and consolidated into large state companies after the exodus of Portuguese settlers in 1975. These companies were now divided up again and their constituent farms privatized. For example, the 33 state-owned coffee plantation companies, which had taken over the *fazendas* (estates) abandoned by the Portuguese coffee farmers, were broken up into about 400 farms, which were sold off to would-be commercial farmers. This happened in other high-value agricultural and livestock-raising areas, such as the ranching country in the south-west, where there had also been large colonial *fazendas* until 1975.

In effect, a new land grab took place, benefiting well-connected families of the politico-military elite at the expense of small peasants, who had been occupying and tilling much of the land of the former state farms on an ad hoc basis, without land titles, since the mid-1980s. These local peasant farmers were never consulted and their interests were not taken into account when state land was sold off or, in many cases, virtually given away, often to new owners from the cities with no previous experience of farming. Although the insecurity in the rural areas effectively prevented many of these landowners from exercising their newly acquired property rights, even during the period of quasi-peace in 1994–98, there was a growing state of unease and fear for the future among the peasants squatting on former state farms, especially in the coffee-growing areas of Uíge and Kwanza Sul (Hodges and Viegas, 1998).

There was similar anxiety and anger among pastoralists in the south-west. There, local peoples had been able to extend their patterns of transhumance and expand their herds after the departure of the colonial ranchers and the removal of their fences in 1975 (Carvalho, 1997). During the 1990s, however, they once again found land being cordoned off by landowners, limiting their movement. The first sign that a serious land crisis was brewing in the south-west came in October 1999, when a dispute arose over land rights in the Gambos, in western Huíla.

The manner by which former state farms have been divested aroused considerable controversy and was criticized even by the Ministry of Agriculture and Rural Development. In a comprehensive review of the agriculture sector, completed in 1996 with the assistance of the UN Food and Agriculture Organization (FAO), the ministry criticized the trend towards converting former state farms into private commercial *fazendas.* It argued that the government should give priority in land distribution and agricultural support programmes to small-scale peasant farmers, since this would do more to raise production, alleviate poverty and reduce household food insecurity than the low-wage employment provided by commercial *fazendas.* MINADER and FAO argued that large commercial farms also have the disadvantage of requiring substantial capital inputs such as farm machinery, as well as imported fertilizer and technical expertise, all of which are scarce in Angola, while peasant farms rely mainly on family labour, animal traction and manure (MINADER, 1996). By then, however, it was already too late. Most of the former state farms had already been handed over to commercial farmers. The business aspirations of the politico-military elite had overriden the technical considerations of agronomists or concerns about poverty reduction.

The well-connected have also been able, through similar processes and again at almost no cost, to acquire prime real estate in the cities, sometimes worth hundreds of thousands or even millions of dollars. After independence, almost all housing in the modern 'concrete' part of Luanda and other cities had been nationalized, because of the flight of the Portuguese settlers. The abandoned houses and apartments had been occupied spontaneously by Africans moving in from the poorer *bairros* and *musseques*, while the state became the legal owners, through the State Secretariat for Housing. Because this body collected only nominal rents and received only minor allocations from the state budget, it was unable to invest in new housing or even to maintain the thousands of buildings that had fallen under its responsibility. As a result, the housing stock deteriorated, while no new homes were built, apart from the informal shacks erected by arriving migrants in the expanding shantytowns. When the State Secretariat for Housing began to sell off its apartments and villas in the late 1980s and early 1990s, it did so for nominal payments. The state in effect presided over the transfer of properties for a fraction of their true value, at enormous cost to government revenue. This can only be explained as an act of self-enrichment on the part of the high officials who acquired some of the best properties and, more generally, as a stratagem to cultivate the continuing loyalty of the MPLA's traditional urban constituency. In some cases, those who obtained ownership of prime apartments and villas found that, with investments of $100 or $200, they owned properties that could be rented to foreign companies, diplomats or UN personnel for thousands of dollars a month.

More generally, complaints about the non-transparent procedures used in the initial wave of privatization in 1991–92 brought about a halt in the privatization programme until a new law was enacted in 1994, laying down more rigorous procedures. This included requirements for the valuation of companies and public bidding (law 10/94). However, there has been little progress since then in preparing the larger state companies for sale. A plan to privatize 155 state companies, including several large ones, was approved in 1997 but frozen in 1998 (UNDP, 1999a). The government made new commitments to prepare some large state companies for restructuring and/or privatization in the agreement with the IMF in April 2000.

There are other forms of administrative favouritism that help businesses owned by individuals well-placed in the power structure. In some cases, such as the approval of foreign investment projects, the state can foist hand-picked Angolan business partners on prospective foreign investors. In one well-known case, disputes over the selection of Angolan partners held up the approval of a $26 million investment by Coca-Cola for four years, until agreement was finally reached in 1998.[16] As a result, Angola had to import Coca-Cola and most other soft drinks – a prime example of import dependence for products that could easily be manufactured locally were it not for bureaucratic obstacles resulting from private interests.

Complex import procedures, along with the restrictive access to foreign exchange and the limited scope of domestic production, have created oligopolistic market conditions for many products, making the import trade an especially profitable activity for those licensed to engage in it, especially where access to import licences has been backed by privileged access to 'cheap' foreign exchange and credit. Competition is further restricted by the administrative obstacles that complicate business operations and by the role played by bodies such as the *Polícia Económica* in harassing businesses that find it difficult to comply with or circumvent the regulatory bureaucracy. In some provinces, the governors have effectively established local monopolies by abusing their administrative powers and their control over the police to keep out or close down rival businesses, while also manipulating procurement procedures to channel state contracts to their own firms.

These examples show how there is a nexus of interests which benefit from the opportunities created by non-transparent administrative systems for the allocation of foreign exchange, import licences, credit, mining concessions, privatized state assets, contracts and other benefits. While these interests remain entrenched within the system, and patronage is used as a strategy for buying loyalty and cementing alliances,

---

[16] See *Africa Confidential*, 29 November 1996.

it will be difficult to move decisively towards more transparent, accountable systems of resource management, even though conjunctural economic imperatives or financial necessities may dictate periodic bursts of reform.

6
Oil ▊ & the 'Bermuda Triangle'

In the period since independence, oil has acquired a quite exceptional significance in the political economy of Angola, affecting not only the nature of the economy, but also the course and likely outcome of the war, the quality of governance, the country's international relations and even its culture. This has happened because of the rapid increase in the volume of oil production, which has outweighed the long-term decline in oil prices since the early 1980s, giving the state control of unparalleled oil revenues. Oil production has risen almost sixfold since 1983 and the trend is set to continue following a series of major discoveries in the 1990s which, in the words of one analyst, has made Angola 'indisputably the most promising place in the world for oil exploration'.[1]

Oil has been a mixed blessing, even in purely economic terms. Angola's extreme dependence on this single commodity has left the country dangerously exposed to the ups and downs of the international oil market, sometimes with serious consequences for the rest of the economy, as in 1985–86 when the steep fall in oil prices triggered Angola's debt crisis. Perhaps even more important is the fact that, despite periodic falls in the oil price, the general trend of rising production and rising real oil revenues has tended to lull the country's rulers into a state of complacency about the decline of the non-oil sectors of the economy.

To all intents and purposes, the state has lapsed into living off the revenue from oil, which is ultimately a non-renewable resource even though the country's reserves promise many years of production. The oil revenue has basically been used to finance large military expenditures and sustain basic government operations, while providing some minimal services and subsidies for the country's largely unproductive but swollen urban enclaves and thus helping to maintain social peace in the cities. By contrast, very little public money has gone to investments in infra-

---

[1] EIU, *Angola Country Report*, 3rd Quarter, 1998.

structure and human capital, which are critical for development and economic diversification.

The huge rents accruing to the state from oil exploitation have also had far-reaching implications for governance. They have provided the resources for a system of presidential patronage or, to return to Messiant's phrase, clientelist redistribution, which profoundly affects the relations between state and society. Earlier chapters have discussed how part of the rent from oil has been transferred to the leading families of the regime through such mechanisms as the rationed allocation of subsidized foreign exchange, the selective provision of subsidized credit by state banks and opportunities for kickbacks on oil-financed contracts for military procurement.

It is also widely suspected that the oil resources have provided opportunities for enrichment on a fabulous scale at the summit of the system. However, it has been impossible in practice to track exactly where all the oil revenue has gone because so much of the revenue and expenditure is off-budget. The lack of transparency in government finances, discussed in the previous chapter, is intertwined with a system of oil-collateralized financing of imports, under which, to cope with the country's low international credit rating, loans and credit lines for the government are tied to future shipments of oil by the state oil company, SONANGOL. This chapter takes its title from the fact that the complex triangular relationship between SONANGOL, the Treasury and the central bank has created a 'black hole' for the country's oil revenues, akin to the famed Bermuda triangle where shipping would disappear without trace.

Oil has also affected how foreign countries deal with the Angolan state. The competition among international companies for oil blocks has made governments in the industrialized countries wary about being too critical of government policies. Oil wealth has in any case reduced the leverage of Western creditors and the international financial institutions to influence economic policies through the normal mechanisms of 'conditionality', the strings attached to IMF and World Bank loans. There have been exceptions, during brief periods of financial crisis such as that which followed the crash in oil prices in the closing months of 1998 and the beginning of 1999. But on the whole the government has managed to keep afloat on a rising cushion of oil earnings, despite its heavy debt burden.

The military strength made possible by oil has also enabled Angola to become a sub-regional 'power', capable of intervening in the civil wars in the two Congos in 1997 to advance its geo-strategic interests. In both cases, it helped to install friendly governments and end these neighbouring territories' previous role as rear bases for UNITA and FLEC.

This international and regional stature has affected the national psyche. Although their country has been virtually destroyed by war and its human development indicators are among the worst in the world, many

Angolans believe that oil has made their country one that is respected, solicited by and listened to in the wider world, or at least one that cannot be bullied and knocked around like other poorer African countries. This is a trait common to many oil-producing countries, including some like Nigeria that are in an almost equivalent state of social and economic decay.

The rise of the oil industry

Oil production started in Angola in 1955, following the discovery of oil onshore in the Kwanza basin. This was followed, during the 1960s, by the discovery and development of oilfields off the coast of Cabinda, where production began in 1968. By 1973, oil had become the country's largest source of export earnings, overtaking cofffee.

In the immediate post-independence period, the government set up a national oil company, the *Sociedade Nacional de Combustíveis* (SONANGOL), in 1976, and promulgated a petroleum law (law 13/78) in 1978. This made the state the sole owner of the country's petroleum deposits and established SONANGOL as the exclusive concessionaire for oil exploration and development, while permitting the state company to enter into associations with foreign companies to obtain the resources needed for oil exploration, development and production. SONANGOL subsequently set up joint ventures with the oil companies which had already been producing oil in Angola, namely the Cabinda Gulf Oil Company, which became a subsidiary of Chevron in 1984, and Petrofina and Texaco, which had been producing onshore in the Kwanza and Congo basins.

Apart from Cabinda, where Cabinda Gulf was already active, the continental shelf was then divided into 13 blocks, which were offered in stages for bidding by international oil companies. Production-sharing agreements (PSAs) were signed with several companies, and from the early 1980s exploration began in shallow waters, mainly along the northern part of the Angolan coast. During the 1980s and 1990s, successful shallow water exploration, particularly by Chevron in Cabinda and by Elf and Texaco off the estuary of the Congo river, led to substantial new investments in development and a steady rise in production. By 2000, Angola's production was approaching 800,000 barrels a day (b/d), or almost six times higher than it had been in 1980, and Angola was by far the largest oil producer in Sub-Saharan Africa, apart from Nigeria.[2]

---

[2] By comparison, Nigeria produced 2.15 million b/d in 1998. Chevron, operator of Block 0 in Cabinda, accounted for about 60 per cent of Angolan production in 1999. The other two major producers are Elf in Block 3 (24 per cent) and Texaco in Block 2 (12 per cent). Onshore production, by Petrofina, is only about 20,000 b/d, or 2 per cent of production. SONANGOL and its Canadian partner, Ranger Oil, produce about 12,000 b/d, or 1 per cent of national production, from Block 4.

Figure 6.1: Oil production, 1980–2000
(thousand barrels per day; actual 1980–99; projected 2000)

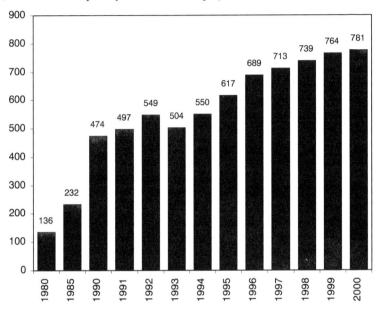

Sources: Ministry of Petroleum; SONANGOL; IMF, 1999a, 1999c, 2000

In the early 1990s, the Angolan oil industry entered a new stage of its development: the application of the new deep water technology, pioneered in oil provinces like the North Sea, to exploit resources further off the Angolan coast. Deep water exploration began after the government awarded the first of 17 new blocks demarcated in water depths of 150–600 metres (Blocks 14–30). The drilling in these blocks has proved extraordinarily successful. Since 1996, almost 20 large deep water discoveries have been made by Chevron, Exxon, Elf and BP Amoco and, overall, two thirds of deep water exploration wells have struck oil, compared with a historical world average closer to 15 per cent.[3] Four of the fields discovered so far (Girassol, Dalia, Kuito and Hungo) have reserves of between 1 and 2 billion barrels, comparable in size to the North Sea's giant Brent and Ninian fields. Indeed, during the 1990s, Angola was the most successful non-Opec country in the world for oil exploration, raising its proven oil reserves almost fourfold (EIU, August 2000).

Indeed, this exploration success, along with the relatively low operating costs in Angola's offshore industry, meant that even the steep decline in world oil prices in 1998–99 did not dent the enthusiasm of the

---

[3] *Financial Times*, 7 January 2000

international oil companies. In the midst of the downturn, they engaged in intense competition to obtain stakes in the first three 'ultra-deep water' blocks put up for bidding by the government (Blocks 31–33). To back up their bids for these blocks, which are adjacent to the northern deep water blocks where exploration has proved the most successful, they offered the government unprecedented 'signature bonuses', up-front one-off payments for exploration rights. Between them, the three successful consortia, led respectively by BP-Amoco, Elf and Exxon, paid over $900 million in signature bonuses for Blocks 31–33, thereby helping the government extract itself from the acute financial crisis that followed the fall in oil prices.[4]

The importance attached to deep water discoveries has also been borne out by the very high levels of development expenditure being earmarked to bring some of the new fields into production. For example, Elf planned to spend $2.5 billion to bring Girassol into production. SONANGOL has estimated that, overall, investment in the Angolan oil industry will average between $4 and $5 billion a year in 2000–2003.[5]

Development of the new deep water fields will bring a new upward surge in Angola's oil production. Chevron's Kuito field in Block 14 was the first to come on stream, in January 2000, and this will be followed by Elf's Girassol field in Block 17 in 2001. The oil consultancy company Wood Mackenzie has projected that, on the basis of discoveries to date, production should rise to about 1.4 million b/d by 2005.[6] This roughly corroborates official forecasts made in 1998 by the country's former oil minister, Albina de Assis, that output would reach 1.3 million b/d in 2003 and 1.6 million b/d in 2008.[7] Extrapolating from the past exploration success and assuming oil prices remain above $14 a barrel, one senior oil company executive in Luanda interviewed by the author in mid-1999 projected that production, including from deposits yet to be found, would rise to about 2.5 million barrels a day by 2010–15. At that rate, Angola would be close to or even above Nigerian levels of production.

Institutional structure

The petroleum sector is dominated by international companies. The role of the state oil company, SONANGOL, is essentially to establish partnerships

[4] According to the Dow Jones Energy Service (13 April 1999), the signature bonuses were $350 m. for Block 31, $200 m. for Block 32 and $370 m. for Block 33. A total of 38 companies bid for stakes in the three blocks. A fourth ultra-deep water block, Block 34, was earmarked for a consortium led by SONANGOL and Norsk Hydro in October 1999.
[5] *Financial Times*, 7 January 2000.
[6] Ibid.
[7] *África Hoje*, Lisbon, June 1998.

with these companies, both through the PSAs and, in a few blocks, through direct stakeholdings in contractor groups or joint ventures. Under the PSA contracts, foreign companies serve as contractors to SONANGOL, finance the costs of investment and then recoup their investments and operating costs with what is known as 'cost oil'. As costs are recovered, they then go on to share 'profit oil' with SONANGOL on a sliding scale linked to the level of cumulative production or, in the case of the deep water blocks, the internal rate of return.

Where SONANGOL has a direct stakeholding, as a partner in a joint venture or in the contractor group under the PSA system, it is responsible for raising its share of the capital for the development of new fields and also receives a share of production in accordance with the size of its shareholdings. SONANGOL's involvement in the industry as an equity partner has increased over the years, its portfolio currently including stakeholdings in ten offshore blocks, including one deep water block and two ultra-deep water blocks.

SONANGOL's technical and organizational capacity to offer blocks for bidding, negotiate with interested oil companies and manage its stake-holdings has been strengthened significantly since the company was set up in the late 1970s. It has been able to attract some of the most highly educated Angolans entering the labour market by offering relatively high salaries, and it has invested heavily in training programmes. However, it is likely to face increasing difficulties in competing with the foreign oil companies, which will need to recruit large numbers of qualified Angolans in the coming years, due to the expansion of oil operations and the obligations on foreign companies to indigenize their labour force.

Since the early 1990s, SONANGOL has been restructured, becoming a holding company with autonomous subsidiaries, including SONANGOL *Pesquisa e Produção,* for exploration and production, and SONANGOL *Distribuição* for marketing of refined products. Despite the creation of SONANGOL *Pesquisa e Produção,* the company has so far had little experience as an operator for oilfield exploration, development and production, although it is formally the operator for production from one small field, Kiabo, in Block 4. In this capacity, it is receiving technical assistance from the Canadian company Ranger Oil. A similar arrangement has been made for ultra-deep water block 34, where SONANGOL became the formal operator in 1999, with technical assistance from Norsk Hydro. Downstream, SONANGOL has a small shareholding in the Luanda refinery, along with the government itself and Petrofina, and enjoys a virtual monopoly in the distribution market, directly through its own network of service stations and through a joint venture known as Sonangalp, set up with the Portuguese company Petrogal. Plans for liberalization of the distribution industry, which have been on the drawing board since the early 1990s, have not yet been implemented.

SONANGOL has also secured for itself a pivotal role in the supply and service sector of the oil industry, by establishing a nexus of joint venture companies (with foreign partners and Angolan business interests). These companies, which provide such services as helicopters, supply boats, support bases, seismic studies, civil construction and drilling, give SONANGOL enormous leverage, amounting in some fields to a virtual monopoly in the local market.

An enclave industry

The petroleum industry in Angola is an extreme case of an enclave sector, with minimal linkages to the rest of the economy, except through the redistributive mechanisms of government revenue and expenditure. As a capital-intensive industry, it creates few local jobs: in all it employs about 10,000 Angolans, half of whom work for SONANGOL. Backward and forward linkages are weak, between crude oil production and other industries, either downstream (refineries) or with respect to the supply of goods and services for exploration, development and production.

With the exception of about 40,000 b/d delivered to the country's sole refinery, in Luanda, all oil production is exported. The refinery produces a small surplus over and above national needs for most refined products, adding marginally to petroleum sector exports. Its capacity will begin to fall short of national needs, however, if a broad-based economic recovery begins following the ending of the war and an improved business environment. There are plans to build a second, much larger, refinery at Lobito, a port city on the Atlantic coast and the terminus of the Benguela railway, which, prior to the outbreak of the war in 1975, linked the coast with the rich agricultural hinterland of the central *planalto* and with the Copperbelt of south-eastern DRC (ex-Zaire) and northern Zambia. The government has stated that the refinery will have a capacity of 200,000 b/d, but construction will depend on securing foreign markets and financing. It could only serve inland markets if lasting peace is restored in both Angola and the DRC, permitting the rehabilitation of the Benguela railway and trans-national highways.

Almost all the equipment and materials and many of the services required by the oil industry have to be imported. In the 1980s, the first steps were taken to develop a support industry, by setting up a construction yard for production platforms and other equipment at Ambriz (through a joint venture known as Petromar involving SONANGOL and the French company Bouygues Offshore) and an oil industry supply base at Soyo. However, these investments were destroyed when both Ambriz and Soyo were occupied by UNITA in 1993–94. The Petromar yard had been limited to the assembly of equipment manufactured abroad. The base at Soyo has largely been rebuilt and there are now similar facilities in Luanda and Lobito.

The petroleum sector is not only an economic enclave, but a geographic and social enclave as well. More than 97 per cent of Angola's oil is pumped from fields offshore, so there is almost no direct contact between the industry and local communities, and little risk of attack by rebels, whether from UNITA or, in the case of Cabinda, from FLEC. Only once, in 1993 at Soyo, at the mouth of the Congo estuary, were onshore oil installations, including onshore production facilities, occupied and destroyed by UNITA. As Le Billon (1999) has put it, this location has made the oil industry an economic sanctuary as well as a geographic enclave.[8] In theory, the government could still survive by living off its offshore oil revenues, even if almost the entire country was overrun by UNITA.

The industry's largely offshore location, along with the extremely small size of the population in the coastal provinces where oil production is concentrated, means that there is also a low risk of disputes between the oil companies and local communities, of the type seen in the Delta region in Nigeria. The two provinces responsible for all of Angola's current oil production, Cabinda and Zaire, have a combined population of only 350,000, less than 3 per cent of the country's total population (IOM, 1996).

Environmental impact

The oil industry poses two main types of environmental risk. The first is that oil will pollute fishing resources in the offshore production areas. The Angolan/Namibian coast has historically been one of the richest fishing zones in Africa, along with the coast from Senegal to southern Morocco, although the fish resources are more important off southern Angola than in the northern coastal areas where petroleum activities have so far been concentrated.

The other environmental challenge facing the industry is to find a solution to the problem of flaring gas. Gas is associated with almost all the oilfields discovered in the Lower Congo basin and Cabinda. Although small amounts of liquefied petroleum gas are exported and some gas is used for enhanced recovery in the oilfields, most associated gas is flared. In some cases, the architecture of the oil reserves rules out gas reinjection. The government would also like to find a productive use for several deposits of non-associated gas which have been discovered. It has stated that in future the flaring of gas in newly developed oilfields will be illegal.

---

[8] By contrast, as Le Billon has noted, the Mobutu regime in former Zaire did not have the same geographical advantage. Most of that country's mineral resources are located inland, at great distance from the capital, and were quickly overrun by the rebels led by Laurent Kabila.

However, there will be a strong temptation to circumvent this restriction in the absence of viable uses for the gas.

This presents a genuine quandary. The potential for using gas for power generation is limited by the low level of domestic (and regional) industrial development and by the substantial hydroelectric resources provided by the country's many rivers. The new 520 mw hydroelectric dam under construction at Capanda on the River Kwanza will more than double Angola's total electricity-generating capacity. Gas is thus unlikely to provide a competitive source of energy for industrial development, even if domestic energy demand increases quite rapidly in a post-conflict context of economic recovery and investments in industrial development.

The only major potential source of demand in the region for imported gas or electricity is South Africa, whose GDP is larger than that of all the other member states of the Southern African Development Community (SADC) combined. However, due to its distance from South Africa, Angola is poorly placed to compete in this market. Mozambique and Namibia, which border South Africa, have large gas reserves and are already exploring opportunities to export gas by pipeline to South Africa (in addition to Mozambique's exports of electricity from the Cabora Bassa hydroelectric dam). Some companies are considering the option of liquefying gas for export to international markets, but Angola may not be competitive with countries like Algeria and Venezuela that are much closer to the main markets in the industrialized countries.

The economic impact of oil

If properly managed and harnessed for the long-term economic and social development of the country, oil wealth would give Angola a considerable advantage over most other developing countries. The scale of its earnings from oil has become impressive. In 1996–98, annual oil exports averaged almost $4.1 billion and total exports $4.6 billion, more than any other country in Sub-Saharan Africa apart from South Africa and Nigeria.

It should be borne in mind that these figures are for gross exports and, in Angola's case, the net foreign-exchange earnings from oil are considerably less because of the oil industry's own dependence on imported goods and services and the repatriation of oil company profits.[9] Historically, the net contribution of the sector to the current account of the balance of payments has been around half of its gross export earnings (BNA, 1998a).

This net foreign-exchange revenue from oil approximates the total fiscal contribution received by the state from petroleum taxes and

---

[9] These imports tend to be particularly high during a period of expansion of the industry, when large expenditures are made for exploration and development.

royalties, which averaged $2.2 billion a year in 1996–99. These are still very substantial resources by comparison with those available to most other African governments. However, even in purely economic terms, oil has in some respects become more of a liability than an asset.

The first problem is that Angola has become over-dependent on this single commodity, making it perilously exposed to the sharp price fluctuations that affect the oil market. Over the past two decades, oil has become almost the only vibrant, dynamic sector of the Angolan economy, while the stagnation or decline of the rest of the economy has amplified the country's dependence on oil. Even in 1998, when oil prices were exceptionally low, the petroleum sector accounted for 32.9 per cent of Angola's GDP, 70 per cent of fiscal revenue and 87 per cent of export earnings (see Figure 6.2 and Table 6.1).

Figure 6.2: Role of oil in the Angolan economy, 1998

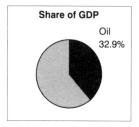  

Sources: IMF, 1999a, 2000

Table 6.1: The economy's dependence on oil, 1993–99

	1993	1994	1995	1996	1997	1998	Est 1999
Oil production ('000 b/d)	504	550	617	689	713	739	764
Oil exports (million barrels)	170	184	206	228	243	252	…
Average oil export price ($ per barrel)	16.1	15.3	16.6	20.4	18.6	12.0	17.4
Value of oil exports ($ m.)	2,750	2,822	3,425	4,651	4,507	3,038	…
Total petroleum sector exports ($ m.)	2,826	2,901	3,522	4,854	4,630	3,091	4,694
Petroleum share in total exports (%)	97.4	96.2	94.6	93.9	92.5	87.2	87.8
Fiscal revenue from petroleum sector ($ m.)	1,780	1,518	1,324	2,625	2,475	1,215	2,366
Petroleum share of total fiscal revenue (%)	81.9	88.9	87.2	89.2	83.2	69.6	87.6
Oil sector share of GDP (%)	40.2	56.6	55.8	58.0	48.3	32,9	…

Sources: IMF, 1999a, 1999b, 1999c, 2000, derived from BNA, Ministry of Finance and Ministry of Planning.

The petroleum sector has accounted for over 80 per cent of export earnings since the early 1980s and for well over 90 per cent of exports throughout the 1990s, except in 1998 (BNA, 1998a). This is almost entirely accounted for by crude oil, with refined petroleum and gas contributing very little. In stark contrast with the situation before independence, diamonds are now the only other export commodity of any consequence. In 1997, crude oil accounted for 90 per cent of exports, diamonds for 7 per cent, refined petroleum for 2 per cent, and all other products, including gas, for 1 per cent.[10]

The oil sector's share of GDP had been much higher (58 per cent in 1996) before the fall in oil prices in 1998 and is likely to have risen well above 50 per cent again in 1999–2000 due to the price recovery and the further expansion of production. Likewise, the sector's contribution to fiscal revenue rose to 88 per cent in 1999.[11]

Even though the rise in production has more than offset the long-term decline in prices since the early 1980s, thereby ensuring that both the value of oil exports and government oil revenue have risen considerably in the past two decades, macroeconomic management has been made more difficult by fluctuations in prices. When oil prices rise or fall, government revenue from oil is disproportionately affected, since both the PSA and royalty systems tend to exaggerate the fiscal effects of movements in prices.[12] There have been two particularly severe external shocks as a result of large and sudden falls in oil prices in the past two decades (see Figure 6.3).

The first external shock, in 1985–86, which marked the end of the period of high oil prices ushered in by OPEC in the 1970s, caused a 38 per cent fall in Angola's petroleum sector exports in 1986, plunging the country into a debt trap from which it has yet to extract itself. Previous levels of borrowing had been premised on a level of oil prices that proved unrealistic. The country began building up external arrears from 1986, destroying its previously high credit rating in international financial

---

[10] The share of diamonds would be significantly higher if exports from UNITA-controlled areas were included.

[11] As Chapter 5 has indicated, data on fiscal revenue should be treated with considerable caution, because of the large extra-budgetary operations (on both the revenue and expenditure sides) and their linkages to cross-debts involving the government, the central bank and SONANGOL.

[12] Fiscal revenue decreases when prices fall, first, because of the impact on companies' net revenue. Second, under the PSA system, the proportion of oil retained by the companies as 'cost oil' rises when prices fall, although this proportion cannot exceed 50 per cent of the oil produced. The impact of oil prices on the revenue of SONANGOL (and ultimately the government as 'owner' of 90 per cent of SONANGOL's oil from the PSAs) will increase further as production rises in the deep water blocks, since in those blocks the share of 'profit oil' between SONANGOL and the contractor group is determined by a sliding scale linked to the nominal rate of return: the lower the oil price and thus the rate of return, the lower the percentage share of profit oil that will be due to SONANGOL.

Figure 6.3: Crude oil export value and average prices, 1980–98

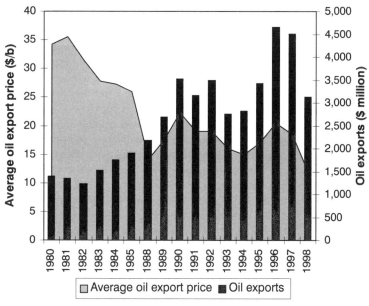

Sources: IMF, 1999a, 1999b; Ministry of Petroleum; SONANGOL; BNA

markets and creating the situation which led to the mortgaging of oil resources for import financing in the 1990s.

A similar external shock occurred in 1998, when the average price of Angolan crude fell to $12 a barrel and the value of oil exports fell by 33 per cent. International reserves were almost completely exhausted by the beginning of 1999, when prices briefly dipped below $10 a barrel, and it became difficult for the government even to meet its commitments for the servicing of its oil-collateralized loans. This happened at a particularly unfavourable time, just as the country was returning to war and the government was engaging in major new military procurement contracts. The situation had eased by the end of 1999, however, as a result of the dramatic recovery in oil prices, which rose above $30 a barrel in mid-2000, and the timely windfall that accrued to the government in the form of signature bonuses from the leasing of the first ultra-deep water blocks.

A second major problem resulting from the prominence of oil in the economy has been its negative impact on the development of other sectors. This is the Angolan version of the 'Dutch disease'. In its pure form, the concept of the Dutch disease refers to the harmful effects on the non-oil sectors of the economy which result from the appreciation of the exchange rate due to the scale of a country's oil earnings. This is not an automatic consequence: by means of fiscal or monetary adjustments, governments can counteract the tendency to exchange rate appreciation. In Angola, where until May 1999 there was not a market-driven fluctuating exchange rate regime, except in the parallel market, the Dutch disease took a slightly different form. By maintaining an administratively fixed official exchange rate, the currency tended to increase in value in real effective terms, because of the high rate of domestic inflation, although there were periodic devaluations during the 1990s to try to close the gap between the official and parallel exchange rates. This tended to place domestic businesses at a competitive disadvantage vis-à-vis importers with access to foreign exchange at the official rate, and also to make most non-oil exports (apart from diamonds) uncompetitive in international markets.

In reality, however, the Dutch disease phenomenon goes far beyond the exchange rate effects of a large oil sector. Possibly more important are the economic consequences that arise from the effects of oil wealth on the vision and attitudes of a country's rulers. Angola provides a particularly striking example of this. To put matters in a nutshell, high and rising oil revenues have tended, despite the occasional adverse price shocks, to encourage complacency about the dismal state of the rest of the economy.

Despite the large fiscal deficits, the scale of oil revenues seems to have made the government unaware of the importance of halting and reversing the decline in the contribution of non-oil fiscal receipts to government revenue. The low level of non-oil revenue (about $500 million a year or approximately 7 per cent of GDP in 1997–98) has been due partly to the impact of the war and the decline in non-oil economic activity, but it is noteworthy that little has been done to modernize the tax system, widen the tax base, remove the large number of unjustified tax exemptions, improve the tax and customs administration or crack down on tax evasion.

The state of complacency has also been demonstrated by the low priority the authorities have given to investment in the development of physical and social infrastructure. According to the IMF, capital expenditure was on average less than 7 per cent of actual budget expenditure and 4 per cent of GDP between 1996 and 1998 (IMF, 2000). Even the existing infrastructure has been poorly maintained and has consequently decayed, compounding the impact of the damage and destruction wrought by the war.

The situation has been made worse by the fact that public utilities, such as those responsible for electricity and water supply, have been unable to generate sufficient internal sources of revenue because of their inability to set their own tariffs. These have been kept at ludicrously low levels by government decree, with the result that the utilities have remained almost totally dependent on transfers from the government budget. These subsidies have been inadequate to permit routine maintenance, let alone carry out the new investments required to meet the needs of a growing population or economy. Electricity generation and distribution, water supply, the road network, railways and ports have all suffered, raising the costs of production and transport and discouraging investment in the non-oil sectors of the economy. Likewise, the low level of investment in education and health has resulted in a poorly educated and often unhealthy workforce with low levels of productivity.

Partly due to the war-related disruption, the government has never had a long-term economic and social development strategy, identifying key public expenditure priorities. In some cases, sectoral strategies have been drafted, but rarely have they been approved and implemented. Furthermore, the capacity for preparing a coherent public investment programme and integrating it into the budget is extremely weak.[13]

In effect, Angola has been drawing down a non-renewable resource. Without a much greater focus on using the proceeds from oil to diversify the economy, the country risks eventually depleting these resources with no long-term gain. Government revenue has been allocated primarily to military expenditure, the running costs of the public administration (government consumption) and transfers for subsidies to keep ailing state companies afloat or to subsidize official prices, notably for petroleum products, water and electricity. Data on budget outturns indicate that on average between 1996 and 1998, expenditure on defence and internal security accounted for 32 per cent of total government expenditure. Following the resumption of the war, this proportion rose to 41 per cent in 1999 (IMF, 2000).

As we have seen in Chapter 5, some of the foreign exchange obtained by the government from oil has been sold to the private sector at a subsidized rate, implicitly depriving the state of a substantial amount of revenue in local currency terms. The state-owned banks' provision of subsidized credit to the politically connected elite has likewise amounted to a transfer of government resources. However, the beneficiaries have rarely used these funds to undertake long-term investments, preferring instead to make quick profits from import operations and the related opportunities for arbitrage between the official and parallel markets. Furthermore, no bank credit has been available to the private sector for long-term investment: the primitive banking system provides credit for a maximum of two years, giving a strong bias to the financing of import operations. The uncertain macroeconomic climate, the high production

---

[13] The great majority of projects are submitted by sectoral ministries to the Ministry of Planning with little or no data, and without any prior appraisal or cost-benefit analysis, while capital expenditures for the Ministry of Defence do not enter the planning process at all. Furthermore, there are insufficient qualified personnel in the Ministry of Planning to undertake project appraisal, and so the Public Investment Programme (PIP) becomes little more than a wish-list of proposed projects.

costs resulting from the poor state of the infrastructure, the negative impact of an overvalued official exchange rate on businesses' potential competitiveness in international markets or vis-à-vis imports, and the maze of arbitrarily enforced regulations affecting business operations, have also discouraged long-term private investment.

The World Bank has aptly described this state of affairs as follows (World Bank, 1993):

> Angola has been consuming future generations' wealth. Public policies have encouraged misuse of the proceeds from non-renewable resources (petroleum and diamonds) for non-developmental activities. The bulk of the country's revenue is supporting a bloated civil service, consumption, and military expenditure, rather than investing for long-term growth.

This assessment highlights the need for a major shift in the use of the country's oil earnings, away from consumption and military expenditure, so as to permit increased investment, aimed at diversifying the economy and reducing long-term dependence on oil. The World Bank has suggested that the government should set aside a proportion of oil revenues for an investment fund that would allow the net income stream (total revenue minus the contribution to the fund) to be permanently sustained.

The role of oil in the war

Control of the country's oil resources is the ultimate prize of the Angolan war. Power for power's sake or fear of the consequences of defeat may be part of the motive for fighting to win or retain control of the state. However, holding state power also gives access to resources which, as noted above, have generated an annual oil rent averaging $2.1 billion in the second half of the 1990s.

In the specific case of Cabinda, its strategic importance as the source of about 60 per cent of Angola's current oil production is almost certainly the main motive for separatism and also an iron-clad reason why the government, whether controlled by the MPLA, UNITA or any other party or ruler, would never consider letting the province secede. For the Cabindans, the material benefits of secession would be quite staggering. With a population of only about 110,000 and oil exports of $2.5 billion (at the level of production and prices recorded in 1995–97), Cabinda would be one of the richest countries in the developing world in per capita terms. Its net annual earnings from oil might well be close to $11,000 per capita, making it a sort of tropical mini-Kuwait.

This dazzling prospect is almost certainly a far more powerful motive for secession than any sense of ethnic identity or economic injustice. The Cabindans are related to the other Bakongo peoples of north-western Angola and they are no worse off than the population of any other Angolan province. In fact, to assuage separatist feelings, the government has been allocating to Cabinda a far higher level of government expenditure in per capita terms than to any other province. Although the government has never lived up to a pledge made in the early 1990s to allow Cabinda to retain 10 per cent of the oil revenue generated in the province, it has been quite generous: in 1996, for example, Cabinda received 20.5 per cent of the budgetary resources transferred to the 18 provinces, despite having one of the smallest populations. On a per capita basis, the transfers to Cabinda were 26 times higher than the average for all provinces (MINFIN, 1997).

Oil is not just a prize or a motive, however. For the government, it provides the means to wage war. On average during the period from 1996 to 1999, 18 per cent of the country's GDP was devoted to defence and security expenditure (IMF, 2000). This is an extraordinarily high proportion by any standards, especially for a country which for most of that period was technically at peace, following the Lusaka Protocol in November 1994. By comparison, developing countries as a group devoted 2.4 per cent of their GDP to military expenditure in 1996, or eight times less than Angola in the same year (UNDP, 1999b).[14] In dollar terms, IMF estimates of Angola's budget expenditure indicate that the government spent on average $1.2 billion a year on defence and security between 1996 and 1999 (IMF, 2000).

Clearly, expenditure on defence and security at these levels has only been possible because such a high proportion of GDP (on average 34 per cent during 1996–99) accrues to the government in the form of oil rent. In particular, the fact that this rent accrues in the form of foreign currency has made it possible for the government to engage in high levels of overseas military procurement, despite the halt to Soviet bloc military assistance since the end of the 1980s. Throughout, Angola has built up a capital-intensive war machine to confront the threats from South Africa (until the latter's disengagement) and UNITA.

Due to its external arrears and consequent low credit rating in international financial markets, Angola cannot obtain credits for military procurement through normal banking facilities or from official export

---

[14] The figures given here for Angola and developing countries are not strictly comparable, since the data for Angola include expenditure on 'public order', which refers to the police. However, much of the police, in particular the *Polícia de Intervenção Rápida* (PIR), is in effect an auxiliary military force. Even if expenditure on the police was excluded, the share of GDP spent on the armed forces would probably still be at least four times higher than the average for developing countries.

credit agencies. Instead, as the next section discusses in greater detail, it has to purchase military equipment by using either current oil revenues to make cash payments or future oil revenue as collateral for loans. The latter option is only possible where oil is physically available to the government through SONANGOL as a result of its equity stakes in certain fields and its share in the production of oil from fields governed by PSAs.

A new mechanism for financing military procurement appears to have been devised in 1999 through the arrangements for equity stakes in the first ultra-deep water blocks. For the first time, small companies with links to arms trading and financing, and with very little, if any, experience in the oil industry, were given stakes in the successful consortia. This was particularly strange in view of the intense competition among *bona fide* oil companies for stakeholdings and the huge resources that would be required of consortium partners for the development of fields in ultra-deep water blocks in the event of commercial discoveries. Almost inevitably there was suspicion that the holdings were an alternative means of payment in kind for arms contracts.[15]

Overall, the scale of oil earnings available to the government, along with the steep decline in UNITA's revenue from diamonds since 1998 (see Chapter 7), had created a major imbalance in their relative military strength by 2000. While 'oiling the wheels of war', the rent from petroleum might eventually create a situation in which the government has a decisive military edge. In this scenario, discussed further in Chapter 8, oil would help restore peace in the long run.

Oil, governance and debt

Oil revenues have also had profound consequences for the nature of the state and the system of governance. First, the rent from oil has given Futungo de Belas far larger resources with which to dispense patronage than would have been the case in a non-oil state. The term 'oil *nomenklatura*' has been used generically to encompass the nexus of elite families, inter-related through marriage and political allegiance, who have benefited from this 'manna'. It would be redundant here to return once more to the various mechanisms by which a part of the resources generated by oil are transferred, legally or illegally, to those who are members of this charmed circle. Suffice it to say that oil-financed patronage has been a fundamental part of the strategy pursued by Futungo

---

[15] According to the British-based NGO Global Witness (GW, 1999), one company with a 20 per cent stake in Block 32 (Prodev) and two companies with 10 per cent and 5 per cent stakes respectively in Block 33 (Falcon Oil and Naptha) had links to arms trading.

de Belas for the consolidation and conservation of political power. This has extended even to the pressures placed on international oil companies to make donations to FESA, which, as Chapter 4 described, has become a new vehicle for the dispensation of presidential providence and the cultivation of the President's popular standing.

However, the system of governance has also been profoundly affected by another consequence of the rent from oil: the diversion of a large proportion of oil revenues outside the approved budget, creating a system of parallel finances not subject to public scrutiny or even the purview of senior officials in the Ministry of Finance. This has been closely related to the special ways in which the regime has had to use part of the oil rent to secure loans to finance the procurement of military equipment and other imports.

To understand how this has arisen, it is necessary first to look at how oil has become a crucial instrument for the negotiating of trade finance in the context of a heavy debt burden and substantial external arrears, which have damaged Angola's external credit rating and closed off more traditional forms of commercial borrowing. Modest until the early 1980s, when it amounted to less than $3 billion, Angola's external debt rose rapidly between the mid-1980s and the mid-1990s, reaching more than $11 billion by 1995. At first, the main factors driving this surge in debt were the large loans negotiated with the former USSR in the 1980s for military procurement and ill-conceived capital projects, notably the $2 billion Capanda dam and the mausoleum for the late Agostinho Neto in Luanda. Later, after Angola began to default on its debt-service payments from the late 1980s, the stock of debt increased further as a result of the capitalization of interest arrears and the use of oil collateralized credits to finance imports of military equipment and consumer goods.

Since the steep fall in oil prices in 1985–86, the Angolan government has honoured only part of the debt service falling due, as the accumulation of arrears has been the principal way of financing deficits. Between 1987 and 1995, external arrears soared from $166 million to $5.6 billion. To ease its external financial difficulties, the government negotiated a series of bilateral rescheduling agreements with the USSR, its largest creditor, between 1986 and 1996, the last such agreement including a substantial element of debt write-off, amounting to some $4 billion. There have also been small bilateral rescheduling arrangements with Brazil and Portugal and two multilateral reschedulings, agreed exceptionally by the Paris Club of official Western creditors in 1987 and 1989 in the absence of an IMF agreement (normally a pre-condition for rescheduling) because Angola was then in the process of joining the Fund.[16] There was no

---

[16] Angola applied to join the Fund following the launching of the SEF in August 1987 and was finally admitted in September 1989. For a detailed account of these debt rescheduling arrangements in the late 1980s, see Hodges, 1993.

element of debt reduction in these 'first-generation' Paris Club re-schedulings. As a result of the debt relief provided by Russia, however, total external debt fell from \$11.7 billion at the end of 1995 to \$8.5 billion at the end of 1996, while external arrears were halved, to \$2.5 billion (IMF, 2000).

During the 1990s, Angola has been unable to obtain access through the Paris Club to further debt rescheduling or to the more recent opportunities for debt reduction because it has failed to reach an agreement with the IMF on a full-scale adjustment programme.[17] Instead, the government has circumvented its external financial constraints by building up new arrears, which had risen again to \$4.4 billion by the end of 1999, and by using the share of oil production received by SONANGOL to guarantee loans for the financing of imports. Most of these loans have been arranged with international banks, although some have been insured or provided directly by official export credit agencies. Without the collateral provided by future oil shipments, neither the banks nor the export credit agencies would have continued providing or insuring trade finance for Angola.[18] Consequently, these oil-backed loans, most of which were contracted on behalf of the state by SONANGOL, have become virtually the only form of external financing available to the government during the 1990s.

Due to the country's rock-bottom credit rating, these loans carry onerous terms. They have short maturities (usually four years or less) and high interest rates, usually about 2 percentage points above the London inter-bank offered rate (Libor), the benchmark rate for international lending. However, Le Billon (1999: 27) has argued that extra interest charges of \$50–100 million a year were a small price to pay for avoiding an agreement with the IMF and so 'keeping international auditors and conditionality at bay'.[19]

As Figure 6.4 illustrates, the loan agreements are tied to contracts with oil trading companies, for the lifting of oil from the share of production accruing to SONANGOL. The receipts from these oil shipments are then

---

[17] The staff-monitored programmes agreed with the IMF in 1995 and 2000 did not make Angola eligible for Paris Club negotiations.

[18] Only three official export credit agencies, those of Brazil, Portugal and Spain, have been prepared to provide Angola with lines of credit for general imports in the 1990s. These have been repaid with oil deliveries, like the commercial bank credits. Some agencies, such as the US Export-Import Bank and the Korean Export Insurance Corporation, have provided loans to SONANGOL to finance its share of development costs for oilfields in which it has equity stakes, again requiring repayment through the proceeds of oil deliveries. Some other agencies, notably the UK's Export Credit Guarantee Department, have refused to provide any export insurance cover for sales to Angola.

[19] Le Billon's figure is based on World Bank estimates, assuming a stock of \$1.6 billion in oil-guaranteed loans and a 3–6 per cent spread compared with loans that would otherwise be available from the Bretton Woods institutions and London Club banks.

Figure 6.4: Typical structure of oil-guaranteed loans

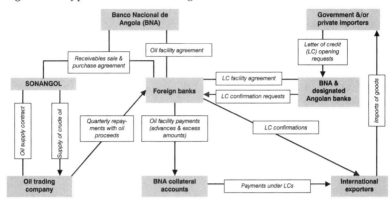

paid into designated accounts in foreign banks, to service loans to the *Banco Nacional de Angola* (BNA) for the financing of imports into Angola. Most of the proceeds are paid through two trusts, known as the Cabinda Trust and the Soyo-Palanca Trust, which are administered by foreign banks and serve as offshore accounts.

By the late 1990s, almost all the oil physically available to the government through SONANGOL (amounting to almost half of the government's total oil revenue) was committed to the servicing of oil-guaranteed loans.[20] The secure repayment arrangements for these loans also meant that Angola has had less scope for accumulating external arrears in recent years.

Thus, it is the nature or composition of the debt, rather than its total value, that has increasingly become the main problem for Angola. In fact, the decision by Russia to cancel much of the debt contracted by Angola from the former USSR in the 1980s resulted in a sharp fall in the debt/exports ratio from 342 to 156 per cent between 1994 and 1996. Although the total external debt rose again in the late 1990s, to \$9.6 billion in 1999, this was equivalent to 175 per cent of exports, much less than in the early 1990s. Ironically, however, the Russian write-off did not make any real difference to the payments situation, as the debt to Russia was not being serviced anyway. In contrast, the commercial oil-

---

[20] Data obtained by the author on SONANGOL's oil shipments in the first quarter of 1999 indicate that more than 95 per cent of oil sold by the state oil company (or about \$260 m. worth of oil shipments) was used to service oil-guaranteed debts. At a minimum, actual debt service for oil-guaranteed loans was therefore running at slightly over \$1 billion in 1999. This is almost certainly an underestimate, as oil prices were exceptionally low in the first part of the year resulting in the deferment of some debt repayments to later oil shipments. IMF projections for 2000 put the debt service due on oil-guaranteed debt at \$954m., assuming no further oil-guaranteed borrowing in the course of the year (IMF, 2000).

guaranteed debts, which have come to the fore in the 1990s, have to be serviced.[21] By 1999, the oil-guaranteed debts amounted to $2.7 billion, or 28 per cent of total external debt (IMF, 2000).

Because of the scale of these loans and the resulting cross-debts between SONANGOL, the government and the BNA, the oil-collateralized loans have important implications for the management of government finances as a whole. In recent years, much of the fiscal revenue due from SONANGOL has not been paid to the Treasury or recorded in the budget execution accounts, since SONANGOL has in effect been servicing debts on behalf of the state through its oil shipments. The oil-backed loans are thus closely inter-related with the problem of extra-budgetary operations and with the central issues of transparency and accountability in government finances.

Further complications have arisen from SONANGOL's deduction from its tax payments of other claims on the government, such as unpaid subsidies for petroleum products, which until February 2000 were sold on the domestic market at officially set prices that were a fraction of market rates. Problems relating to SONANGOL's ability to pay its required share of development costs in oil blocks where it has an equity stake may also have resulted at times in the deferment of tax payments. In addition, SONANGOL appears not to have communicated full information to the BNA on the debts it has contracted on behalf of the state, resulting in lack of comprehensive information on the external debt. In such a confused situation, affecting expenditure, revenue and debt, the lack of transparency also makes it relatively easy for fraud to go undetected.

The oil-backed loans only concern the oil available to SONANGOL through its equity stakes and the sharing of 'profit oil' under the PSAs. The government also obtains fiscal revenue, through tax payments, from the foreign oil companies. As this is not physical oil, it cannot be used for oil-collateralized loans. In the absence of other means of financing imports, due to the lack of creditworthiness, the foreign exchange available to the government from this source has mainly been used for cash purchases of imports, in particular for military equipment. To the limited extent that there has been a surplus of funds above the government's own import requirements, some foreign exchange has been sold to the private sector – to the privileged beneficiaries of the official exchange rate until May 1999 and, since then, through an inter-bank

[21] Even when oil prices fall so low that it is impossible to meet the obligations to all creditors on schedule, as happened in the early months of 1999, payments can be deferred to later shipments with penalties, or re-financing can be arranged. *Union des Banques Suisses* (UBS) did this in May 1999, providing a $575 million syndicated loan to refinance earlier loans over a four-year period. For details, see GW, 1999. Arrears built up in 1999 on some oil-guaranteed debt owing to official bilateral creditors, as oil deliveries to private creditors were given priority. These arrears totalled $450m. at the end of 1999 (IMF, 2000).

foreign-exchange market. The distribution of oil production and revenues, and the respective ways in which oil resources are used for the financing of imports, are presented graphically in Figure 6.5.

The problems resulting from the lack of fully comprehensive, transparent data about oil transactions, fiscal revenue from oil, off-budget government expenditures, oil-backed loans and the interlocking claims of the government, SONANGOL and BNA have been recognized repeatedly by senior government officials. Again and again, the annual budget statements have decried the extra-budgetary operations, and stressed the importance of honouring budget execution procedures, only to return to the same theme, with similar admissions of failure and renewed calls for rigour, at the end of each budget year. Ritually, IMF missions to Angola have made proposals for an audit of the petroleum and diamond sectors, as well as other measures to instil greater transparency and discipline in the management of government finances.

In March 1999, an IMF mission was informed that the government would finally go ahead with a 'diagnostic study' of the petroleum sector. The Fund commented as follows, spelling out in some detail what it expected the study to cover (IMF, 1999b):

> At a minimum, the study would aim at evaluating the current situation of the oil sector and developing a framework for systematically reporting data on crude reserves, output, and exports of the petroleum sector and on tax and other oil sector payments to the Treasury. In this vein, there would also be full disclosure of the accounts of SONANGOL, including its operations with the Treasury and the National Bank of Angola (BNA), in accordance with internationally accepted accounting norms. In addition to the diagnostic study of the oil sector, it would be important that the authorities identify and record all government revenue and expenditure, improve the budgetary accounting and treasury systems, and ensure that the BNA does not make payments on the government's behalf without payment orders. Furthermore, it would be desirable to initiate promptly an independent external audit of the National Bank of Angola, and to undertake a diagnostic study of the diamond sector as soon as the security situation in the diamond-producing regions permits.

By mid-2000, neither the audit of the BNA nor the diagnostic studies of the petroleum and diamond industries had yet begun, although terms of reference for the petroleum sector study had been agreed with the IMF and a bidding process for that study was under way, as a prerequisite for the staff-monitored programme agreed with the Fund in April. The strategic and politically sensitive nature of these studies is all too evident.

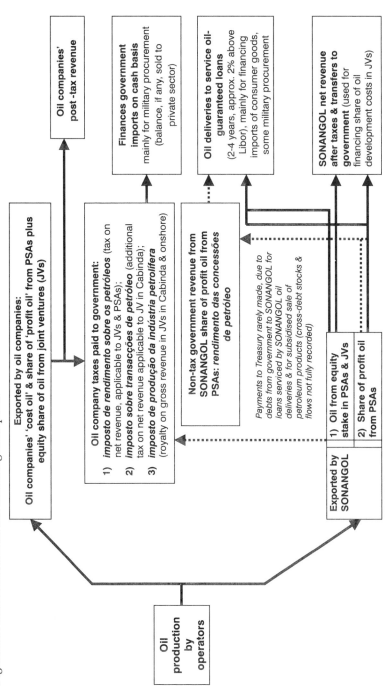

Figure 6.5: Oil revenues and the financing of imports

For Futungo de Belas, they risk exposing the murky way in which public resources have been managed up to now. But for many Angolans, including frustrated technocrats within the state bureaucracy, as well as the donor community, the studies were seen as a key first step towards achieving greater transparency in public finances. Without such transparency, there could be no real basis for effective accountability. Comprehensive and readily available data on the finances of strategic state companies such as SONANGOL and ENDIAMA, on the accounts of the central bank, on government revenue and expenditure, and on public debt stocks and flows, are a prerequisite for meaningful reporting on the management of public finances to the National Assembly or, if it is one day set up in practice, to the *Tribunal de Contas*. Achieving such improvements in economic governance is thus the key to improved resource management and ultimately to Angola's socio-economic recovery and development. Without such transparency and accountability, the country's resources are likely to continue being mismanaged, not only in a technical sense, but also with respect to the fundamental choices about whether resources are used to meet the needs of Angolan society as a whole or those of the privileged few.

7

Diamonds | **UNITA's War Economy & State Patronage**

While the government has bankrolled its war machine with the proceeds from oil, UNITA was able to secure control of lucrative diamond mines, generating revenues that would substitute for the loss of foreign military assistance in the early 1990s. Because of their strategic economic importance, the north-eastern provinces of Lunda Norte and Lunda Sul, where the main diamond deposits are located, have been among the most fought-over parts of the hinterland. The UN eventually imposed a ban on the purchase of UNITA diamonds in July 1998, in a belated attempt to deprive the movement of the funds needed to sustain its armed forces, but it came too late to salvage the crumbling peace process and proved relatively easy for UNITA to flout.

On the government side too, the country's diamond wealth has a special importance, even though the current official revenues from diamonds come a distant second to the earnings from oil and so have been far less important as a means of military financing than in UNITA's case. The government is well aware that diamonds could one day earn Angola a lot more, not just because of the potential benefits of peace for the industry's future development, but also because the country has huge underground deposits, or kimberlites, that have yet to be exploited. Meanwhile, diamonds have played a pivotal role in the process of enrichment of the new *nomenklatura* and in the system of patronage that has been at the heart of the presidency's strategy for conserving power.

Complicating the situation still further, the struggle by 'outsiders' (the Kimbundu/urban elite and the Ovimbundu-based UNITA) for control of the country's diamond resources has stirred simmering discontent among the local Lunda-Chokwe, adding a new regionalist/ethnic dimension to the conflict and raising fears of a 'second Cabinda'.

Origins and development of the industry

Diamond mining is one of Angola's oldest industries, dating back to 1912, when seven diamonds were discovered in a stream in the Lunda region of north-eastern Angola. Five years later, the *Companhia de Diamantes de Angola* (DIAMANG) was set up. It focused its attention on the alluvial and eluvial deposits found in river beds, former river courses and valley hillsides, particularly in the Lunda region (now constituting the provinces of Lunda Norte and Lunda Sul). As the industry developed, DIAMANG used river diversion techniques, involving dykes and canals, to drain rivers and then mine the diamond-bearing gravel on the river beds and banks (Helmore, 1984; Hodges, 1987).

Diamonds became Angola's main export for almost three decades, until the coffee boom following the Second World War, which encouraged widespread coffee planting. After 1973, when oil became the leading export, diamonds fell back to third place. However, diamond production had continued to increase, reaching 2.4 million carats in 1974, and in value terms Angola was one of the world's largest producers. Angola's diamonds are almost all of gem or near-gem quality rather than industrial diamonds, and they fetch among the highest prices per carat in the world.[1] Until the mid-1980s, all the diamonds mined in Angola were marketed through the Central Selling Organization (CSO), the international cartel operated on behalf of diamond producers by De Beers, which controls about 70 per cent of the world trade in rough diamonds.

During the latter decades of colonial rule, DIAMANG became the largest commercial enterprise in Portugal's African empire. Initially it had prospecting rights to the whole of Angola, but in 1970 this was reduced to a 50,000 square kilometre area in the Lundas. This is where the main mining sites had been developed and the company ran its concession area like a state within the state. In addition to running the mines, DIAMANG operated a wide range of support services; it produced its own power supply and owned a series of commercial farms to provide food for its workforce.

After independence, the Angolan government took a majority share-holding in DIAMANG, and then in 1986 replaced it with a new wholly state-owned company, the *Empresa de Diamantes de Angola* (ENDIAMA). In its marketing arrangements, the government became more independent, ending its contract with the CSO in 1985, although, when the diamond market slumped later in the decade, it rediscovered the benefits of the price supports provided by the CSO and began a rapprochement with De Beers in 1989. However, it never again reverted to marketing all official production through the CSO.

---

[1] In 1995–97, Angola's official diamond exports had an average sales price of $287 per carat.

Following independence, diamond production had been seriously disrupted by the exodus of managers and other skilled workers in 1975 and then by growing security problems, which increased operating costs in the remote mining areas of the north-east. From the mid-1980s, when UNITA extended its guerrilla operations into the north of the country, making use of logistical facilities and sanctuaries across the border in southern Zaire, the guerrillas began to threaten the diamond mines. On occasion they raided the mines, seizing expatriate miners as hostages. In the most dramatic of these raids, in February 1984, against the mining town of Cafunfo, in Lunda Norte, UNITA seized 77 Portuguese, Britons and Filipinos and marched them hundreds of miles across the bush before releasing them. The numerous raids resulted in the periodic destruction of mine equipment and closure of mining operations. The risk of ambush also made it difficult to transport mine equipment and supplies by road from the coast, forcing the mines to depend on air transport, which significantly raised the costs of production. In addition, as lawlessness spread in the north-east, theft of diamonds from the mining sites, illegal mining operations and smuggling became wide-spread.

As a result of these growing difficulties, officially recorded exports of diamonds declined sharply, reaching their lowest level, less than 200,000 carats, in 1986 (see Figure 7.1). There was a partial recovery in the late 1980s, as the government reinforced security in the mining areas. In 1992, benefiting from the improved security that followed the Bicesse Accords, officially recorded exports reached their highest level in a decade, about 1.4 million carats, although this was still considerably below the level in the early 1970s, which had averaged about 2 million carats a year. Following the resumption of the war at the end of 1992, official sales collapsed to less than 300,000 carats in 1993, but there was a gradual recovery thereafter, as security conditions in the official mining areas improved. By 1997, official diamond exports had recovered to 1.2 million carats (IMF, 1999a). In 1998–99, there was a rapid expansion of production, reaching 2.7 billion carats in 1998 and 3.7 billion carats in 1999, due to much improved security and the commissioning of a major new mine at Catoca in Lunda Sul.

In value, officially recorded diamond exports recovered from a low of $63 million in 1993 to an estimated $614 million in 1999 (EIU, August 2000). However, the government's fiscal revenue from diamonds has been insignificant, due to low earnings or losses by some companies (related to the high costs of security and dependence on air transport) and, in other cases, tax evasion and fraud resulting from the weak tax administration and the ease of smuggling.

The global value of Angola's diamond production and exports has been far higher than the official figures cited above. Large numbers of illegal

Figure 7.1   Official diamond exports, 1973–97
(thousand carats)

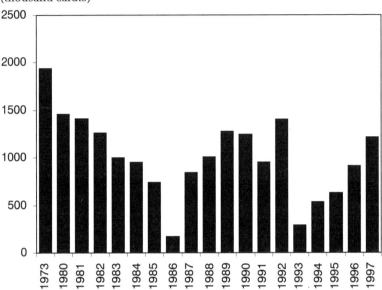

Sources: IMF; Ministry of Geology and Mines; ENDIAMA

miners and smugglers, as well as UNITA, have been active in the 'informal' diamond industry, generically known as *garimpo*, and even much of the output in government-controlled areas is not reported and taxed. The *garimpeiros* first became active in the Lundas when the strict security regime enforced there by DIAMANG and the authorities began to crumble in the 1980s. However, it was after the Bicesse Accords that illegal mining took off in a big way. The improved security conditions encouraged thousands of fortune-seekers to head for the Lundas and, by mid-1992, industry sources estimated that there were between 30,000 and 40,000 *garimpeiros* at work in the region (Hodges, 1993).

Unlike in the petroleum industry, technological sophistication or large capital outlays are not required to mine diamonds from alluvial deposits. It was possible for UNITA and the *garimpeiros* to exploit deposits with quite simple open-cast methods, sometimes making use of abandoned investments such as river diversions made in earlier years by industrial mining companies. As Figure 7.2 shows, illegal sales are thought to have amounted to some $600 million a year in much of the period between 1992 and 1997, dwarfing official sales. They then fell off sharply to around $200 million in 1998, following the restoration of government control over many of the mining sites previously controlled by UNITA.

Figure 7.2 Estimated global diamond sales, 1992–99 ($ million)

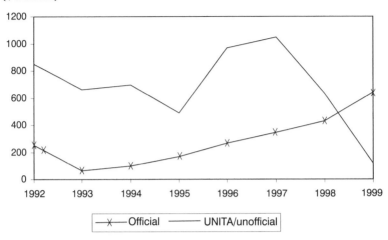

Sources: derived from EIU, Global Witness and industry sources.

Even so, Angola's global exports of diamonds are estimated to have amounted to some $600–700 million in 1998.[2] This would be close to 10 per cent of the value of world diamond production (almost $7 billion in 1998), and equivalent to about 20 per cent of the value of Angolan oil exports. Including both official and unofficial sales, Angola is currently the world's fourth largest diamond producer, in value terms, after Botswana, Russia and South Africa.

In the longer term, the restoration of peace and security would enable mining companies to invest in the development of Angola's major kimberlite deposits. These primary deposits are large underground diamond-bearing shafts of volcanic origin. Several such deposits have been found in Angola and they are expected to become a major new source of foreign-exchange earnings in the twenty-first century, alongside the earnings from oil.

UNITA's war economy and UN sanctions

Until the early 1990s, UNITA's capacity to wage war depended mainly on military assistance from South Africa and, after the repeal of the Clark amendment in 1985, the United States. This external military assistance was supplemented by weapons seized from the FAPLA. UNITA's revenue

---

[2] EIU, *Angola Country Report*, 1st Quarter, 1999.

from commercial exports was minimal, although there was some trafficking in diamonds, timber and ivory, with the help of South African
troops and foreign businessmen. Fred Bridgland, the biographer of Jonas
Savimbi, claims that UNITA was generating between $50,000 and $4
million a month from diamonds by 1986–87 (Bridgland, 1988). When it
established control over much of the coffee-growing north-west in the late
1980s, the movement also generated a small income from coffee, which
was sold to traders from Zaire. The amounts involved were very small,
however, and generally the areas under UNITA control in the 1980s
reverted to a low-level subsistence economy, although some long-
distance traders brought in exchange goods from Namibia, Zambia and
Zaire and there was some localized petty trade across military lines.

By the end of the 1980s, however, UNITA had secured control of several
important diamond areas in the north-east and had begun to exploit a few
sites abandoned by industrial mining companies and to tax independent
garimpeiros. Thus, even before the loss of US and South African support
in the early 1990s, it had already taken steps to rely on its own resources
(Le Billon, 1999). During the post-Bicesse period, it was able to take
advantage of the influx of diggers into the diamond-rich zones under its
control. Then, following the resumption of the war in late 1992, it rapidly
secured control of almost all of Lunda Norte and Lunda Sul, including the
entire Cuango valley, the source of Angola's most valuable alluvial
diamond deposits.[3] UNITA was able to acquire diamonds by three means.
It directly exploited some mines, using its own troops and civilian labour
requisitioned for this purpose. Another mechanism was to extract a tax
(normally in the form of a share of production) from independent diggers
working sites in the territory under its control. Finally, it obtained
revenue by selling licences to diamond buyers to operate within its
territory. To defend and monitor its diamond mining operations, it
organized a special mines protection force (UN, 2000).

UNITA was able to accumulate unparalleled resources from the mining,
taxation and sale of diamonds, although the scale of unofficial mining
fluctuated from year to year, depending on the military situation and
weather conditions, which affect mining along river courses. Overall,
according to one source (Global Witness, 1998), UNITA's revenue from
diamonds amounted to $3.7 billion between 1992 and 1998. The figure
may be too high because it appears to be based on the market value of all

---

[3] The government retained control only of enclaves in the extreme north-east of Lunda Norte
(around ENDIAMA's headquarters at Dundo and the mining sites of Andrada and Lucapa) and
around the capital of Lunda Sul, Saurimo. The FAA succeeded in recapturing the important
mining centre of Cafunfo, in the Cuango valley, with the help of mercenaries from the South
African firm, Executive Outcomes, in 1993, but, even after the Lusaka Protocol, this remained
an isolated outpost surrounded by UNITA-held territory until 1997.

Angolan rough diamonds sold in what the industry calls the 'outside market'. UNITA's net revenue from diamonds, while substantial, would have been less, both because of the large cut taken by middlemen and because a significant proportion of unofficial goods is smuggled out of government-controlled as well as UNITA areas. Industry sources put UNITA's cumulative net revenue in 1992–98 at around $2 billion, still a substantial sum and far more than the movement ever received from the United States and South Africa, its main external patrons, prior to the Bicesse Accords in 1991.[4]

Given the importance of diamonds to UNITA's ability to sustain its military capability, it seems odd in retrospect that the international community took no action to stop it until 12 June 1998, when the UN Security Council imposed its worldwide ban on the purchase of unofficial Angolan diamonds and ordered the freezing of UNITA bank accounts and other financial assets.[5] On 8 July 1998, the European Union announced its formal adoption of the sanctions, which thereby became mandatory for all 15 member states. This was especially important because of the role of Belgium, an EU member, in the world diamond trade: approximately 80 per cent of the trade in rough (uncut) diamonds takes place in the Belgian city of Antwerp. In another follow-up move, De Beers announced that the CSO fully supported 'both the letter and spirit of the UN resolution 1173' and was refusing to buy Angolan diamonds without official certificates of origin. Previously, the CSO's buying offices had been systematically buying up illegally exported Angolan diamonds, including those mined in UNITA areas, in order to prevent the 'outside market' from depressing world prices. Angolan diamonds have been the main source of supply to that market over the past decade.

Nonetheless, the new UN sanctions proved difficult to implement, due to the ease with which diamonds could be smuggled out of Angola via neighbouring states and then sold in the major diamond trading centres, either with forged Angolan certificates of origin or with documents obtained in other states to disguise their Angolan origin. Although more bulky, some arms and fuel sales to UNITA also continued in violation of the earlier UN sanctions and, despite the growing risks, several foreign air-freight companies continued to lease aircraft to fly into UNITA areas to deliver arms and fuel and take out parcels of diamonds.

---

[4] The value of the military assistance received from the United States during the Reagan Administration reportedly reached a peak of $40–60 million a year in 1989–91 (Minter, 1994).
[5] UN Security Council Resolution 1173 (1998) required states to 'take the necessary measures...to prohibit the direct or indirect import from Angola to their territory of all diamonds that are not controlled through the Certificate of Origin regime of the GURN'. States were also to prohibit 'the sale or supply to persons or entities in areas of Angola to which State administration has not been extended...of equipment used in mining or mining services'. It also required states to freeze all UNITA 'funds and financial resources' within their territories.

These violations became a cause of growing concern within the UN Security Council, as Angola drifted back to war towards the end of 1998. Under a new chairman, Ambassador Robert Fowler of Canada, the Security Council's previously rather somnolent Angolan Sanctions Committee became more active and, in January 1999, proposed in-depth studies on the trafficking of armaments and oil supplies to UNITA and the movement of UNITA funds.[6] The proposal was accepted by the Security Council which, by Resolution 1237 on 7 May 1999, set up an expert panel, headed by Ambassador Anders Möllander of Sweden, to carry out the investigations.

In the course of its work, the expert panel visited almost 30 countries, to gather information from government officials, diplomats, police and intelligence agencies, commercial companies, NGOs and journalists. It also held long interviews with a number of high-ranking defectors from UNITA, some of whom had personal knowledge of UNITA's methods of trading diamonds for arms and fuel. Through these inquiries, the panel was able to piece together a comprehensive picture of the methods used to evade the sanctions, which it detailed in a report to the Security Council on 10 March 2000 (UN, 2000).

The panel found that, despite the sanctions on arms supplies to UNITA, which had been in place since 1993, the movement had been able to import a wide range of military equipment, including mechanized vehicles such as tanks and armoured personnel carriers, landmines and explosives, a variety of small arms and light weapons, anti-tank weapons, anti-aircraft systems and artillery pieces. Most of these weapons had been sourced in Eastern Europe. As a result of the end of the Cold War and the dissolution of the Warsaw Pact, international arms markets were saturated in the 1990s with surplus Eastern European weaponry, much of it being offered at knock-down prices. Economic difficulties in some of these countries, as well as the arms reduction requirements of the Conventional Forces in Europe Treaty, had fuelled the sell-off. Much of the equipment went to Africa, where demand was high because of civil wars and the general climate of insecurity. Some East European countries had weak export control procedures, making it quite easy for weapons to be acquired with falsified end-user certificates.

In UNITA's case, most of the weapons came from Bulgaria, often using Zairean, Togolese and Burkinabe end-user certificates. Zaire was the main conduit until the overthrow of Mobutu in May 1997.[7] According to the expert panel:

---

[6] Fowler described the embargoes on UNITA as being 'like traffic rules'. However, 'nobody enforced them, people drove where they wanted and parked all over the place. It was a complete disaster' (Address to the International Development Committee, House of Commons, London, 6 July 1999, cited in HRW, 1999).

[7] This relationship even made it possible for UNITA officers masquerading as Zaireans to obtain training in Bulgaria in 1996 in the use of the SAM-6 anti-aircraft missile system.

UNITA used Zaire as a base for the stockpiling of weapons, and it used Zairean end-user certificates as the means by which arms brokers working for UNITA were able to obtain the weapons Savimbi wanted. Mobutu provided Savimbi with the Zairean end-user certificates, and in return Savimbi gave Mobutu diamonds and cash. (UN, 2000: para 20)

Fearful about the future of Zaire, however, Savimbi sought to diversify his sources of end-user certificates and find alternative logistical bases. In 1993, he reached an agreement to this effect with President Gnassingbe Eyadema of Togo, who also agreed to host some of Savimbi's children. As the Mobutu regime crumbled in the early months of 1997, UNITA relocated to Togo some of its more valuable equipment, including SAM-6 anti-aircraft missiles, which had previously been kept in Zaire during the period after the Lusaka Protocol to avoid detection by UNAVEM. The panel reported that, following Mobutu's downfall, President Eyadema replaced the Zairean dictator as the primary supplier of end-user certificates for arms and military equipment destined for UNITA. The panel also obtained evidence suggesting that it was highly likely that arms legally sold and transported to Burkina Faso had been diverted by the Burkinabe authorities to UNITA, and it stated that Ouagadougou had been serving as the base of operations for the central figure in UNITA's external procurement and diamond trade operations, Marcelo Moisés Dachala, also known as Karriça.

The panel summarized its findings on the arms traffic to UNITA by noting that it had been made possible by four key factors:

First has been the willingness of certain countries in Africa to provide their end-user certificates to UNITA and to facilitate the passage of arms and military equipment through their territory to UNITA – most notably Zaire under Mobutu, Togo and Burkina Faso. Second has been the willingness of some arms supplying countries, officially or unofficially, to sell weapons with little or no regard for where those arms would actually end up – in this case most notably Bulgaria. Third has been the eagerness of international arms brokers and air transport carriers to act as intermediaries between UNITA and the suppliers of the arms and military equipment. A fourth factor has been the capacity of UNITA to continue to pay for what it wants (para 51).

The fourth factor highlighted the crucial role of diamonds. Because of their very high value, small weight and size, easy marketability, indestructibility and general availability to UNITA, the panel noted that diamond stocks were almost ideally suited to the movement's operational needs, playing a threefold role in its war economy:

First, UNITA's ongoing ability to sell rough diamonds for cash and to exchange rough diamonds for weapons provide the means for it to sustain its political and military activities. Second, diamonds have been and continue to be an important component of UNITA's strategy for acquiring friends and maintaining external support. Third, rough diamond caches rather than cash or bank deposits constitute the primary and the preferred means of stockpiling wealth for UNITA (para 77).

According to the panel's findings, UNITA has mainly employed a system of barter, by which arms, fuel and other supplies are exchanged directly for diamonds. UNITA has contracted brokers, who in turn procure military equipment, fuel and other supplies, arrange for their transportation and delivery (and sometimes training, maintenance and spare parts) and receive payment in parcels of diamonds. Diamond experts provided by the arms brokers and UNITA would agree on the value of each parcel based on the number and quality of stones presented.

At times, UNITA has sold diamonds for cash, in order to raise funds for operational expenses, in particular for travel and the maintenance of offices, personnel and family members outside the country. To avoid the seizure of assets under the financial sanctions imposed by the Security Council, only small amounts of funds have been deposited in foreign bank accounts. The organization's assets are held in the form of rough diamonds, controlled by Savimbi personally and released by him to UNITA officials, as and when required, for purchases of weapons, fuel and other commodities and to raise cash for the payment of stipends for senior UNITA personnel and family members living abroad.

First-hand testimony provided to the panel alleged that UNITA also made large gifts of diamonds to several African heads of state, including the President of Burkina Faso, Blaise Compaoré, the President of Togo, Gnassingbe Eyadema, and the former President of Zaire, Mobutu Sese Seko, in exchange for their logistical and other assistance. By 'buying' these heads of states' co-operation, UNITA was able to obtain end-user certificates, transit rights and temporary storage for military equipment purchased in Eastern Europe, as well as safe havens for diamond deals with arms brokers, the safe keeping of cash and sanctuaries for UNITA leaders' families. When the agreement with Eyadema was sealed in 1993, for example, Savimbi's envoy, Colonel Alcides Lucas Kangunga (known as 'Kallias'), gave Eyadema a 'passport-sized' packet of diamonds.

The panel found that it was easy for UNITA to market its diamonds. As noted above, in many cases it would exchange diamonds directly for weapons and other goods, the traders travelling to Andulo to make the deal. In other cases, the traders and UNITA officials would meet in a 'safe haven', such as Zaire (during the Mobutu era), Burkina Faso and Rwanda, which provided such facilities after 1998 when UNITA and Rwanda became de facto allies in the war in the DRC against President Kabila. Other diamonds were smuggled through Southern African countries, including Namibia, South Africa and Zambia, sometimes corrupting individual local officials but without the knowledge or approval of the governments concerned. In some cases, the diamonds were taken directly to Antwerp and sold there. Most of the rest of UNITA's diamonds would end up there indirectly.

The ease with which diamonds originating from UNITA territory could be sold to traders and cutters in Antwerp was one of the major holes in the UN sanctions. The panel found that 'the extremely lax controls and regulations governing the Antwerp market facilitate and perhaps even encourage illegal trading activity' (para 87). It acknowledged the intrinsic difficulties of policing the trade: the ease with which diamonds can be smuggled, the sheer size of the Antwerp market, which has an annual turnover of around $5 billion and thousands of dealers, jewellers, manufacturers and brokers, and the difficulties of identifying the precise origin of a parcel of diamonds, particularly if stones from several areas have been mixed together. However, it accused the Belgian authorities of failing to establish an effective import identification regime for diamonds and to monitor, sanction or blacklist traders known to be dealing in UNITA diamonds.

Lax controls within the broader diamond industry make these problems worse. To import diamonds into most countries, it has traditionally been necessary only to indicate provenance, rather than origin. Furthermore, it has been claimed (Global Witness, 1998) that large quantities of diamonds from UNITA territory have been smuggled through third countries, such as Zambia, where they have been issued with false certificates of origin by corrupt officials.

Despite the widespread sanctions busting revealed by the panel, it would be erroneous to conclude that the sanctions have been without any effect at all. The panel's report indicated that in some critical respects they were biting. In particular, UNITA was finding it extremely difficult to obtain and fly in fuel. Fuel stocks were very low, posing a severe constraint on UNITA forces' mobility and military capability.

The increased international publicity given to sanctions busting in 1998–2000, as a result of the efforts of Ambassadors Fowler and Möllander as well as a high-profile campaign by the British-based NGO, Global Witness, prompted governments and companies to take measures to appear clean. As was to be expected, the governments accused in the UN expert panel's report claimed that they were innocent of sanctions violations. Globally, the diamond industry itself began to take measures in 2000 to clean up its act, notably by endorsing proposals for international controls that would tag legal diamonds from mines to the retail market, in order to reassure consumers that they are not purchasing 'conflict diamonds' from war zones such as Angola and Sierra Leone. Fears of exposure and of the possible future costs of being caught (industry blacklists, forfeitures of aircraft or criminal proceedings) made UNITA's direct and indirect partners more wary of buying its diamonds, selling it arms and fuel or leasing aircraft. To compensate for the higher risks, the brokers, traders and airfreight companies still willing to deal with UNITA demanded higher fees. In addition, in mid-2000 the UN Security Council was considering new, tougher actions in the light of the panel's findings and recommendations.

For UNITA, the rise in its transaction costs and the increasing difficulties of procurement could not have come at a worse time. The war had started again and, by the end of 1999, the movement had also lost its principal airport at Andulo in the Central Highlands, making its air communications much more difficult. In addition, its access to diamonds has greatly diminished. There have been two main reasons for this. First, in the mid-1990s, UNITA and the *garimpeiros* in its territory gradually exhausted most of the alluvial sites to which they had ready access. In the absence of new prospecting or investments such as river diversions, it would have been difficult to sustain the level of production. To a large extent, UNITA had been living off the pickings from sites identified and prepared in previous years by industrial mining companies, and this could not go on for ever. Secondly, towards the end of 1997, UNITA agreed, under intense pressure to fulfil its commitments under the Lusaka Protocol, to return its main mining areas to government control. Possibly, the fact that these sites had already been largely exhausted made the handover less difficult to accept. In any case, the CSO reported a steep decline in the supply of Angolan rough diamonds from unofficial/UNITA sources entering the market in 1998. With the resumption of the war at the end of 1998 and the government's subsequent military successes, this trend is likely to have continued into 1999 and 2000. The implication is that, since 1998, not only have UNITA's transaction costs increased, but its stockpile of diamonds has been significantly depleted.

Diamond concessions and the *nomenklatura*

Ironically, the lack of meaningful controls on the diamond trade within Angola has also facilitated the smuggling of diamonds, including from UNITA-controlled areas. The expert panel described the market within Angola as 'wide open', with virtually anyone legally able to posssess, buy or sell diamonds, and observed that it would have been 'relatively easy for

UNITA to "launder" its diamonds through official channels' (UN, 2000: para 94).

This situation arose because of radical changes in the legislation governing the production and trading of diamonds in the early 1990s. Until then, all officially sanctioned diamond mining had been carried out by large industrial mining companies, acting as contractors to ENDIAMA, which was responsible for all marketing. Beginning in 1991, the government undertook a series of legislative changes which appeared to be an attempt to respond to the spreading *garimpo* phenomenon by creating legal opportunities for small-scale private mining and trade in diamonds.

The first step was a law in December 1991 which legalized the possession and trading of rough diamonds acquired outside the mining companies' concession areas and provided for the establishment of licensed trading offices where diamonds could be bought and sold for foreign currency (law 30/91). The rationale was that this would channel the informal trade in rough diamonds into official circuits, thus generating revenue for the government. By the late 1990s, there were five officially licensed buyers, which in turn sub-contracted to a large number of local buyers. Because most of these sub-contracted buyers operated on a commission basis, they had a financial incentive not to ask questions about the origin of the goods. As a result, some diamonds produced in UNITA-controlled areas ended up being marketed through these buying agents and then exported through legal channels in Luanda, with official certificates of origin. The UN panel confirmed this, stating that 'a quantity of diamonds coming from UNITA areas (and from which UNITA had already extracted its cut) were undoubtedly sold through official channels' (UN, 2000: para 95).

In 1998, Global Witness drew attention to the fact that it was also easy to forge Angolan certificates of origin, or to bribe officials to sign them. Another source claimed that official certificates of origin were available for sale in Luanda (HRW, 1999). Ambassador Fowler called in July 1999 for the re-design of the certificates of origin, to make them more difficult to forge. It was doubtless because of the laxity of the marketing system in Angola that, in January 2000, De Beers' CSO decided that it would cease to buy any Angolan diamonds, including even those bearing government certificates of origin, except for the output of one particular mine which it was contractually obligated to purchase.

Given the strategic nature of diamonds for UNITA's military procurement, it seems on the face of it extraordinary that the government should have allowed such a situation to have continued for so many years. The only plausible explanation is that the vested interests of government officials and their partners were strong enough to hold off reform. Trading diamonds has been one of the principal avenues for enrichment by the elite and profits were to be made by making deals across politico-military lines.[8]

The liberalization of the marketing system in the 1990s was accompanied by new legislation governing the mining of diamonds, to allow small producers to participate legally in the industry, in addition to large mining companies. It would be much more difficult to monitor and tax the sales of numerous small mine owners than in the days when there were only two or three large mining operations.

Following the enactment of a new mining law in 1992 (law 1/92), the government adopted a new law on the diamond industry in 1994 (law 16/94). As its preamble explained, the main innovation of this law was

> to allow artisanal mining of diamond deposits selected according to their special characteristics, in a rational and controlled manner. This type of mining will occur on those deposits which are not minable on an industrial scale and will only be allowed within areas surrounding present or future areas demarcated for industrial mining...

This provision amounted to the legalization of what had been a de facto situation before, namely, the exploitation of alluvial diamond resources by *garimpeiros* using artisanal methods. Mining permits were supposed to be granted only to local people, who had lived for at least ten years in the surrounding *comunas*, as certified by the local chiefs and headmen. Subsequently, the government launched a special scheme entitled the *Programa para Estabilização do Sector Diamantífero em Angola* (PROESDA), to put this provision into effect. In practice, however, PROESDA strayed from its declared goal, allocating about 30 small concessions to government officials and other well-connected individuals along the Rivers Luachimo and Chicapa.

Law 16/94 also brought important changes with respect to the concessions for industrial mining. While vesting all mining rights over the whole national territory in ENDIAMA, it allowed the state company to participate with foreign and Angolan companies in mixed companies, joint ventures and other contractual arrangements for prospecting and

---

[8] According to Human Rights Watch, Angolan government officials, including military officers, regularly engaged in deals with UNITA in the Lundas in 1995–98, arranging local transactions while claiming in Luanda that the diamonds were obtained from mines in government areas. Human Rights Watch also stated that it had reason to believe that in 1998 senior Angolan government officials also assisted UNITA in its procurement of fuel, thereby breaking the UN embargo. A number of truck drivers told Human Rights Watch that, on the orders of the governor of Malange, Flávio Fernandes, SONANGOL trucks delivered fuel to UNITA in Quela, eastern Malange. This appears to have continued for several months until the city came under siege from UNITA in December 1998, whereupon the sub-commissioner of police in Malange was arrested on charges of facilitating oil sales to UNITA (HRW, 1999).

production in specific concession areas. More than 20 concessions, involving 30 to 40 companies, were awarded in 1994–99. Significantly, and for the first time in Angolan mining legislation, law 16/94 made a special point of referring to the 'participation of Angolan companies (which) should be encouraged, as long as they possess the required technical and financial conditions' (Article 2.6). This opened the way for the involvement of small private Angolan companies in the industry. Several such companies (*Lumanhe, Esplendor, Anglo Sul, Consórcio Mineiro do Lucula, Mombo, Opala Negra* and *Transcoi*) had obtained concessions by 1999.

Along with the profits to be made from diamond trafficking, the diamond concessions awarded since 1994 have become one of the new *nomenklatura's* main avenues for accumulating wealth, while the shadowy procedures for awarding the concessions provide another prime example of the non-transparency of resource management and the role of presidential patronage in building and cementing alliances. The tendering process has been opaque and it is well known that the final decisions on diamond concessions are taken at Futungo de Belas. Significantly, several concessions have gone to companies set up by army generals and other high state officials, apparently for nominal licence fees, suggesting that the diamond concessions have been one of the main ways of rewarding military loyalty.

In 1996–97, President dos Santos offered the same type of benefits to UNITA, as a 'peace-building' measure. He calculated that UNITA would be unlikely to relinquish its control of the main diamond-mining areas, despite its commitments to do so under the Lusaka Protocol, unless it was assured a share in future diamond revenues from a legalized concession. Discussions on the subject continued for about two years, notably during the summit meetings held by dos Santos and Savimbi in Zambia, Gabon and Belgium in 1995–6. Various government officials, including the director-general of ENDIAMA, visited Bailundo for technical discussions.[9] Eventually, in November 1996, the government and UNITA signed a memorandum of understanding, which indicated that UNITA would obtain the right to control and explore certain diamond areas through a legally registered company (Hare, 1998).

Although the UN was not directly involved in these negotiations, the United States, which played a key role in the peace process as a member of the troika, actively encouraged the 'peace for diamonds' proposal, on the

---

[9] Savimbi, in an interview with a Portuguese radio station, *Rádio Renascença*, on 27 June 1996, acknowledged the visit had taken place and underscored the importance of diamonds for UNITA. 'Yes, he paid a visit. We acknowledge that there are ongoing discussions, very realistic discussions. The fact is, UNITA cannot be left without resources. It cannot, you cannot ask for everything: let us have your army! Here, take it. Let us have your weapons! Here, take them. Let us have your money! Oh, come on, get real! Nobody will accept that.'

realpolitik presumption that UNITA's need for an independent source of funding had to be taken into account if the peace process was not to unravel. As a result, it became an accomplice to a type of bargaining over mineral rights that set the worst possible example of resource management and an incentive for future rebels to seek mining rights the same way.

In the end, the proposed deal collapsed, as the government grew tired of UNITA's procrastinating in the peace process. Government forces went on the offensive in the Lundas, overrunning much of the eastern part of Lunda Norte in May 1997 and, as we have seen, UNITA subsequently withdrew peacefully from the Cuango valley at the end of the year. As the country returned to full-scale war at the end of 1998, no more was heard of sharing diamond resources with UNITA.

As a more general form of patronage, however, diamond concessions have been one of the most attractive, influential gifts that Futungo can arrange on behalf of loyal officials. Relatively small investments are required for alluvial diamond mining. To compensate for their lack of capital and technical experience, the Angolan concessionaires have no shortage of potential partners among the foreign mining companies eager to gain a stake in the industry. Technically, law 16/94 required companies to have the financial and technical means to prospect and develop their concessions, but in practice the small Angolan concessionaires have invariably turned to foreign partners for the financing of investments and to conduct mining operations. For example, *Lumanhe*, a company owned by several senior army oficers, operates its mines at Calonda and Chitotolo in partnership with ITM, an international company whose origins are in the Zambian copper mining industry, and which has been involved in diamond mining in Angola since the 1980s. Most of the part-nership arrangements encourage typical rent-seeking behaviour on the part of the Angolan concessionaires, as the foreign partners normally have to bear all the prospecting, development and operating costs and take all the risks, while sharing their profits with the concessionaires, who are effectively 'sleeping partners'.[10] As has been noted above, the government itself has earned almost nothing from the diamond industry, less than 1 per cent of its fiscal revenue coming from diamonds in the period between 1992 and 1996.

Only after the resumption of the war in 1998, and as a result of the growing international concern about the seepage of UNITA diamonds into the world market through official Angolan channels, did the government finally take steps to begin reforms of the diamond industry. In May 1999, the director-general of ENDIAMA was dismissed and a new board was

---

[10] Under one contract, seen by this author, the foreign partner is responsible for all mining activities and, after deduction of costs and fiscal obligations, shares the rest of the production with the Angolan concessionaires on a 50–50 basis.

subsequently appointed, headed by a FAA general. The government intro-duced new certificates of origin, which were said to be harder to forge and easier to verify. Steps were taken to restructure ENDIAMA, which lost its role in the sale of diamonds to a new marketing company, Angola Selling Corporation (ASCORP), which was given sole rights to market all diamonds produced in Angola. Meanwhile, pressure from the IMF for greater trans-parency about the earnings from diamonds resulted in the government agreeing to commission an independent audit of the diamond industry, as one of the conditions for the new 'staff monitored programme' agreed with the Fund in April 2000. At the time of writing, it was too early to tell how far the reforms would go in practice or what would be their impact.

Lunda-Chokwe discontent

The scramble for diamond wealth by outsiders has exacerbated a smoul-dering discontent among the local population of Lunda Norte and Lunda Sul, who are from the Lunda-Chokwe ethnic group. This is a small minority in national terms (6 per cent of Angolans speak the Chokwe language), but is numerically the fourth largest group after the Mbundu, Ovimbundu and Bakongo. Chokwe speakers constitute the overwhelming majority of the sparse population of the three eastern provinces of Lunda Norte, Lunda Sul and Moxico: 73 per cent according to a 1996 survey (INE, 1999). They also have strong ethno-linguistic ties across the border with the Lunda population of the Shaba region of the DRC.[11]

During the colonial period, the development of diamond mining had a profound impact on the local population in the north-east. Not only did DIAMANG have a large concession area but, because of the high value of diamonds and the risk of theft and smuggling, it also had its own police force. It enforced tight security, restricting entry into its concession area and limiting the movement of local people. However, it also provided considerable employment opportunities, both in the mines and in a range of ancillary services, company farms and other industries. In the early 1970s, the company employed 18,000 workers. Along with their families, they constituted a substantial proportion of the relatively small population of the then unified Lunda province.[12] As a result, much of

---

[11] In the nineteenth century, the Chokwe spread their influence among the Lunda and other neighbouring peoples through inter-marriage and conquest and, in 1885, they sacked the capital of the Lunda kingdom, overthrowing its ruler, the Mwata Yamvo. As a result of the intermingling of these peoples, most Lunda in eastern Angola largely became assimilated into Chokwe culture. For an analysis of the Lunda Kingdom and the rise of the Chokwe, see Birmingham, 1992.

[12] More recent estimates from the International Organization for Migration put the population of Lunda Norte at 338,000 and Lunda Sul at 201,000 in 1996 (IOM, 1996).

the local population became proletarianized, losing its peasant traditions. In particular, small-scale family farming declined, as DIAMANG's salaried workforce was supplied with food from the company's own large farms.

Conditions for DIAMANG's workers and their families deteriorated after independence, in particular from the mid-1980s, as security conditions worsened, transport links with the coast were disrupted and mine output fell. ENDIAMA, which replaced DIAMANG in 1986, found it difficult to sustain many of the commercial farms, schools, hospitals and other institutions it inherited, and its employees suffered a sharp decline in their standard of living. The gradual collapse of the commercial farms resulted in food shortages, in the absence of significant local peasant production. Then, during the early 1990s, ENDIAMA's workers saw their salaries almost wiped out by inflation. Discontent grew and there was anger at the lack of government action to address local problems, reflected in the almost permanent absenteeism of the provincial governors of both Lunda Norte and Lunda Sul, who spent most of their time in Luanda.[13]

The provinces presented great extremes of wealth and poverty. Some local people benefited from the opportunities to engage in informal diamond digging and trading, as well as employment in the mining companies. However, large numbers of Angolans from other parts of the country, along with Zaireans and West Africans, arrived in the Lundas at the height of the *garimpo* boom in the 1990s. The largest profits were going to outsiders — namely to UNITA and its Ovimbundu leaders from the Central Highlands, to the government officials and FAA officers who won diamond concessions and to the *garimpo* bosses and traders who came from other parts of Angola or from abroad to join in the bonanza.

The troops deployed in the provinces were also primarily from outside the region, and they often treated the local people with disdain, pillaging their goods and, in UNITA's case, using forced labour to work some of the mining sites. As a result of the FAA offensive in the eastern *comunas* of Lunda Norte in May 1997, several villages were burned down and thousands of civilians were forced to flee for safety to the cities. This may have been a deliberate act of clearance, to secure areas granted as concessions to mining companies. As in the colonial period, the legislation governing the diamond sector gives sweeping powers to the authorities to move

---

[13] Symbolic of the insensitivity of the authorities was a decision by ENDIAMA to build an expensive but well-equipped clinic in the early 1990s for its Luanda-based employees and fee-paying private patients on the Ilha de Luanda, while the hospital in Dundo and other health facilities in Lunda Norte were in a state of collapse, with no drugs or equipment.

local populations compulsorily from their homes and to prevent free movement in areas reserved for mining.[14]

The discontent brewing among the Lunda-Chokwe as a result of their economic difficulties and the spectre of outsiders fighting for control of the wealth in their territory has given rise to a regionalist party, the *Partido de Renovação Social* (PRS), which did well in the 1992 parliamentary elections, coming second to the MPLA and well ahead of UNITA in both provinces. The party obtained 28 per cent of the votes cast in Lunda Sul and 14 per cent in Lunda Norte, and as a result won five seats in the National Assembly, more than any other party apart from the MPLA and UNITA. The PRS retains considerable support in the two provinces and, although it has been a non-violent party, the frustration and anger that lie behind its localized success are a warning of the potential for new sources of conflict.

---

[14] Article 13.1 of law 16//94 states that 'access, circulation of people and goods, residence and the exercise of economic activities may be controlled, limited or prohibited within the mining production areas or those reserved for the same...' Articles 21.1 and 21.2 state that 'residence in restricted areas and in protected areas is forbidden, except for people linked with the mining operations' and that 'the population residing in restricted areas or in protected areas at the time they are established must be regrouped outside such areas...' The concessionaires are supposed to provide suitable alternative accommodation and infrastructure in the areas of relocation. Article 21.3 specifies that the provincial governor is responsible for approving the relocation of populations proposed by concessionaires. Article 23 left the responsibility for controlling the movement of people in restricted and protected areas to the concessionaires, who were authorized to contract specialized security companies for this purpose.

Conclusions **8**

During the 1990s, Angola was simultaneously trying to grapple with a quadruple transition: from war to peace and reconciliation; from humanitarian emergency to rehabilitation, recovery and development; from an authoritarian, one-party system of governance to pluralist democracy; and from a command economy to an economy based on the laws of the market. Munslow (1999: 552) has commented that each one of these transitions on its own would represent a major challenge. 'Occurring together (they) would test to the utmost the capacity of a country possessing the most effective and well endowed human and institutional resources.' Angola, for all the resilience of its people, has neither.

It is questionable, however, whether the core causal problem is the weakness of institutional capacity and human resources. Mozambique, which undertook a similar multi-faceted transition following the Rome Accords in 1992, has proved far more successful, despite arguably having even weaker capacity. It has not only avoided returning to war, but has managed to develop a genuine democracy and to rebuild its economy, growth averaging more than 7 per cent a year since 1994 and 11–12 per cent, one of the highest rates in the world, in 1997–98.

No one factor alone fully explains this difference in outcome. In Angola, personal factors, particularly in the case of Savimbi, have played a role. However, there does seem to be an overwhelming body of evidence to suggest that a large part of the answer lies in Angola's endowment of mineral resources. This, is the central thesis of Munslow and also of other students of Angola, notably Le Billon (1999). By contrast, Mozambique is a much poorer country and its political factions do not have access to mineral rents.

Angola in the 1990s was a story of incomplete transition, replete with contradictions and setbacks. While it would be quite wrong to conclude that there has been no transition at all, there have been inconsistencies and setbacks. Almost a decade after the Bicesse Accords and the democratic reforms of 1991, Angola does still have a multi-party system and a diverse civil society, albeit in many respects weak and circumscribed. There has been no return to the overtly totalitarian one-party system that preceded the reforms. However, the National Assembly does not yet provide a really effective system of parliamentary accountability. There have been no elections for eight years. The democratization of local and provincial government has been postponed *sine die*. Legal restrictions and political intimidation, as well as market limitations, have held back the development of the mass media, which hardly yet constitute a real 'fourth estate'. A continuing climate of fear pervades Angolan society. Human rights abuses occur on a large scale, committed by both sides in the conflict, and the justice system is too weak and corrupted to uphold the rule of law even in the parts of the country where it formally functions.

The lack of transparency in the management of public resources, symbolized by the infamous Bermuda triangle, has made accountability even more difficult to achieve. A large proportion of public revenue and expenditure is off-budget, in a murky world of presidential directives and beyond the purview even of the core economic ministries, let alone of auditors. Angola has not returned to a command economy, but certain features of that system remain and distort the type of market economy which has emerged in the 1990s.

The presidential system that developed under the mantle of the one-party system continued after the 1991 reforms. The marginalization of the party, which had in practice long lost its 'leading role', was confirmed constitutionally. Now in power for more than two decades, dos Santos has remained an executive President, appointing and chairing the Council of Ministers and at times dispensing altogether with the pretence of having a Prime Minister. He is commander-in-chief of the armed forces and, in the provinces, the governors act as his personal representatives, unencumbered by any form of electoral accountability. On top of all this, the head of state directly controls a substantial part of government revenue through extra-budgetary accounts.

It is the transition to peace and reconstruction which has proved most disappointing of all. Despite the hopes raised by the Bicesse Accords in 1991 and then, with greater circumspection on the part of most Angolans, by the Lusaka Protocol in 1994, Angola never achieved much more than a shaky quasi-peace, a state of 'neither peace nor war', and twice slipped back to full-scale war. At the time of writing, the country is still in the grip of war and its attendant humanitarian crisis.

The four dimensions of transition (to peace, reconstruction, pluralist democracy and a market economy) have been intertwined, the degree of progress in one depending at least in part on one or more of the others. In particular, the failure to restore a sustainable peace has directly derailed attempts at economic and social reconstruction (the return of IDPs and refugees, demining, the recovery of the rural economy) and cast a dark shadow over other aspects of the transition. The war has provided a rationale for the high levels of government expenditure on the armed forces, the postponement of elections and the failure to implement democratic reforms in local and provincial government, and served as an alibi for government failures, notably in the management of the economy.

A possible hypothesis is that the regime accepted democratic reforms in 1991 under duress. It needed to find a way to end the conflict with UNITA, which could only be accommodated in a pluralist political system. This proposition implies that, as the peace process broke down, so too would the adherence to democratic principles. The war would then be used as a pretext to cut short the still incomplete process of democratic transition and to restrict democratic freedoms (highlighted, for example, by the attacks on the media), in order to defend the interests of an elite whose wealth depended on the absence of strong democratic checks and balances.

There is much truth in this, but the argument should not be extended to suggest that the regime is bent on returning to the overt totalitarianism of the past. On the contrary, the regime values the legitimacy it gains, at home and abroad, from the trappings of pluralist democracy, while having at its disposal an armoury of techniques for the subtle subversion of the democratic forms established in 1991. Repression is only a tool of last resort. As we saw in Chapter 4, Futungo's strategy for conserving power has rested on patronage as well as strong security forces. Employed to buy the loyalty of army officers and tame potential political opponents, patronage has come in many forms: the award of diamond concessions, the transfer of state companies and properties to private owners, the allocation of commercial contracts and business licences, the allocation of rationed foreign exchange at the official exchange rate and subsidized credit from state-owned banks, subsidies to the political parties, generous Christmas bonuses to members of parliament and even the largesse distributed through the FESA to national NGOs.

These privileges mainly benefit the circle of closely inter-related Luanda-based creole families who were active in or identified with the MPLA and, after taking over the administrative and military positions vacated by Portuguese administrators and officers, developed capitalist aspirations during the 1980s. When the market system was instituted in the early 1990s, these families took advantage of the new opportunities to accumulate capital, while manipulating their political connections and residual administrative mechanisms to gain privileged access to resources.

To a limited extent, clientelist redistribution has also benefited a wider layer of the urban population, through such mechanisms as state or parastatal employment and subsidies for fuel, water and electricity. At times of hyperinflation, as in 1996, state resources have also been used to finance imports of food and other basic commodities at a subsidized exchange rate to head off the risk of urban protest. However, these benefits have been heavily outweighed by the decline in real purchasing power and the decay of social service provision by the state. Some of the benefits are limited to the residents of the 'concrete city', rather than the urban majority of more recent migrants, packed into the shantytowns and dependent almost exclusively on the informal market. Even less does clientelist redistribution reach the rural population.

The system is one that cultivates cronyism and arbitrariness, and requires opaqueness in the management of state resources. Tenders are not used for state contracts. In so far as they exist at all, rules for public procurement are ignored. Privatization has taken place without proper valuations or any form of bidding. Diamond concessions are allocated as favours or rewards. Land titles are transferred without taking into account the interests of local peasant farmers or pastoralists. Until 1999, banks allocated rationed credit and foreign exchange to beneficiaries in response to directives from political authorities. Government payments are often made without the required Treasury payment orders, bypassing the established procedures, and the state accounts are not open to full inspection, either by the government's own internal auditing department or by an external body, such as the long promised but never implemented *Tribunal de Contas.*

Cronyism on the scale that it is practised depends on the state's access to the rent from oil wealth, running at well over $2 billion a year. In short, part of the oil rent is transferred, legally or illegally, to the elite or 'oil *nomenklatura*' (Ferreira, 1995), although some forms of patronage make use of other resources available to the state (diamond deposits, farmland). In addition, the oil rent is used to finance large, capital-intensive armed forces, maintain some basic operations of the state and provide subsidies for prices and parastatals on behalf of urban beneficiaries.

Most of the net foreign exchange earnings from oil are retained by the state for its own imports, although a part is transferred to the private sector through the sale of foreign exchange. Ultimately, however, the resources are used almost entirely for non-productive purposes, that is, mainly for military expenditure and for consumption. Very little of the rent from oil is used for the social sectors, for which budgetary allocations have been far lower than in most African countries, or for investment in physical infrastructure, such as roads, railways, ports, electricity supply and water systems, all of which are in a deplorable state. Both public investment and non-oil private investment are extremely low relative to GDP. The poor physical infrastructure and low levels of human capital combine with other factors that discourage private sector investment, such as the unstable macroeconomic environment, the maze of bureaucratic regulations, a primitive financial services sector, the lack of safe-guards resulting from a weak judicial system and the effects of an over-valued exchange rate on competitiveness.

Employing the typology of Bergesen and Haugland (2000), these characteristics combine to give Angola many of the features of a 'predatory' rather than 'developmental' state. The rent from oil is used primarily to satisfy elite interests and finance the means of retaining power, through expenditure on security and patronage, rather than to promote social and economic development.

The rent from oil has also shielded the state from external pressure, except in temporary periods of financial difficulty caused by sudden sharp falls in world oil prices. By and large, the Angolan regime does not need donor aid, while the donors themselves are anxious to avoid damaging their relations with the regime and thus endangering the interests of their oil companies.[1] Above all, the regime was able to avoid reaching an agreement on structural adjustment measures with the international financial institutions throughout the 1990s, except for the single agreement with the IMF on a staff-monitored programme in 1995 which tellingly was abandoned within a few months. Despite the heavy external debt burden, the regime has been able to use rising levels of oil production to continue negotiating oil-guaranteed loans to sustain its imports and, as Le Billon (1999) has noted, it has been willing to bear the disadvantageous terms (higher interest charges and short maturities) to keep conditionality and auditors at bay. At the time of writing, it is too early to tell whether the new staff-monitored programme agreed with the IMF in April 2000 will mark a radical break with the pattern of the 1990s.

Above all, the huge resources generated by oil provide a powerful motive to fight to win or hold on to power, illustrating what Collier and Hoeffler (1999) call the 'loot-seeking' motive for civil wars. This is not to say that mineral wealth originally 'caused' the Angolan conflict, which it did not. The war began as a nationalist revolt against an obdurate colonial power and continued, from 1975, as a struggle between rival nationalist factions headed by leaders unwilling to share power and able to mobilize their respective ethno-regional constituencies and the support of external patrons. The escalation of the conflict depended to a very large extent on the geo-strategic motives of the apartheid regime in South Africa and the Cold War rivalries of the United States and the USSR. Since the beginning of the 1990s, however, the nature of the war has fundamentally changed.

---

[1] Munslow (1999: 552) has remarked that 'the wealth of the country is such that it has proved impossible to create a sufficiently strong consensus and commitment within the international community to encourage both a longstanding peace between the two sides and the adoption of a macroeconomic stabilization package that can restore some sanity to the Angolan economy, to the eventual benefit of its people. The mineral wealth has corrupted all those involved.'

The protagonists no longer have powerful external backers, due to the end of the Cold War and the demise of apartheid, nor any real social base within the country. There are no clear political or ideological differences between the two sides, at least since the MPLA's abandonment of Marxism. It is difficult to avoid the conclusion that the conflict has become a raw struggle between rival elites for the control of the resources generated by oil and to a lesser extent by diamonds. This is without doubt the main motive of the Cabindan separatists as well.

The assessment must be qualified, however, by taking into account personal factors, particularly in the case of Savimbi. The failure of the peace process can be explained in part by Savimbi's failure to convert from military to political leader and his psychological inability to accept short-term defeat and build a long-term base of support outside his traditional Ovimbundu constituency by exploiting the failures of the incumbent regime. A different disposition on the part of Savimbi would probably have overcome the mutual distrust that overshadowed implementation of the Bicesse and Lusaka agreements. The personal factors prevented compromise and reconciliation (among elites rather than 'national'), even though dos Santos offered UNITA a share in the 'looting', in the form of a legally recognized front company for diamond mining. The prospect of inclusion within the circuits of state patronage could not satisfy the expectations and aspirations of the UNITA leader, nor perhaps by this stage overcome his personal fear of returning to Luanda. Savimbi revealed the limits of clientelist redistribution.

Access to mineral wealth provided for both sides the means to wage war and, until the end of the 1990s, created a certain military equilibrium. As Le Billon (1999) has stressed, geography played a crucial role. While UNITA was able to overrun parts of the remote diamond-bearing northeast, taking advantage of the complicity of neighbouring Zaire under Mobutu, the oil industry acted as an offshore economic sanctuary as well as an economic enclave for the regime in Luanda. However, although UNITA was able to earn perhaps $2 billion from diamonds in 1992–97 (after the cuts of diamond dealers, arms brokers, airfreight companies and other intermediaries), its hold on the diamond areas was much less secure than the government's control of the oilfields. Since the government's reoccupation of the main diamond mining zones, there has been a growing imbalance in the resources available to the two sides. In addition, despite the shortcomings of the international sanctions against UNITA, they have increased the movement's transaction costs. The disproportion in access to mineral rent, which by the end of the 1990s was at least ten to one, can only increase in the long term, due to the rising level of oil production and the gradual rundown of UNITA's stockpiled diamond caches.

During 1999, it was becoming clear that the imbalance in resources was giving the government a clear military advantage. The FAA's victories in the closing months of the year marked a watershed in the conflict, closing the period since 1992 when UNITA had been strong enough to hold fixed positions, including rural towns, using semi-conventional means of warfare. With the loss of Bailundo and Andulo, along with most of its heavy weaponry, UNITA reverted to rural guerrilla warfare – but, unlike in the past, with no powerful external allies, and with diminishing resources, growing logistical and supply problems and spreading demoralization within its ranks, demonstrated by numerous defections of political cadres, military officers and rank-and-file troops. This assessment does not, however, underestimate the difficulties of eliminating a rural guerrilla movement or its potential to continue disrupting rural life and block the recovery of the hinterland economy, possibly for many years.

In the final analysis, the disproportion in resources may mean that, instead of fuelling the conflict, the rent from oil will bring it to an end, either through outright victory or through new negotiations in which the government can bring to bear its overwhelming superiority. This would provide further confirmation of the hypothesis of Collier and Hoeffler (1999), who postulate that, while the risk of civil war increases with the taxable base of the economy, this risk decreases again at the highest levels of resource endowment, due to the greater financial capacity of the state to defend itself.[2]

The resolution or diminution of the threat from UNITA would not, in and of itself, guarantee improvements in governance. The vested interests associated with access to the oil rent flowing to the state remain a powerful obstacle to reform. However, there would be new opportunities for progress. The definitive ending of the war would remove an alibi to justify mismanagement and a pretext to curb democratic freedoms. It would raise expectations of a better life and loosen the psychological shackles of fatalism and fear. Finally, it could change the political landscape, by ending the bipolarism in Angolan politics that has barred the emergence of a credible civilian opposition with an agenda for progressive change.

---

[2] Collier and Hoeffler found that the highest risk is reached when primary exports represent 28 per cent of GDP. In Angola's case, oil has accounted for more than 50 per cent of GDP in recent years, except in 1998 due to the temporary fall in oil prices.

Table A-1 Distribution of human resources in the public administration by category of post and gender, March 1998

	Number	% of total	Gender distribution (%)	
			Female	Male
Senior professionals				
(*técnicos superiores*)	6,803	3.5	27.4	72.6
Professionals (*técnicos*)	664	0.3	22.3	77.7
Mid-level professionals				
(*técnicos médios*)	45,070	23.0	34.4	65.6
Administrative staff	67,650	38.6	41.9	58.1
Administrative officials	22,058	11.3	42.9	57.1
Typists	37,319	19.1	40.4	59.6
Support staff	75,599	38.6	43.2	56.8
Administrative support staff	32,514	16.6	37.8	62.2
Cleaning staff	18,526	9.5	76.4	23.6
Skilled workers	12,717	6.5	21.5	78.5
Unskilled workers	9,439	4.8	35.9	64.1
Drivers	2,253	1.2	0.6	99.4
Total	195,786	100.0	40.0	60.0

Source: MAPESS, 1999a

Table A-2 Distribution of human resources in the public administration by level of education, March 1998

	% of total		
	All staff	**Female**	**Male**
Less than 4 years primary school	16.6	21.1	13.5
4 years *(I nível ensino de base)*	13.6	11.7	14.8
6 years (*II nível ensino de base*)	20.5	19.7	21.1
8 years (*III nível ensino de base*)	29.9	31.6	28.8
Completed technical college (*ensino médio*)	13.2	11.6	14.2
Completed upper secondary school (*ensino pre-universitário*)	2.7	1.8	3.3
University qualifications:	3.6	2.4	4.3
Bachelors degree (*bacharelato*)	1.5	1.0	1.8
Licenciatura	2.0	1.3	2.4
Masters (*mestrado*)	0.12	0.04	0.17
Doctorate (*doutoramento*)	0.03	0.03	0.03

Source: MAPESS, 1999a

Table A-3 Distribution of human resources in the public administration by province, March 1998

	Number	**% of total**
Bengo	2,536	1
Benguela	20,007	10
Bié	8,360	4
Cabinda	10,810	4
Cuando Cubango	2,802	9
Cunene	4,194	1
Huambo	13,563	1
Huíla	17,092	7
Kwanza Norte	6,147	3
Kwanza Sul	9,506	5
Luanda	63,032	32
Lunda Norte	2,765	1
Lunda Sul	3,158	2
Malange	7,597	4
Moxico	5,807	3
Namibe	6,744	3
Uíge	8,093	5
Zaire	2,763	1
Total	195,786	100

Source: MAPESS, 1999a

Table A-4   Distribution of human resources in the public administration by sector, March 1998

Sector	% of total
Social sectors (education, health, social welfare & relief, war veterans, youth & sports, family, employment & social security)	57
Economic sectors (industry, agriculture, petroleum, trade, geology & mines, fisheries, hotels & tourism)	16
Political/administrative (Secretariat of Council of Ministers, finance, planning, public administration, justice, foreign relations, territorial administration, information)	16
Infrastructure (public works, transport, post & telecommunications, energy & water, housing)	6
Defence and security (civilian personnel)	4
Presidency, National Assembly & courts	1

Source: MAPESS, 1999a

Table A-5   Salaries in the public administration, 1991–98 (average monthly salaries converted to US dollars at parallel exchange rate)

	Nov 1991	Apr 1992	Mar 1993	Mar 1994	Mar 1995	Mar 1996	Jan 1997	Aug 1997[a]	Nov 1998[a]
Directors (*directores*)	401	209	190	32	11	263	164	294	107
Managers (*responsáveis*)	209	107	96	11	6	148	60	n.a.	n.a.
Senior professionals (*técnicos superiores*)	337	174	142	24	8	190	77	170	75
Mid-level professionals (*técnicos médios*)	170	84	69	13	5	93	38	98	43
Low-level professionals (*técnicos básicos*)	73	37	30	6	2	33	13	…	…
Skilled workers	71	46	45	8	3	50	20	72	31
Unskilled workers	19	13	15	2	1	14	6	38	16
Minimum wage	15	10	11	1	1	12	5	22	13

[a] Categories not entirely consistent with period prior to August 1997, due to reclassification of civil service posts.

Sources: MAPESS, INE and BNA (for exchange rates)

Table A-6   Internally displaced population, by province, June 1999

| | New IDPs 1998–99 | | IDPs from | Total confirmed |
	Reported	Confirmed	1992–97	IDPs
Bengo	33,037	33,037	0	33,037
Benguela	71,158	54,597	34,357	88,954
Bié	99,561	65,016	8,646	73,662
Cabinda	0	0	0	0
Cuando Cubango	66,493	63,393	34,000	97,393
Cunene	5,171	2,871	3,118	5,989
Huambo	180,638	175,098	0	175,098
Huíla	95,534	76,307	70,368	146,675
Kwanza Norte	77,553	54,524	10,990	65,514
Kwanza Sul	75,300	45,567	23,000	68,567
Luanda	287,000	72,000	0	72,000
Lunda Norte	23,747	17,957	101,000	118,957
Lunda Sul	43,559	27,336	34,000	61,336
Malange	134,820	128,601	4,500	133,101
Moxico	95,955	91,715	55,614	147,329
Namibe	7,098	6,409	5,584	11,993
Uíge	71,800	34,824	20,000	54,824
Zaire	2,950	2,950	22,000	24,950
Total	1,371,374	952,202	427,177	1,379,379

Source: United Nations, Humanitarian Assistance Co-ordination Unit (UCAH)

Table A-7   Access to primary education, 1996
(1st six classes of basic education)

| | Urban areas | Rural areas | Boys | Girls | Overall | Averages for Sub-Saharan Africa | |
						Boys	Girls
Net enrolment ratio in 1st class[a]	40.0	25.1	32.8	28.6	30.5	…	…
Net enrolment ratio in classes 1–6[b]	63.7	39.6	51.8	48.0	49.7	59	51
Gross enrolment ratio in classes 1–6[c]	109.5	75.0	97.7	82.1	89.4	82	67

[a] Percentage of 6-year-olds entering Class 1. [b] Percentage of children aged 6–11 in classes 1–6.
[c] Children of all ages in Classes 1–6 as % of children aged 6–11.
Sources: Multiple Indicator Cluster Survey (MICS), a household survey conducted in all provinces, including in UNITA-controlled areas, in 1996 (INE, 1999); average data for Sub-Saharan Africa from UNICEF, 2000

Table A-8 Enrolment in education, 1980/81–1995/96
('000 pupils)

	1980/81	1985/86	1990/91	1991/92	1992/93	1993/94	1994/95	1995/96
Pre-primary	404	228	164	189	110	169	101	109
Basic education	1,519	1,136	1,150	1,179	846	1,090	1,159	1,028
1st level (classes 1–4)	1,332	971	990	989	697	907	967	836
2nd level (classes 5–6)	150	131	125	147	107	132	131	130
3rd level (classes 7–8)	36	35	35	42	41	50	61	63
Technical secondary education (*ensino médio*)	5	9	20	23	11	22	23	…
Technical	3	5	11	12	8	13	15	…
Teacher training	2	4	9	11	3	9	9	16
Pre-university (PUNIV)	2	4	6	7	…	…	…	…
Higher education	2	5	7	6	…	…	4	…
Total	1,933	1,381	1,347	1,403	…	…	…	…

Sources: UNICEF, 1999; MED, 1996; UNESCO/UNICEF/MED, 1993

Table A-9 Vaccination coverage, 1996
(% of children aged 12–23 months vaccinated, according to vaccination cards and history)

	Urban areas	Rural areas	Overall	Averages for Sub-Saharan Africa[a]
BCG (TB)	74.2	47.0	59.5	63
DPT 3 (diphtheria, pertussis & tetanus)	35.3	14.2	23.9	48
OPV 3 (polio)	36.6	19.8	27.5	48
Measles	49.2	42.4	45.5	48
All of above	25.6	9.5	21.1	…
Yellow fever	27.2	17.0	16.7	…

[a] Data for 1995–98.
Sources: Multiple Indicator Cluster Survey (MICS), a household survey conducted in all provinces, including in UNITA-controlled areas, in 1996 (INE, 1999); average data for Sub-Saharan Africa from UNICEF, 2000

Table A-10 Nutrition data, 1996
(% of children under 5 with moderate or severe malnutrition)

	Low weight for height (wasting)		Low height for age (stunting)		Low weight for age (underweight)	
	Moderate & severe[a]	Severe[b]	Moderate & severe[a]	Severe[b]	Moderate & severe[a]	Severe[b]
Urban areas	5.2	1.3	46.8	19.6	31.6	10.0
Rural areas	7.1	1.8	57.5	32.5	48.5	16.8
Overall	6.4	1.6	53.1	27.2	41.6	14.0
Average, Sub-Saharan Africa	9	…	41	…	32	10

[a] < –2 standard deviations from median. [b] < –3 standard deviations from median.
Sources: Multiple Indicator Cluster Survey (MICS), a household survey conducted in all provinces, including in UNITA-controlled areas, in 1996 (INE, 1999); average data for Sub-Saharan Africa from UNICEF, 2000

Table A-11 Access to safe water and adequate sanitation
(% of population)

	Angola, 1996			Sub-Saharan Africa, 1990–98		
	Urban	Rural	Overall	Urban	Rural	Overall
Access to safe water	46	22	31	77	39	50
Access to adequate sanitation	62	27	40	70	35	45

Sources: Multiple Indicator Cluster Survey (MICS), a household survey conducted in all provinces, including in UNITA-controlled areas, in 1996 (INE, 1999); average data for Sub-Saharan Africa from UNICEF, 2000

Table A-12   Gross domestic product by sectors, 1993–98
(% share of total)

	1993	1994	1995	1996	Est. 1997	Est. 1998
Agriculture, forestry & fisheries	11.6	6.6	7.7	7.3	9.5	12.3
Mining	41.0	58.6	58.5	61.3	52.1	40.2
Oil and LPG	40.2	56.6	55.8	58.0	48.3	32.9
Diamonds	0.8	2.0	2.7	3.3	3.8	7.3
Manufacturing	5.7	4.9	4.0	3.4	4.4	5.7
Electricity and water	0.1	0.0	0.0	0.0	0.0	0.1
Construction	4.5	3.4	3.4	3.1	4.1	5.5
Trade and commerce	20.3	18.1	17.6	14.8	16.2	20.7
Non-tradeable services	14.4	6.5	7.3	8.1	11.3	13.9
Import duties	2.5	1.8	1.4	1.9	2.4	1.7
GDP at market prices	100.0	100.0	100.0	100.0	100.0	100.0

Sources: IMF, 1999c, from Ministry of Planning

Table A-13   Real growth of gross domestic product, 1993–99 (%)

	1993	1994	1995	1996	1997	1998	Est. 1999
GDP at market prices	–23.8	1.4	10.3	10.0	6.2	3.2	2.7
Petroleum sector	–8.4	9.2	12.0	10.4	4.7	3.5	4.1
Non-petroleum sector	–31.4	–3.8	8.1	9.4	8.4	2.9	1.8
GDP at market prices ($ m.)	...	4,060	5,059	6,535	7,690	6,449	5,606

Sources: IMF, 1999a, 1999c, 2000, derived from Ministry of Planning

Table A-14   Consumer price inflation, Luanda, 1995–99 (%)

	Monthly inflation					Annual inflation				
	1995	1996	1997	1998	1999	1995	1996	1997	1998	1999
January	38.6	36.0	7.9	5.4	10.6	1,084	3,710	2,013	59	146
February	32.4	22.5	2.2	3.1	12.1	1,304	3,425	1,680	62	168
March	28.9	34.9	–3.5	2.9	6.5	1,480	3,589	1,151	72	177
April	16.8	51.9	3.2	5.0	7.8	1,478	4,699	750	75	185
May	14.2	84.1	0.9	6.2	10.3	1,511	7,639	356	84	196
June	16.5	61.8	0.6	3.7	11.2	1,654	10,649	170	90	217
July	22.3	38.1	1.4	10.6	13.3	1,738	12,035	113	108	225
August	43.3	9.5	6.5	26.0	16.8	2,040	9,171	107	146	201
September	52.7	5.0	6.0	4.4	28.9	2,549	6,277	109	142	272
October	30.4	2.1	7.4	4.7	20.2	2,592	4,892	120	136	327
November	82.0	0.7	6.2	7.2	9.4	3,596	2,661	132	138	335
December	66.4	5.5	12.9	11.3	9.6	3,784	1,651	148	135	329

Source: INE

Table A-15   Oil balance, 1993–98[a]

	1993	1994	1995	1996	1997	1998
Crude oil (millions of barrels)						
Production	184.1	200.9	225.0	248.6	254.9	280.8
Domestic refinery	12.6	14.1	14.3	14.5	15.5	…
Exports[b]	170.4	184.3	206.4	231.7	231.7	251.9
Net change in stocks	1.1	2.5	4.3	2.4	7.7	
Derivatives (thousand tons)						
Supply	1,581	1,811	1,817	1,815	1,815	…
Domestic production	1,522	1,710	1,760	1,776	1,776	…
Imports	58	101	57	39	39	…
Uses	1,581	1,811	1,817	1,815	1,815	…
Domestic sales	979	1,114	1,070	932	932	…
Exports	611	709	727	784	784	…
Net change in stocks	–9	–13	20	99	99	…

[a] Data for 1997–98 not fully consistent with oil production data in other tables. [b] As reported in balance of payments (except 1998, from *Revista Energia*); other sources differ slightly.
Source: IMF, 1999a, derived from Ministry of Petroleum, SONANGOL and BNA

Table A-16   Mining production, 1993–98

	1993	1994	1995	1996	1997	1998
Crude oil						
in millions of barrels	184	201	225	249	255	281
in thousand barrels per day	504	550	617	689	713	739
LPG						
in thousand barrels	1,282	1,481	1,616	1,580	1,581	…
Diamonds (recorded exports)						
in thousand carats	295	537	628	917	1,212	2,716

Sources: IMF, 1999a, 2000 derived from Ministry of Petroleum and ENDIAMA; EIU

Table A-17 Balance of payments, 1996–99
($ million)

	1996	1997	1998	Est. 1999
Exports fob	5,169	5,007	3,543	5,344
Oil	4,854	4,630	3,091	4,694
Non-oil	315	377	452	650
Imports fob	2,040	2,477	2,079	3,267
Trade balance	3,129	2,529	1,464	2,077
Services and transfers (net)	−3,378	−3,399	−3,487	−3,874
Interest payments	−767	−442	−454	−326
Current account balance	−249	−869	−2,023	1,797
Direct investment (net)	588	492	1,115	2,520
Medium and long-term borrowing (net)	−306	267	−965	−705
Drawings	907	1,601	603	812
Amortization	1,213	1,334	1,568	1,517
Short-term capital (net)	−257	−668	−172	−263
Capital account	24	91	−22	1,552
Errors and omissions	−121	−32	673	4
Overall balance	−346	−810	−1,372	−240
Financing	346	810	1,372	240
Change in reserves (− = increase)	−1,520	184	317	−534
Change in arrears (− = decrease)	−3,871	596	988	774
Rescheduling	1,704	29	…	0
Debt cancellation	4,033	0	…	0

Memorandum items

	1996	1997	1998	Est. 1999
Current account as % of GDP	−3.8	−11.3	−31.4	−32.1
Overall balance as % of GDP	−5.3	−10.5	−21.3	−4.3
Gross international reserves ($m.)	558	392	201	481
Import coverage (in months of next year's imports)	1.3	1.0	0.4	0.9
External debt ($m.)	8,449	8,570	8,782	9,591
External debt as % of exports of goods and services	156	164	240	175
Debt-service ratio (%)	34	15	24	17
Export price of oil ($ per barrel)	20.4	18.6	12.0	17.4

Source: IMF, 2000

Table A-18   Main trade partners, 1993–97
(% of total exports and imports)

	1993	1994	1995	1996	1997
Exports					
United States	71.3	70.3	66.0	58.0	63.6
China (People's Republic)	5.8	1.5	3.8	5.0	12.9
Belgium & Luxembourg	0.3	4.3	4.4	4.9	6.0
France	4.3	3.9	2.4	2.9	3.8
Taiwan	0.6	0.4	2.6	6.1	2.8
Spain	2.7	4.6	3.3	4.2	1.9
Italy	4.0	3.9	3.2	3.9	0.4
Brazil	1.0	0.5	1.1	3.1	0.9
Canada	0.6	0.1	0.3	2.7	0.0
Rest of world	6.6	5.4	6.0	6.1	7.2
Imports					
Portugal	26.6	22.5	20.4	21.4	20.6
United States	12.9	15.6	15.4	14.5	13.2
South Africa	6.2	6.7	8.0	18.6	14.1
France	7.3	10.5	22.7	8.2	5.6
Spain	10.0	2.4	3.5	5.0	8.2
United Kingdom	3.2	2.8	2.9	3.9	6.2
Italy	4.7	2.5	2.5	3.1	2.6
China (People's Republic)	0.9	1.0	1.3	1.5	1.4
Brazil	2.9	11.9	1.2	1.9	3.8
Germany	2.3	1.8	1.7	1.7	2.2
Rest of world	23.1	22.4	20.4	20.2	22.1

Source: IMF, Direction of Trade Statistics; data provided by partners

Table A-19 Merchandise exports, by commodities, 1993–98

	1993	1994	1995	1996	1997	1998
Crude oil						
Volume (millions of barrels)	170	184	206	228	243	252
Average price ($ per barrel)	16.1	15.3	16.6	20.4	18.6	12.0
Value ($ m.)	2,750	2,822	3,425	4,651	4,507	3,038
Refined petroleum products						
Volume (thousand tons)	611	709	727	784	833	...
Average price ($ per ton)	103	101	107	133	121	...
Value ($ m.)	63	72	78	105	101	...
Gas						
Volume (thousand barrels)	1,270	677	1,512	1,633	1,543	...
Average price ($ per barrel)	10.5	10.7	12.2	15.6	14.5	...
Value	13	7	18	25	22	...
Diamonds						
Volume (thousand carats)	295	537	628	917	1,212	...
Average price ($ per carat)	213	181	268	291	287	...
Value ($ m.)	63	97	168	267	348	...
Coffee						
Volume (tons)	2,333	498	2,434	2,894	3,039	...
Average price ($ per ton)	917	2,083	2,367	1,546	1,506	...
Value ($ m.)	2.1	1.0	5.8	4.5	4.6	...

Source: IMF, 1999a, from BNA

Table A-20 Government finances, 1994–99
(in % of GDP)

	1994	1995	1996	1997	1998	Prelim. 1999
Revenue	42.1	30.0	45.0	38.7	27.0	48.2
Oil revenue	37.4	26.2	40.2	32.2	18.8	42.2
Non-oil revenue	4.7	3.8	4.8	6.5	8.2	6.0
Current expenditure	...	...	53.3	51.3	40.4	53.6
Capital expenditure	...	...	4.9	4.5	1.4	4.2
Total expenditure	62.1	57.3	58.2	55.8	41.8	57.7
Overall balance, commitment basis	−20.1	−27.3	−15.8	−17.8	−15.1	13.1
Overall balance, cash basis	−7.9	−17.6	−1.8	−13.8	−7.6	1.1

Source: IMF, 1999a, 1999c, 2000

Table A-21 Government expenditure by functions, 1996–99

billions of kwanzas

	1996	1997	1998	Prelim. 1999
Total expenditure	0.49	0.98	1.06	8.94
General public services	0.06	0.17	0.19	1.44
Defence and public order	0.16	0.34	0.29	3.67
of which: unrecorded	0.13	0.18	0.15	0.00
Peace process	0.00	0.01	0.00	0.01
Social spending	0.05	0.13	0.12	0.84
Education	0.02	0.05	0.07	0.43
Health	0.01	0.03	0.04	0.25
Economic affairs and services	0.04	0.17	0.14	0.84
Interest (commitment basis)	0.10	0.10	0.18	0.96

% of total government expenditure

	1996	1997	1998	Prelim. 1999
Total expenditure	100.0	100.0	100.0	100.0
General public services	13.3	17.8	18.3	16.1
Defence and public order	33.5	34.9	27.2	41.0
of which: unrecorded	26.3	18.2	13.8	0.0
Peace process	0.8	0.6	0.0	0.1
Social spending	9.3	13.4	11.8	9.4
Education	4.4	5.0	6.2	4.8
Health	2.9	3.1	3.3	2.8
Economic affairs and services	8.1	17.7	13.4	10.3
Interest (commitment basis)	20.0	10.0	16.6	10.7

% of GDP

	1996	1997	1998	Prelim. 1999
Total expenditure	57.5	56.0	41.7	52.9
General public services	7.6	9.9	7.7	8.5
Defence and public order	19.2	19.5	11.4	21.7
of which: unrecorded	15.1	10.2	5.8	0.0
Peace process	0.4	0.3	0.0	0.1
Social spending	5.4	7.5	4.9	4.9
Education	2.5	2.8	2.6	2.5
Health	1.6	1.8	1.4	1.5
Economic affairs and services	4.7	9.9	5.6	5.4
Interest (commitment basis)	11.5	5.6	6.9	5.7

Source: IMF, 2000

Table A-22 Public external debt, end 1999
($ million)

	Debt outstanding	of which, arrears
Total public external debt	9,591	4,440
Medium and long term debt	8,782	3,749
Multilateral creditors	251	98
Bilateral creditors	5,344	2,351
Private creditors	3,630	1,300
Short term debt	809	691
Oil guaranteed debt	2,689	450
Bilateral creditors	1,718	445
Private creditors	971	5

Source: IMF, 2000

BIBLIOGRAPHY

ACR, 1976/77, *Africa Contemporary Record, Annual Survey and Documents, 1976–77*, ed. Colin Legum, Rex Collings, London.

ACR, 1977/78, *Africa Contemporary Record, Annual Survey and Documents, 1977–78*, ed. Colin Legum, Rex Collings, London.

ACR, 1978/79, *Africa Contemporary Record, Annual Survey and Documents, 1978–79*, ed. Colin Legum, Rex Collings, London.

Adauta, Mário, 1997, 'Contribuição para o Conhecimento do Sector Informal em Luanda, Angola', unpublished paper.

Aguilar, Renato, and Mario Zejan, 1991, *Angola: A Long and Hard Way to the Marketplace*, Macroeconomic Studies 19/91, Department of Economics, University of Gothenburg, Sweden.

Aguilar, Renato, and Mario Zejan, 1992, *Angola: The Last Stand of Central Planning*, Macroeconomic Studies, 33/92, Department of Economics, University of Gothenburg, Sweden.

Aguilar, Renato, and Asa Stenman, 1994, *Angola 1994: Trying to Break through the Wall*, Department of Economics, Gothenburg University, Sweden.

Aguilar, Renato, and Asa Stenman, 1996, *Angola 1996: Hyper-Inflation, Confusion and Political Crisis*, Department of Economics, Gothenburg University, Sweden.

Amado, F., F. Cruz and R. Hakkert, 1992, 'Urbanização e Desurbanização em Angola', *Cadernos de População e Desenvolvimento,* Vol. 1, No. 1, January–June 1992, Ministry of Planning and United Nations Population Fund, Luanda.

Amado, F., and J. Van-Dúnem, 1996, *"Position Paper": A Família*, Centro de Ensino e Investigação em População, Universidade Agostinho Neto, Luanda.

Amnesty International (AI), 1992, *Angola: An Appeal for Prompt Action to Protect Human Rights*, Amnesty International, London and New York.

AI, 1999, *Angola: Freedom of Expression under Threat*, Amnesty International, London.

Anstee, Margaret, 1997, *Orphan of the Cold War*, Macmillan, London.

Bender, W., and S. Hunt, 1991, *Poverty and Food Insecurity in Luanda*, Relatório 1, Inquérito sobre as Despesas e Receitas dos Agregados Familiares em Luanda, Ministry of Planning, UNICEF and Food Studies Group, University of Oxford.

Bergesen, Helge, and Torleif Haugland, 2000, 'The Puzzle of Petro-States: A Comparative Study of Azerbaijan and Angola', draft.

Birmingham, David, 1992, *A África Central até 1870*, ENDIPU UEE, Luanda.

Birmingham, David, 1995, 'Language is Power: Regional Politics in Angola,' in Keith Hart and Joanna Lewis (eds), *Why Angola Matters*, African Studies Centre, Cambridge University, and James Currey, London.

BNA, 1998a, *Balança de Pagamentos 1997*, Direcção de Estudos e Estatística, Banco Nacional de Angola, Luanda.

BNA, 1998b, *Boletim Estatístico-Económico,* 1ˢᵗ half, No. 4, October, Banco Nacional de Angola, Luanda.

BNA, 1998c, *Boletim Estatístico-Económico*, No. 5, September, Banco Nacional de Angola, Luanda.

BNA, 1998d, *Boletim Estatístico, Outubro de 1998*, No. 7, November, Banco Nacional de Angola, Luanda.

BNA, 1998e, *Boletim Estatístico*, No. 8, November, Banco Nacional de Angola, Luanda.

Boudreau, T., 1996, *Risk Mapping Report*, Save the Children Fund (UK), Luanda.

Bravo Manuel (ed.), 1996, *Angola, Transição para a Paz, Reconciliação e Desenvolvimento*, Hugin Editores Lda, Lisbon.

Bridgland, F., 1988, *Jonas Savimbi: A Key to Africa*, Hodder and Stoughton, London.

Carvalho, R., 1997, 'Um Estudo de Caso: Os Kuvale e o Futuro Pastoril em Questão', paper presented to workshop on Angolan communities and Community Institutions in the Post-war Situation, sponsored by Acção para o Desenvolvimento Rural e Ambiente, Luanda, April.

CCF, 1996, *Sexual Abuse and Exploitation of Children in Time of War: The Case of Angola*, Christian Children's Fund, Luanda.

Christoplos, I., 1997, *Local Service Institutions and the Humanitarian Imperative in Relief and Rehabilitation: A Case Study of the Angolan Red Cross*, Department of Rural Development Studies, Swedish University of Agricultural Sciences, Uppsala.

CIES, 1997, *Cada Um Fala a Sua Verdade: Histórias do Maralhão*, Projecto Kandengues Unidos, Centro Informazione e Educazione allo Sviluppo, Luanda.

Collier, Paul and Anke Hoeffler, 1999, 'Justice-Seeking and Loot-Seeking in Civil War', paper for Conference on Economic Agendas in Civil Wars, London, 26–27 April.

Coopers & Lybrand, 1997, *Luanda Urban Water Supply and Sanitation Project*, 3 volumes, Coopers and Lybrand, Luanda.

Da Rocha, Alves, 1996, 'Le passage de l'Angola à l'économie de marché: enrichir qui est déjà riche', *Antipodes*, Brussels, 134–5, December.

Da Rosa, Bravo, 1998, 'Angola – Exportações de Petróleo (1998)', *Revista Energia*, 53, April.

DW, 1995, *Water Supply and Sanitation in Luanda: Informal Sector Study and Beneficiary Assessment*, study for the World Bank, Development Workshop, Luanda.

DW, 1997, 'Estudo nas Zonas Peri-Urbanas de Luanda', paper presented to workshop on Angolan Communities and Community Institutions in the Post-War Situation, sponsored by Acção para o Desenvolvimento Rural e Ambiente, Luanda, April.

EIU, 1998, 1999 and 2000, *Country Report, Angola*, quarterly, The Economist Intelligence Unit, London.

FAO and WFP, 1997, *FAO/WFP Crop and Food Supply Assessment Mission to Angola, May 1997*, Food and Agriculture Organization of the United Nations and World Food Programme, Rome.

Ferreira, E.S., 1977, *O Fim de uma Era: o Colonialismo Português em Africa*, Sá da Costa, Lisbon.

Ferreira, M.E., 1995, 'La reconversion économique de la nomenklatura pétrolière', *Politique Africaine*, 57.

FESA, 1997, *Fondation Eduardo dos Santos, Overview*, Luanda.

Global Witness, 1998, *A Rough Trade, The Role of Companies and Governments in the Angolan Conflict*, Global Witness, London.

Global Witness, 1999, *A Crude Awakening: The Role of the Oil and Banking Industries in Angola's Civil War and the Plunder of State Assets*, Global Witness, London.

GURN, 1999, *Memorando sobre as Medidas de Política, Institucionais e Estruturais no âmbito da Estratégia Global para a Saída da Crise*, Governo da Unidade e da Reconciliação Nacional, Luanda, March.

Hare, P., 1998, *Angola's Last Best Chance for Peace: An Insider's Account of the Peace Process*, United States Institute for Peace, Washington, DC.

Helmore, Richard, 1984, 'Diamond Mining in Angola', *Mining Magazine*, June.

Henderson, Lawrence W., 1979, *Angola: Five Centuries of Conflict*, Cornell University Press, Ithaca, NY, and London.

Hodges, Tony, 1987, *Angola to the 1990s, The Potential for Recovery*, EIU Economic Prospects Series, The Economist Intelligence Unit, London.

Hodges, Tony, 1993, *Angola to 2000, Prospects for Recovery*, Research Report, The Economist Intelligence Unit, London.

Hodges, Anthony, 1996, 'O Desafio do Pós-Guerra: Reintegração Sócio-Económica de Deslocados, Refugiados e Soldados Desmobilizados,' in Manuel Bravo (ed.), *Angola, Transição para a Paz, Reconciliação e Desenvolvimento*, Hugin Editores Lda, Lisbon.

Hodges, Anthony, and Walter Viegas, 1998, *Country Strategy Study*, Norwegian People's Aid, Luanda.

Hodges, Anthony, and Fernando Pacheco, 1999, *Avaliação do Programa de Micro-Realizações, 1995–99*, Study for the European Commission and Government of Angola, Projectos de Consultoria Austral Lda, Luanda.

Hoygaard, Laurinda, 1995, *Angola, Planificação da Economia Nacional e Gestão dos Recursos Públicos*, Swedish Embassy and Swedish Authority for International Development, Luanda.

HRW, 1989, *Angola: Violations of the Laws of War on Both Sides*, Human Rights Watch, New York.

HRW, 1994, *Angola: Arms Trade and Violations of the Laws of War since the 1992 Elections*, Human Rights Watch, New York and London.

HRW, 1996, *Angola: Between War and Peace, Arms Trade and Human Rights Abuses since the Lusaka Protocol*, Human Rights Watch, New York and London.

HRW, 1999, *Angola Unravels: The Rise and Fall of the Lusaka Peace Process*, Human Rights Watch, New York and London.

IMF, 1995, *Aide-Mémoire da Equipa do Corpo Técnico do FMI, Luanda, 5 de Dezembro de 1995*, International Monetary Fund, Washington, DC.

IMF, 1996a, *Angola, Staff Visit of April 22–26, 1996, Aide-Mémoire*, International Monetary Fund, Washington, DC.

IMF, 1996b, *Angola – Missão de Consulta para o Artigo IV e Negociação dum Programa de Emergência, Aide-Mémoire, 25 de Novembro de 1996*, International Monetary Fund, Washington, DC.

IMF, 1997, *Angola – 1997 Article IV Consultation Mission, Aide-Mémoire, June 1997*, International Monetary Fund, Washington, DC.

IMF, 1999a, *Angola, Statistical Annex*, African Department, International Monetary Fund, Washington, DC, February.

IMF, 1999b, *Concluding Statement of the IMF Mission to Angola, March 17*, Luanda.

IMF, 1999c, *Concluding Statement of the IMF Mission to Angola, September 7*, Luanda.

IMF, 2000, *Staff Report for the 2000 Article IV Consultation and Discussions on a Staff Monitored Program*, African Department, International Monetary Fund, June, Washington, DC.

INE, 1996, *Perfil da Pobreza em Angola*, Instituto Nacional de Estatística, Luanda.

INE, 1999, *O Inquérito de Indicadores Múltiplos (MICS)*, Instituto Nacional de Estatística, Luanda.

INE, undated, *Perfil Estatístico Económico e Social, 1992–1996*, Instituto Nacional de Estatística, Luanda.

IOM, 1996, *Séries de Mapas: Movimentos Populacionais Pós-Guerra em Angola*, 2nd edition, International Organization for Migration, Luanda.

Karl, Terry Lynn, 1997, *The Paradox of Plenty: Oil Booms and Petro-States*, University of California Press, Berkeley, CA.

Le Billon, Philippe, 1999, *A Land Cursed by its Wealth? Angola's War Economy (1975–1999)*, United Nations University/WIDER, Helsinki.

Legum, Colin, and Tony Hodges (1976), *After Angola: The War over Southern Africa*, Rex Collings, London.

Maier, Karl, 1996, *Angola: Promises and Lies*, Serif, London.

MAPESS, 1997, *Legislação sobre a Administração Pública, II Volume (1995–1996)*, Ministry of Public Administration, Employment and Social Security, Luanda.

MAPESS, 1999a, *Perfil dos Recursos Humanos da Administração Pública*, Ministry of Public Administration, Employment and Social Security, Luanda.

MAPESS, 1999b, *Programa de Reforma Administrativo do Governo de Angola*, Ministry of Public Administration, Employment and Social Security, Luanda.

Marcum, J., 1969, *The Angolan Revolution, Vol. I: Anatomy of an Explosion (1950–1962)*, MIT Press, Cambridge, MA.

Marcum, J., 1978, *The Angolan Revolution, Vol. II: Exile Politics and Guerrilla Warfare (1962–1976)*, MIT Press, Cambridge, MA.

Martin, Phyllis, 1980, *Historical Dictionary of Angola*, The Scarecrow Press, Metuchen, NJ, and London.

MED, 1996, *Situação Educacional em Angola, Ano Lectivo 1994/95*, Ministry of Education, Luanda.

Messiant, C., 1992, 'Social and Political Background to the "Democratization" and the Peace Process in Angola', Paper for Seminar on Democratizaton in Angola, Leiden, The Netherlands.

Messiant, C., 1999, 'La Fondation Eduardo dos Santos: A propos de l'investissement de la société civile par le pouvoir politique', in *Politique Africaine*, 73, March: 82–101.

MINADER, 1996, *Agricultural Recovery and Development Options Review*, Ministry of Agriculture and Rural Development, Luanda.

MINARS and UNDP, 1997, *Directório das ONGs*, Ministério da Assistência e Reinserção Social and United Nations Development Programme, Luanda.

MINFIN, 1993, 1994, 1995, 1996, *Contas do Exercícios de 1992, 1993, 1994 & 1995*, Direcção Nacional de Contabilidade, Ministry of Finance, Luanda.

MINFIN, 1997, *Relatório da Execução Orçamental e Financeira, Exercício de 1996*, Direcção Nacional de Contabilidade, Ministry of Finance, Luanda.

MINPLAN, 1996, *O Financiamento do Programa de Reabilitação Comunitária e Reconciliação Nacional desde a Mesa Redonda de Bruxelas*, Ministry of Planning, Luanda.

MINSA, 1997, *Boletim de Vigilância Nutricional*, No. 13, August, Programa Nacional de Nutrição, Ministry of Health, Luanda.

MINTAPSS, 1990, *Inquérito aos Recursos Humanos na Função Pública, Principais Resultados (Síntese)*, Ministry of Labour, Public Administration and Social Security, Luanda.

Minter, William, 1994, *Apartheid's Contras, An Inquiry into the Roots of War in Angola and Mozambique*, Zed Books, London, and Witwatersrand University Press, Johannesburg.

Mogalakwe, M., and F. Lima, 1996, *Avaliação do Sistema de Comunicação Social de Angola*, Media Institute of Southern Africa, Windhoek.

Munslow, Barry, 1999, 'Angola: the Politics of Unsustainable Development', *Third World Quarterly*, 20(3): 551–68.

Pereira, Anthony W., 1994, 'The Neglected Tragedy: The Return to War in Angola, 1992–3,' *Journal of Modern African Studies* 32(1).

República de Angola (RA), 1994, *Lei Constitucional da II República*, Luanda.

RA, 1995, *Programa de Reabilitação Comunitária e Reconciliação Nacional*, Luanda, presented to the donors round-table conference in Brussels, 25–26 September.

RA, 1999, *Orçamento Geral do Estado para 1999, Anexo 1, Relatório de Fundamentação*, Luanda, March.

RPA, 1991, *Lei Constitucional e Outras Leis Complementares*, República Popular de Angola, Edição Minfa, Luanda.

Saferworld, 1996, *Angola: Conflict Resolution and Peace-Building*, Saferworld, London.

Sanches, A., 1966, *Avaliação da Capacidade Institucional do Ministério da Assistência e Reinserção Social (MINARS)*, World Bank, Luanda.

SCF-UK and ADRA, 1997, 'Estudo Caso: Comunidades Rurais do Huambo', paper presented by Save the Children Fund (UK) and Acção para o Desenvolvimento Rural e Ambiente (ADRA) to a workshop on Angolan Communities and Community Institutions in the Post-war Situation, sponsored by ADRA, Luanda, April.

Sebastião, Sidónio, 1999, 'O Brent e as Ramas Angolanas', *Revista Energia*, 53, April, Luanda.

Simão, Pinda, 1995, 'Education in Angola in the Post-Apartheid Era: Overcoming Physical and Spiritual Destruction', in *Transcending the Legacy, Children in the New Southern Africa*, African European Institute, Amsterdam, Southern African Research and Documentation Centre, Harare, and UNICEF, Nairobi.

Somerville, Keith, 1986, *Angola: Politics, Economics and Society*, Frances Pinter, London, and Lynne Rienner Publishers, Boulder, CO.

Tvedten, Inge (1997), *Angola: Struggle for Peace and Reconstruction*, Westview Press, Boulder, CO, and Oxford, UK.

UN, 1998, *United Nations Consolidated Inter-Agency Appeal for Angola, January-December 1998*, United Nations, New York and Geneva.

UN, 1999a, *United Nations Consolidated Inter-Agency Appeal for Angola, January-December 1999*, United Nations, New York and Geneva.

UN, 1999b, *Report of the Secretary-General on the United Nations Observer Mission in Angola*, UN Security Council document S/1999/49, 17 January, New York.

UN, 1999c, *Report of the Secretary-General on the United Nations Observer Mission in Angola*, United Nations Security Council document S/1999/202, 24 February, New York.

UN, 2000, *Report of the Panel of Experts on Violations of Security Council Sanctions against UNITA*, in UN Security Council document S/2000/203, 10 March, New York.

UNDP, 1995, *Conferência de Mesa-Redonda sobre Angola, Relatório da Conferência, Bruxelas, 25–26 de Setembro de 1995*, United Nations Development Programme, New York.

UNDP et al., 1996, *Education for All, Achieving the Goal, Statistical Document*, United Nations Development Programme, United Nations Educational, Scientific and Cultural Organization, United Nations Children's Fund and World Bank.

UNDP, 1997, *Relatório do Desenvolvimento Humano, Angola*, United Nations Development Programme, Luanda.

UNDP, 1998, *Relatório do Desenvolvimento Humano, Angola 1998*, United Nations Development Programme, Luanda.

UNDP, 1999a, *Angola: Economic Developments in 1998*, United Nations Development Programme, Luanda.

UNDP, 1999b, *Human Development Report 1999*, United Nations Development Programme, New York.

UNDP, 2000, *Human Development Report*, United Nations Development Programme, New York.

UNESCO/UNICEF/MED, 1993, *Angola: Opções para a Reconstrução do Sistema Educativo, Estudo Sectorial,* United Nations Educational, Scientific and Cultural Organization, United Nations Children's Fund and Ministry of Education, Luanda.

UNHROA, 1999, 'Promoting the Respect of Human Rights in Angola: Strengthening Effective Planning and Consolidating Support of the International Community', United Nations Human Rights Office in Angola, Luanda, incomplete draft text.

UNICEF, 1999, *Um Futuro de Esperança para as Crianças de Angola, Uma Análise da Situação da Criança*, United Nations Children's Fund, Luanda.

UNICEF, 2000, *State of the World's Children*, United Nations Children's Fund, New York.

Van der Winden, 1996, *A Family of the Musseque: Survival and Development in Postwar Angola*, One World Action, Oxford.

Venâncio, Moisés, 1994, *The United Nations, Peace and Transition: Lessons from Angola*, Instituto de Estudos Estratégicos e Internacionais, Lisbon.

Vines, Alex, 1998, *Peace Postponed, Angola since the Lusaka Protocol*, Catholic Institute for International Relations, London.

World Bank, 1987, *Angola: Issues and Options in the Energy Sector*, World Bank, Washington, DC, May.

World Bank, 1993, *Angola: Public Expenditure Issues and Priorities during Transition to a Market Economy*, Report No. 11649-ANG, World Bank, Washington, DC.

World Bank, 1996, *Angola: Towards Economic and Social Reconstruction*, World Bank, Washington, DC, August.

Zenos, Anthony, 1996, 'The Role of Ethnicity in the Angolan Conflict, A Synthesis of Critical Perspectives', unpublished paper.

INDEX

195